NONPROFIT BOARDS
OF DIRECTORS

Nonprofit Boards of Directors

Analyses and Applications

Edited by
Robert D. Herman
and Jon Van Til

Transaction Publishers
New Brunswick (U.S.A.) and Oxford (U.K.)

Copyright (c) 1989 by Transaction Publishers, New Brunswick, New Jersey 08903.
Originally published 1985 by the Association of Voluntary Action Scholars.

Library of Congress Catalog Number: 88-15617
ISBN: 0-88738-216-9
Printed in the United States of America

Library of Congress Cataloging-in-Publication Data

Nonprofit boards of directors: analyses and applications / edited by Robert D. Herman and Jon Van Til.
    p. cm.
    Articles originally appeared in 1985 in Journal of voluntary action research.
    Includes bibliographies and index.
    ISBN 0-88738-216-9
    1. Corporation, Nonprofit–Management.   2. Association, institutions, etc.– Management. 3. Directors of corporations. I. Herman, Robert D., 1946– . II. Van Til, Jon. III. Title: Non-profit boards of directors
HD62.6N654 1988
658.4'22–dc19
                                                        88-15617
                                                          CIP

Contents

Board Functions and Board-Staff Relations in Nonprofit Organizations: An Introduction

The voluntary board evokes different and contradictory images. Some see the wealthy and powerful, others citizens making a difference. Some see boards as "rubber stamps," others are social clubs and some see boards as active, effective planning and decision-making bodies. No doubt what is seen depends on where we look and partly on what we are prepared to see.

The composition, functions and actions of nonprofit boards are thoroughly connected to the major issues and questions confronting both voluntary action researchers and the voluntary sector. If voluntary boards meet the political and managerial expectations that are culturally assigned to them, they are carrying very heavy burdens. Advocates of voluntarism and the voluntary sector frequently portray U.S. voluntary and nonprofit institutions as the foundation of democratic pluralism and the source of creative social innovation. What sorts of people, selected by what criteria and methods, holding what values, and operating with what procedures are required of nonprofit boards if they are to meet these expectations? Do nonprofit organizations, by and large, maintain and advance pluralism and democracy; do they encourage and promote social change?

There is a widespread view that nonprofit organizations are generally less well managed than businesses. As Walker (1983) has demonstrated this view rests on the implicit assumption that a "managed systems" model of organizational effectiveness is always the most appropriate. The managed systems model emphasizes maximizing one value, conceives action in strictly instrumentally rational terms, and considers hierarchy as the chief basis for coordination and control. Within the managed systems model boards are conceived as the apex of the managerial system. Boards are expected to review, and if necessary, revise the organization's mission, establish basic policies, determine programs and budgets, raise funds, evaluate the performance of the chief staff officer as well as the performance of individual board members and the board as a collectivity. Do nonprofit boards typically perform such extensive governance and managerial roles?

Savage (1984) has suggested that board trusteeship practices, as popularly described and prescribed, are myths. Trusteeship myths include the notions that (a) there is, or can be found, a clear separation between the responsibilities of the board and those of staff, (b) trustees safeguard the public interest, (c) trustees perform important decision-making as well as ceremonial roles, and (d) that a group of relative strangers, meeting only a few times a year, can adequately direct an organization. Savage also argues that the gap between these myths and reality is becoming clearer and that we are struggling to find some way of closing the gap. Certainly, the apparently increasing number of meetings, conferences, manuals, and books designed to improve the effectiveness of nonprofit boards attest to a generalized sense that there's some distance between what boards are supposed to be and do and what they are.

Given their normative importance, there has been surprisingly little systematic research on nonprofit boards. Research in the power elite tradition has focused on the social class origins of board members of the most prestigious local and national nonprofit organizations. The interest of such research is less on what board members actually do and more on what social origins and patterns of personal and inter-organizational linkages imply about the existence of and social processes perpetuating power elites (e.g., Domhoff, 1967, 1970, 1975; Ostrander, 1980; Perucci and Pilisuk, 1970; Ratcliff, *et al.,* 1979; Salzman and Domhoff, 1983; Useem, 1979).

Though the connections between nonprofit organizations and the encompassing socio-political system are sometimes ignored by those intent only on celebrating the nonprofit sector's virtues, it is certainly true that many nonprofit organizations and their board members are not among the power elite. Hodgkinson and Weitzman (1986) report that as of 1984 the Internal Revenue Service counts 352,884 501(c)(3) tax-exempt organizations as well as 130,344 501(c)(4) tax-exempt organizations. This total of approximately 483,000 voluntary sector organizations excludes many churches and thousands of small nonprofit organizations with annual revenues of less than $5,000. Thus, if one assumes that nonprofit boards average twenty members and if one assumes that half the nation's board seats are held by people who hold other seats, then the *minimum* number of people serving on U.S. nonprofit boards, at a given time, is nearly 5 million. Though this is a very rough estimate, it indicates that the nonprofit sector is large enough and diverse enough to be something more than the preserve of the elite.

Studies investigating what nonprofit boards actually do are rare (see Midddleton, 1987 for an excellent review of the available literature). The organization-and-environment perspective suggests a different conceptualization of the relation between the board and the organization than a managed systems perspective. It may be more fruitful to consider boards as a part of both the organization and the environment. Boards are ultimately legally responsible for the organization, but they typically include many people whose chief interest is not the organization and whose inclusion on the board is an attempt to cope with a source of environmental uncertainty. (See Herman and Tulipana in this volume for a more complete consideration of such a model.) Two studies, both based on the organization-and-environment perspective, have examined the relation between the social composition of nonprofit boards and measures of funding success (Pfeffer, 1973; Provan, 1980). Both support the contentions that board composition varies with environmental differences and that including the prestigious and influential on boards is related to resource acquisition.

Though the subject of a great deal of discussion among practitioners and substantial prescription (O'Connell, 1976, 1985 presents very sound advice) board-chief executive relationships have also not been much researched, especially after the early 1960s. These studies of voluntary social welfare organizations (Kramer, 1965; Nettler, 1958; Senor, 1963; Stein, 1961) found substantial differences between board members and the executive in status, reference groups, welfare values and identification with the organization. The differences may not be as many or as great in other parts of the nonprofit sector (e.g.. in neighborhood organizations or some arts organizations). Much of the practitioner-oriented literature on board-executive relationships use terms such as "partnership" and "team." There are no doubt circumstances in which board-executive relations are of this character, but it is difficult not to suspect that these terms are often polite fictions—cases of "pluralistic ignorance," where to maintain the norms people tacitly agree to ignore what really exists. To what extent is this true? What differences, in personal relationships, in organizational functioning, would occur if the fiction ceased?

The preference for a single model or theory of board functioning and board-executive relations seems to be strong, among both practitioners and scholars. But as Kramer (1983; see also Kramer, 1987) has recently suggested board-executive relations, including influence relations, will vary with characteristics of the organization, executive, board members, situation, issue, and interpersonal role relationships. It is unrealistic to expect one general pattern to describe all or even most board-executive relationships. Contingency theories are required—both in describing board-executive relationships and in describing the roles and functions of boards. It seems likely that the composition, extent to which the board emphasizes internal and external functions, and the extent to which it takes an especially active managerial role will be related to (a) the organization's location in the community's socio-political system, (b) organizational life cycle, (c) organizational size (both financially and numerically) and (d) the nature of the organization's mission.

The proceeding is one interpretation of the state of research on nonprofit boards and a sketch of the importance of the issues involved. Clearly much needs to be done. The pieces included in this volume contribute important evidence and clarification on many of the basic issues. In the first piece Candance Widmer investigates the incentives and expectations that induce voluntary participation on nonprofit boards. She finds that most board members expect to obtain multiple valued outcomes and that social and personal development incentives are much more common and effective than ideological or altruistic incentives.

The chapter by Melissa Midddleton presents a rich and detailed study of the board of directors of an orchestra. This case study examines the inter-relationships among board members and of board members to management. It illuminates the bases and consequences of board groupings, examines problems in organizational and board transitions. The orchestra's board members generally seen to participate in response to social and development incentives, as well as to ensure provision of personally-valued public good. Such similarities of motivation, nonetheless, do not ensure that all members conceive of the board's role in the same terms.

Whereas Widmer focuses on motivation at the individual level, Lucille Covelli considers the class-consistent motivations of uppermiddle and upper class women board members. Covelli finds that board membership on the part of such women is frequently motivated both to legitimize class structure and by personal needs of achievement and leadership. Such motivations are undoubtedly an important element affecting the behavior of many members of prestigious nonprofit boards. While more thorough study of the effect of such board member class-consistent motivations on organizational goals and program activities is desirable, they must usually function as tacit constraints on organizational actions.

If the uses, functions and behaviors of nonprofit governing boards are varied and ambiguous, the position and operation of advisory boards is even more so. Jone Pearce and Judy Rosener examine the performance of advisory boards. Based on a sample of public television stations' community advisory boards they find that establishing objectives and creating subcommittees enhance board performance. In a study of influence and perceived effectiveness in nonprofit organizations Herman and Tulipana also find evidence that the extent to which board members feel informed of their duties and tasks positively affects both their feelings of influence in the organization and their assessments of organizational effectiveness.

A substantial proportion of U.S. nonprofit organizations originated in the period from the mid-1960's to the mid-1970's, as the federal government, and to a lesser extent state and local governments, expanded funding and programs in a wide variety of social services. Rather than carry out such services only through government agencies, contracts were developed with (often) recently created nonprofit organizations (see Salamon, 1987 for an account of the extent of and issues raised by such "third party government"). Justin Fink has been working with and studying such nonprofit organizations. In his contribution to this volume he reports on comparative case studies of twenty community agencies. He finds that the idealized fiduciary role of the board is almost never achieved in these community organizations. Indeed, the gap between prescription and practice is often substantial. His study raises important questions about why there is a substantial gap and about rethinking our expectations of the board's role.

The gap between prescription and practice seems to occur for all board functions. One of the most important board functions is that of linkage to important actors and institutions in the organization's environment. As has been frequently observed, many nonprofit organizations, in a strategy intended to successfully cope with many sources of environmental uncertainty, attempt to attract a community's influential elite as board members. In a study of four United Way organizations Donald Plambeck presents evidence that suggests such a strategy is not always successful. In studying fund-raising success Plambeck compares two more successful United Ways with two less successful United Ways. The more successful organizations had boards with higher attendance at meetings, smaller proportions of male members, younger members, and members with shorter average years resident in their communities. While these variables do not mean that the successful United Ways necessarily included a more representative spectrum of the community, the results are consistent with the view that the top elite do not insure greater funding success. Plambeck also discovered that the more successful United Ways differed in operational procedures, for instance by setting higher goals and use of community needs studies.

If a great many nonprofit organizations are interested in attracting those with influence in the community, including high-ranking corporate executives, how do corporate executives approach service on nonprofit boards? John P. Mascotte, Chairman of the Board for the Continental Corporation, urges executives to take "ownership" for a community problem rather than becoming exclusively interested in the survival of a particular nonprofit organization. He suggests too many nonprofit organizations doing similar things exist and that a community's business leaders ought to take greater responsibility for concentrating voluntary resources on the right problems. Mascotte also presents straightforward prescriptions about the functions and roles of nonprofit boards. While the extent to which his views are shared by other corporate executives and the extent to which his prescriptions are being implemented is unknown, clearly his piece gives important insight on the corporate executive view of nonprofit organizations.

In different ways many of the early pieces in the volume emphasize how role expectations affect board and organizational performance. Virtually every board manual specifies the desirability of clear, unambiguous role expectations for board members. Job descriptions, orientations and board retreats almost always include efforts to develop and clarify expectations. However, much descriptive research finds uncertainty and confusion about what board membes are *really* expected to do. The next three pieces all address issues of expectations. Robert Leduc and Stephen Block, utilizing Mintzberg's (1973) work on managerial roles, suggest a process for helping boards and executives sort out who will do what in each managerial role. A larger point, implicit in their article, is that a written or spoken formulation may be useful, but it is seldom sufficient. Expectations are probably never settled once and always. Expectations must be refined and sometimes modified as people and circumstances change. Thus, while very basic expectations, for example, about attendance at board meetings, level of financial contribution, if any, and service on committees should be clearly specified and accepted, clarifying and agreeing on expectations is a process and requires frequent attention.

As much research makes clear, nonprofit board members are largely dependent on the organization's chief executive for most of their information about the organization. What kinds, how much and in what forms information should be provided to board members has long been a challenge for nonprofit executives. It has been suggested that nonprofit executives sometimes have adapted a strategy of information overload, sending board members highly detailed reports, background papers and the like. Since few board members have the time and inclination to read it all, though they may be reluctant to admit it, the board approves courses of action without real consideration of the information relevant to the course of action. Alternatively, a chief executive may provide brief reports, but which lack context, comparison and trend characteristics. Barry Bader, in a very useful piece that has circulated in photocopies, provides very specific and easily applied advice on the kind of management information boards want and need. Though written explicitly for hospitals, the examples are broadly generalizable.

Standards of sound management practices are yet to be fully developed and widely accepted by professional associations of nonprofit managers and academic institutions with programs in nonprofit management education, though there are signs of movement in that direction. The piece by the late Terry McAdam and David Gies, in effect, provides an initial specification of such standards. The piece presents a list of questions that board members, or prospective board members, should expect information about. The actions required of board members and executives to fully answer these questions will substantially advance achievement of clear and mutually understood expectations. Answering the questions will also advance good management practice in most nonprofit organizations.

The inclusion of minorities on nonprofit boards has long represented a challenge to the picture some advocates of the voluntary sector have sketched as a place of diversity and social innovation. Apparently, almost all nonprofit organizations endorse the ideal of demographic diversity for their boards of directors. The board profiles frequently used by organizations to assess current board strengths and weaknesses typically include racial or ethnic categories. Nonetheless, blacks and other minorities seem to be highly under-represented on most nonprofit boards. A second piece by Candace Widmer contains revealing data about black membership on boards, on how black board members are recruited, who they are, and what stresses they experience on nonprofit boards. Widmer's piece also raises questions about why black people have not been included to a greater extent on nonprofit boards and offers some useful suggestions about ways of enhancing black (and other minority) participation.

Board-staff relations is a frequent topic in most training manuals and workshops. Board-staff relations usually seem to be considered almost exclusively as board-chief executive relations. Indeed, in many nonprofit organizations only the chief executive has important, non-ceremonial interaction with the board. There is apparently a widespread view that "the chain of command" requires that other employees have limited access to the board. Gary Baker's contribution details a different way of organizing board-staff relations. At the Crittenton Center staff (other than the chief excutive) have equal, *voting* representation on important board committees (perhaps the committees should be called organizational committees). Two joint board-staff committees were instrumental in developing a highly innovative and successful participatory-incentive program. Baker's piece both describes the work of the board-staff committees and the operation of the performance-benefit plan the committees created. One of the key features of the performance-benefit plan is the use of a "Trust Committee" (the committee which evaluates the nominations of employees for awards for exceptional performance). The Trust Committee is composed of two board members, the chief executive and two employees elected by their fellow employees. Thus, the plan has been created and is implemented through a participatory board-staff process. The performance-benefit program at Crittenton is a wonderful illustration of non-zero sum (or "win-win") participatory process. Both the board and staff have enhanced their influence in organizational decision-making with concomitant increases in commitment to the organization and its programs. While several of the pieces in this collection call attention to the gap between ideal and reality, Baker's piece, and the process at Crittenton, provide encouraging evidence that nonprofit boards, working closely with those with a central interest in an organization, can creatively contribute to organizational functioning.

This collection combines two important endeavors. First, in various pieces evidence about the behavior and performance of nonprofit boards is reviewed and important additional evidence is presented. Board functions, behaviors and performance have received relatively little research attention. Most of what we "know" about nonprofit boards is based on experience. Much of what has been published is chiefly prescriptive. My judgment is that sometimes the prescriptions are insufficiently attentive to the realities of why boards behave as they usually do and that exhortation and training are unlikely to change those realities. Noting the disparity between reality and widely-accepted beliefs is a long and necessary role for empirical researchers. Such a role, however, is seldom satisfying or useful for practitioners. Thus, the second endeavor in this collection is to present useful and *realistic* ideas and techniques for improving board functioning and board-staff relations. Nearly all the pieces have implicit or explicit applications. In the final selection I attempt to assess the general trend in the pieces and argue for revising the prescriptive model that has long dominated our beliefs about what nonprofit boards do and should do. Though not all will agree with my analysis of why there is often a substantial gap between the ideal and the reality of board behavior nor with my suggestions for modifying the ideal, I hope it will spur advances in both analysis and practice.

I am sure that this collection contains some of the best writing on nonprofit boards. I wish to thank all the authors for their cooperation and I wish that each and every reader finds what she or he is looking for, and more, here.

REFERENCES

Domhoff, C. William
    1967   *Who Rules America?* Englewood Cliff, NJ: Prentice-Hall.
    1970   *The Higher Circles: The Governing Class in America.* New York: Random House.
    1975   "Social Clubs, Policy-Planning Groups and Corporations: A Network Study of Ruling-Class Cohesiveness." *Insrugent Sociologist* 5: 173-184.
Hodgkinson, Virginia A. and Murray S. Weitzman
    1986   *Dimensions of the Independent Sector: A Statistical Profile.* Washington, D.C.: Independent Sector.
Kramer, Ralph M.
    1965   "Ideology, Status, and Power in Board-Executive Relationships." *Social Work* 10: 108-114.

1983   "A Framework for the Analysis of Board-Executive Relationships in Voluntary
         Agencies," pp. 179-201 in F.S. Schwartz (ed.) *Voluntarism and Social Work Practice: A Growing Collaboration.* Lanham, MD: University Press of America.
1987   "Voluntary Agencies and the Personal Social Services," pp. 240-257 in Walter W.
         Powell (ed.) *The Nonprofit Sector: A Research Handbook.* New Haven, CT: Yale
         University Press.

Middleton, Melissa
1987   "Nonprofit Boards of Directors: Beyond the Governance Function," Pp. 141-153
         in Walter W. Powell (ed.) *The Nonprofit Sector: A Research Handbook.* New
         Haven, CT: Yale University Press.

Mintzberg, Henry
1973   *The Nature of Managerial Work*, New York: Harper and Row.

Nettler, Gwynn
1958-9   "Ideology and Welfare Policy," *Social Problems* 6: 203-211.

O'Connell, Brian
1976   *Effective Leadership in Voluntary Organizations.* Chicago: Association Press/Follett.
1985   *The Board Member's Book.* New York: Foundation Center.

Ostrander, Susan A.
1980   "Upper Class Women: The Feminine Side of Privilege," *Qualitative Sociology* 3
         (1) 23-44.

Perucci, Robert and Marc Pilisuk
1970   "Leaders and Ruling Elites: The Interorganizational Bases of Community Power."
         American Sociological Review 35: 1040-1057.

Pfeffer, Jeffrey
1973   "Size, Composition and Function of Hospital Boards of Directors: A Study of
         Organization-Environment Linkage." *Administrative Science Quarterly* 18:
         349-364.

Provan, Keith C.
1980   "Board Power and Organizational Effectiveness Among Human Service Agencies." *Academy of Management Journal* 23: 221-236.

Ratcliff, Richard E., Mary Elizabeth Gallagher, and Kathryn Strother Ratcliff
1979   "The Civic Involvement of Bankers: An Analysis of the Influence of Economic
         Power and Social Prominence in the Command of Civic Policy Positions." *Social
         Problems* 26: 298-313.

Salamon, Lester M.
1987   "Partners in Public Service: The Scope and Theory of Government-Nonprofit
         Relations," Pp. 99-117 in Walter W. Powell (ed.), *The Nonprofit Sector: A Research
         Handbook.*

Salzman, Harold and G. William Domhoff
1983   "Non-Profit Organizations and the Corporate Community." *Social Science History* 7: 205-216.

Savage, Thomas J.
1984   "Not-for-Profit Trusteeship: Salvaging the Myth." Paper presented at the Conference on Research on Volunteerism and Nonprofit Organizations, Blacksburg,
         VA.

Senor, James M.
1963   "Another Look at the Executive-Board Relationship." *Social Work* 8: 19-25.

Stein, Herman
1961   "Some Observations on Board-Executive Relationships in Voluntary Agencies."
         Journal of Jewish Communal Service 38: 390-396.

Useem, Michael
1979   "The Social Organization of the American Business Elite and Participation of
         Corporation Directors in the Governance of American Institutions." *American
         Sociological Review* 44: 553-577.

Walker, J. Malcolm
1983   "Limits of Strategic Management in Voluntary Organizations." *Journal of Voluntary Action Research* 12: 39-55.

Why Board Members Participate

Candace Widmer

In the United States all legally incorporated non-profit organizations are required to have boards of directors. The members of these boards are unpaid volunteers. This paper examines the reasons board members participate. A triad of data collection techniques—questionnaires, interviews, and observations—was used to study the members of the boards of directors of ten human service agencies. The study is based on an incentive approach to participation, which suggests that participation occurs in response to incentives, the expectation of valued outcomes. Four categories of incentives—material, social, developmental, and ideological—are used to organize the data. The study demonstrates that board members have multiple and complex incentives for participation, that some members achieve an adequate number of incentives and some do not, that few members participate in response to incentives that are dependent on specific policy outcomes and that even fewer serve as consumer representatives, and that there are differences among agencies in board members' reasons for serving. Implications for board recruitment and retention are discussed.

All legally incorporated non-profit organizations are required to have boards of directors. But who are these unpaid directors and why do they serve? These are two of the most basic questions that can be asked about citizen boards.[1] These questions were addressed in a study of the members of the boards of directors of ten human service agencies. A brief summary of the theoretical framework on which this research is based will first be presented. A description of the board members studied and data on members' incentives for participation will follow. Implications for board recruitment and retention and for consumer representation are discussed.

AN INCENTIVE APPROACH TO BOARD PARTICIPATION

Theories of motivation have been applied in a number of studies of participation. For example, needs theory was the theoretical framework for McKensie's (1981) study of involvement in school committees; equity theory was applied in MacNair's (1981) study of the agency-citizen relationship; and expectancy theory was the basis for Young's (1984) study of 4-H volunteers. Particularly useful in establishing the theoretical framework for this study has been Clark and Wilson's (1961) typology of organizational incentives, which analyzes incentives from an organizational perspective; Herzberg's (1959, 1976) distinction between satisfiers and dissatisfiers, which is analogous to the distinction between incentives and barriers; and expectancy valence theory (Nadler and Lawler, 1977), which underlines the importance of both the expectation and the value of incentives. Through the synthesis of data from a variety of sources, including those above, I have developed (and am developing) an incentive-barrier model of citizen involvement. (For a complete description of the model see Widmer, 1984.)

The Incentive-Barrier Model proposes that the motivation to participate in organization-initiated policy-making processes is a function of both incentives and barriers to participation. Incentives are those things which incite or motivate participation through the expectation of valued outcomes. Barriers are those things which obstruct participation. Barriers decrease motivation by reducing the expectation and/or value of outcomes.[2]

The incentive-barrier model proposes four incentives for participation. *Material incentives* are tangible rewards (funds, goods, or services) for one's self (or one's group) that are expected to result from participation. Material incentives include employment-related incentives such as the opportunity to work with an organization or agency that is related to one's work or profession; the chance to develop skills that will help one get or advance in a job; the opportunity to make professional contacts, to become "known"; and client-related incentives such as the opportunity to help insure that the board member or members of his or her family get the services they need from the agency. *Social incentives* are intangible rewards (friendship, status, honor) which are expected to be a consequence of associating with others in the participatory process. *Developmental incentives* are intangible personal rewards (the opportunity to use or acquire knowledge or to assume civic responsibilities) which are expected to accompany participation. *Ideological incentives* are intangible rewards (satisfaction, gratification) which are expected to accompany efforts to achieve goals which do not directly benefit the participant but which rather result from working toward "something one believes in." These incentives provide the conceptual framework for the data presented here.

THE STUDY

The incentive-barrier model was applied to a study of 98 members of ten human service agency boards of directors. The agencies were located in central New York State and were selected to differ in type of service, client population, source of funding, and size of staff, board, and budget.

A triad of data collection techniques—questionnaires, interviews, and observation—was employed. The questionnaire consisted of three parts: Why do you serve on this board? What do you do as a member of the board of directors? Who are you? The interviews followed a similar format, but more open-ended questions were used. Questionnaires were mailed to ten members selected randomly from each of the ten boards. The rate of return of the questionnaires was 69%. Three members of each board were interviewed. Meetings of five of the ten boards were observed.

RESULTS

The Participants

The respondents in this study ranged in age from 20 to 77 years of age; 75% were between the ages of 30 and 54. Eighty-eight percent of the board members had at least four years of college; over half had graduate or professional degrees. Forty-three percent of the board members had incomes in excess of $40,000. There were no secretaries, mechanics, retail salespersons, factory workers, or farmers among these board members. Most were well-paid professionals. More than three-quarters owned their own homes. The majority were married and had children.

These board members were active citizens: 95% reported that they voted regularly; 90% had attended a public hearing; 50% considered themselves part of a social movement; 71% had served on other boards.

The literature indicates that citizens who participate have higher incomes, more education, and better jobs, and that is true of the board members here. These board members are "complete activists" (Verba and Nie, 1972) in every regard. They were active in all facets of community life, and they come disproportionately from upper status groups.[3]

Not all board members were the same, of course, and neither were all boards. Some boards were made up primarily of younger, less-established individuals, while others consisted mainly of older, wealthier, more well-established community members. The differences among boards appear to be related in part to the way board members were recruited and in part to the incentives which motivated participation.

Why They Participated

Board members in this study were asked not only why they participated, but also who first talked with them about joining the board, why they joined, what they wanted to accomplish, and how they've benefited. All of these questions were designed to get at the motives of participants. Each of these questions will be discussed below.[4] More general observations and conclusions will follow.

Question: "Who first talked with you about your willingness to serve on this board?"

A large number of board members, 43%, reported that they talked first with a friend on the board. This finding is consistent with work reviewed by Milbrath. In writing of the transition from "spectator" to "gladiator" Milbrath states: "A person needs an extra strong push from the environment (e.g., earnest solicitation from a friend) or needs to feel very strongly about an issue or a candidate" (Milbrath, 1965:20). A newsletter on citizen participation published by the Mountaineers for Rural Progress puts it this way: "People work for people first, and causes second."

But people work not only for friends, but also, apparently, for agency staff or their own employers. Seventeen percent of the board members were asked to join the board by the staff or the director of the agency. Six percent of the board members were asked to join by their employer or supervisor. In a few cases board membership was simply "part of the job."

Question: "Why did you join this board?"

Most responses to this question fell into a limited number of categories.

Many people joined to serve the community. Half of the board members gave "altruistic" reasons for joining the board. Nineteen mentioned community service or civic duty as reasons for joining. In a number of cases board members indicated that they felt an obligation or responsibility to serve.

"Felt an obligation to give something of myself."
"Feeling or responsibility to do some public service."

Ten board members noted that they participated, at least in part, because they "thought they could help." Eighteen board members wrote or spoke of the value of the agency and its services, or the needs of its clients. Twelve board members mentioned an "interest" in the agency or its issues.

"It represented the type of organization I'm interested in."
"I was interested in the work of the group."
"I'm interested in the workings of the agency."

"Interest" can, however, represent concern or fascination. It is a term used often by both participants and writers on participation. Danaceau (1975) writes of "interest or concern," Lauffer and Gorodizky (1977) speak of the "interest or commitment" of volunteers, and Hartogs and Weber (1974) report that 81% of the board members in their study had a "strong interest in community service." It seems likely that in most cases the interest expressed by the board members in this study represents concern, but in some cases it may reflect curiosity. Interest in "the work of the board" is different than interest in "the workings of the board."

There is a much larger problem in interpreting this data, however, than confusion over the word "interest." The entire category of "altruistic" reasons is problematic. Altruism is generally considered to be concern for others as opposed to concern for self. The "desire to contribute to the community" sounds like an altruistic reason, but what about "felt an obligation" to contribute"? Do these statements represent the same motive? Do some people volunteer in order to relieve themselves of a sense of obligation, as Sills (1957) has suggested? Is this altruism?

Some joined because of their beliefs or ideology. While many board members were apparently motivated by a belief in the importance of community service, others believed not just in service or the good of the agency, but in a political ideology that influenced their decision to serve. When asked why they joined, seven board members spoke of causes and commitments.

"[I wanted] to give my time and energy to a cause about which I feel very strongly. . . . to become more involved in the movement."
"[I have] a political-ethical commitment to use my social science constructively."

It is often difficult, however, to distinguish commitment to a program or an agency from commitment to an ideology or a movement. This is especially true when the agency is a "social movement organization."

Some joined because they had something they wanted to accomplish. Seventeen board members described their reasons for joining in terms of what they wanted to accomplish. Some joined in order to represent their agency, their geographic area, or "the man on the street." Some saw themselves as liaisons.

"[I joined] to act as a liaison between this agency and low income handicapped children in my community."
"[I joined] to provide a liaison to the academic community and the feminist movement."

Others saw themselves as advocates: "Poor people need strong advocates." Some had the interests of specific programs in mind, while others wanted to apply their skills to a specific agency problem.

Some reasons for joining had to do with the board members' employment. For some board members joining was simply "a part of the job" or "in the job description." One explained that looking out for the interests of his agency required that he serve on this board. Another wrote that he joined "per supervisor's request." In other cases, the work of the agency was closely related to the work of the board member.

"The agency is directly related to my work, and its strength benefits my program."
"[I joined] to learn about local services in this area and thought it would be helpful to the agency I was in."

In still other cases, the work of the agency was not directly related to the employment of the board member, but service on the board was expected to benefit the member in his or her work life. There were some professionals and small business people who thought board membership might be useful. One reported: "It's good for me to be associated with this group, to be known in the community." Altogether, sixteen of the board members said their work had something to do with their joining the board.

Some board members had social reasons for joining. Twenty-two board members gave social reasons for joining the board. Four board members joined, at least in part, because they were honored to be asked. Four joined to meet people; two of these had recently moved to the community. Four others joined because they already knew board or staff members and liked or respected them. Three board members reported that they joined because they were asked by friends. Two of these friends were the executive directors of the agencies.

Seven board members in this study mentioned the need to "be involved" as a reason for joining the board. The "desire for involvement" (CAP, 1969) and the "satisfaction of involvement" (Lourden and Zusman, 1975) have been previously reported as incentives for participation.

Some joined for reasons of personal development. Some board members joined for reasons that involved neither friends nor jobs, but the desire to develop personally: to learn, to use skills and experience, to grow.

"I joined as a learning experience for myself."
"[It was] a chance to see how human service agencies function and a chance to exercise business experience."
"It's an excellent way to help the community and it's a growing experience for me personally."

Some board members joined because they or members of their families were or had been clients. Six of these board members were "repaying the agency."

"Joining the board was an opportunity to serve an agency that had been involved with my family."
"It gives me the opportunity to contribute . . . to services . . . which have been of enormous assistance to me and many others."

But not all clients or family members of clients joined to repay the agency, and not all human service professionals joined because of their jobs. The characteristics of board members are only clues to their motives. Incentives cannot always be deduced from characteristics.

Question: "Is there anything specific you want to accomplish in serving on this board?"

Forty-two percent of the board members indicated that they had no specific goals in serving on the board; 58% replied that they had goals. Most of these were service and management goals. Six percent of the board members stated advocacy goals.

"To reduce the stigma still attached to treatment for mental illness."
"To make sure the interests and rights of the juveniles we serve are protected."

Three percent expressed goals for changes in the agencies' operations or services that were based on political ideology.

"To have feminist concerns be a part of the way social services are provided."
"To 'dehierarchize' the agency."

Question: "Has participation on this board benefited you in any way?"

Board members in this study were asked if they had benefited by participation and how they had benefited. Their responses are summarized in Table 1. These benefits may or may not have been incentives for participation. Benefits are valued outcomes, but they may or may not have been expected. When asked if he'd benefited, one board member replied with a grin, "Oh, yes. I met my lover. That was an unexpected benefit." Unexpected benefits are not incentives, but they may increase expectations of valued outcomes from subsequent participation.

TABLE 1
Benefits to Board Members

BENEFIT	BOARD MEMBERS (%)
Have not benefited	13
Job-related benefits	15
Social benefits	29
Learning benefits	50
Personal satisfaction and development benefits	24

Thirteen percent of the board members responded that they had not benefited or were unsure if they had benefited. The remaining board members reported one or more benefits. Fifteen percent of the board members reported professional or job related benefits. They said that they had developed administrative or management skills, that they had made valuable professional contacts, and that they had a better understanding of local government, other human service agencies, and the community. One human service professional felt that he had gained recognition from professional colleagues. Another believed that interagency communication had improved. One human service agency director said participation on the board "reminded me of funding sources my own agency had not applied for." Three members responded that board service "looks good on a resume."

Twenty-nine percent of the board members reported social benefits.

"Have a sense of involvement and enjoy working with different kinds of people."
"It has introduced me to a group of people I like and admire."
"Benefits are relationships with staff and other board members, particularly as I had just moved to town."

Half of all the board members said that they had benefited through learning something.

"I'm learning what it takes to implement ideas."
"I've learned how to deal head to head with people with whom I have no values in common."
"I've seen board members whose skills I've admired and I learn from them."

Two ideologically motivated board members saw this as a chance to practice their ideology. One wrote: "It has provided me with an outlet for living my personal convictions and politics."

Five board members benefited through accomplishing specific goals. One had gotten involved in the local community as he had hoped he would, another had made the contacts she wished, and a third felt that she had been an effective advocate. Two board members reported increased self-esteem.

"Learning I'm good at this has been a boost for my self-esteem."
"It's gratifying—an ego trip."

Nine board members noted a sense of accomplishment, of helping or of being useful.

"It makes me feel useful—that I'm doing some good."
"Satisfaction of helping."
"Paying my dues to society."

Six board members found board membership stimulating and implied that participation broadened their world.

"It's been an education in how boards function and operate—quite foreign to my world."
"It 'rounds out' my life and experiences in a way that my job cannot."

One board member described the personal developmental benefits quite eloquently: "it's a good feeling. I'm a better person, more sensitive, a more mature adult. The results are intrinsic."

REASONS FOR PARTICIPATION

The questionnaire sent to board members listed a number of "reasons people participate on boards" and asked respondents to indicate on a scale of 1 to 4 (1 - not a reason; 4 - a major reason) which were reasons they now served on the board. The results of this question are summarized by category in Table 2.[5]

As is evident, different reasons were rated differently by board members. Some of the reasons, particularly those representing "altruistic" incentives, were highly rated by most of the board members. Some of the reasons, especially employment-related incentives, were not incentives for the majority of board members, but were important reasons for the participation of at least some board members. And some of the reasons were highly rated by only a few board members, but were moderately rated by most. (The latter appeared to be "supporting" or secondary incentives for participation.) In general, the data indicate that board members recognize more than one incentive for their participation.

Board members filling out the questionnaire were given the opportunity also to state their reasons for serving in their own words. The reasons these board members stated were the same as or elaborations of reasons, incentives, and benefits described in answers to other questions. There were no *new* reasons for participation uncovered. Several of the board members responding in their own words stressed that they served for more than one reason. Some typical responses are:

"[This] is an agency whose goals I support, whose area of concern is similar to my own area of work and where I can both contribute to and benefit from public service."
"I believe in the work [the agency] is doing, and they wanted to use the talents and abilities I have to offer. I was also influenced by the business-like approach to the work of the board. They don't waste my time."
"This agency has provided very crucial services for my child . . . Beyond this, I have some skills . . . which I believe, can help this agency use their . . . resources in a better manner."

TABLE 2
Board Members' Reasons for Participating by Category of Incentives

	Rating 1	2	3	4	Mean Rating*
MATERIAL INCENTIVES	NUMBER OF BOARD MEMBERS				
Employment-Related Incentives					
e. The organization, agency, or company I work for encourages me to serve on this board.	50	7	6	6	1.5
j. The agency or organization I work for has an interest in the work of this board.	38	12	9	10	1.9
m. I feel that the skills or experience I can get by participating will help me get a job or advance in my present job.	53	8	7	1	1.4
o. I work in a related field and feel that it is important for my work to serve on this board.	35	15	5	14	2.0
Client-Related Incentives					
b. I want to make sure that I and/or my family receive the services we need from this agency.	61	5	1	2	1.2
SOCIAL INCENTIVES					
d. I like to get out and meet people and participation on this board gives me the chance to do that.	22	25	13	9	2.1
g. I like the members of this board and enjoy spending time with them.	15	30	17	7	2.2
l. I have friends on this board and participation gives us the opportunity to work together.	46	11	9	3	1.6
r. I feel that participation on this board is a good opportunity to make new friends.	38	21	7	3	1.6

"I have a lot to offer—skills that human service agencies often lack—and I get a lot out of it at the same time because I can stay involved in issues and with people that are very important to me."
"Serving on the board gives me the opportunity to both grow personally and to make a significant contribution to the community."

SUMMARY OF RESULTS BY CATEGORY OF INCENTIVE

All of the responses discussed above may be summarized and discussed by type of incentive.

TABLE 2 (cont.)

	1	2	3	4	Mean Rating*
	NUMBER OF BOARD MEMBERS				

DEVELOPMENTAL INCENTIVES

	1	2	3	4	Mean Rating*
a. I feel that participation on this board helps me to develop more fully as a person.	18	24	20	7	2.2
f. I feel that I can learn new things by serving on this board.	3	15	38	13	2.9
h. I feel that this is a job I can do that uses the skills, training, or experience that I have.	5	5	28	31	3.2
t. I feel that participation on this board gives me the opportunity to develop new skills.	16	20	20	13	2.4

"SERVICE INCENTIVES"

Belief in Work of Agency

	1	2	3	4	Mean Rating*
c. I want to contribute to the important work this agency does in our community.	2	6	24	37	3.4
k. I want to support the goals of this agency.	2	7	23	37	3.4

Belief in Service/Civic Duty

	1	2	3	4	Mean Rating*
n. I want to help provide services for those less fortunate than I.	8	10	28	23	3.0
p. I consider it my civic duty to participate in community work.	10	16	27	16	2.7

*In looking at these data it is important to note that comparing incentives by mean ratings alone is likely to be misleading. Reasons may have similar mean ratings, but the distribution of the ratings may be quite different. It should also be noted that many of the reasons are related; e.g., meeting people ("d") is very similar to making friends ("r"). Respondents may have selected one or both as reasons they participate.

Material incentives

Both employment-related and client-related incentives are considered material incentives in this model. Employment-related benefits were reported by 15% of the board members. Employment-related incentives were rated as the most important reason for participation by 12% of the board members. Some of the board members with employment-related incentives had jobs that were unrelated or only marginally related to the work of the agency. These board members were likely to have other incentives as well. But some board members were motivated almost exclusively by employment-related incentives. Milbrath suggests that such participants may care less than participants who see participation as a leisure time activity whether or not participation is enjoyable and satisfying (Milbrath, 1965: 70). Indeed, those board members who considered board membership a part of their jobs made little mention of other benefits or incentives. There were few clients on these boards, and only four of them mentioned client-related incentives. None mentioned client-related benefits.

Although they have been included in the same category, client-related incentives and employment-related incentives are very different, and they have very different implications for policy-making processes. Those who participate at least in part to assure themselves, their families or their groups of services, function as consumer representatives. There were few consumer representatives among these board members. Those who participated to attain employment-related incentives were, in most cases, individuals who were employed by related agencies. Such individuals function in a more or less professional capacity and their participation increases professional rather than client control over agency policy.

Social incentives

In this study board members reported both social benefits and social incentives. Twenty-nine percent of the board members listed some social benefit. Not one board member, however, considered a social incentive the most important reason he or she participated, but 86% of the board members rated at least one social incentive a reason to participate. Social incentives are, apparently, important supporting or secondary reasons for participation. (Or social incentives are perceived as less socially acceptable incentives and are therefore not rated as primary incentives.) Most of the board members were friends or at least acquainted with others on their board. More than half of the board members first talked with someone they knew about joining the board. More than three-quarters see other board members socially at least occasionally.

Developmental incentives

Half of the board members in this study described benefits that involved learning. A quarter reported other personal satisfaction and developmental benefits. All of the board members rated at least one developmental incentive of some importance. Seventeen percent of the board members considered a developmental incentive the most important reason they participated. Developmental incentives were either a primary or a secondary incentive for *all* of the board members in this study.

Ideological incentives

Although there were no "ideological reasons" for respondents to rate, some board members indicated ideological incentives. Seven reported ideological reasons for joining. Three stated ideological goals. For these board members ideological incentives seemed quite important. Indeed, some of the least satisfied board members were those who found that their political, social or economic beliefs were not widely shared by others on their boards.

"Service incentives"

Those reasons for participating that I have labeled "service incentives" (see Table 2) were clearly important reasons for many board members. Only one board member did not include an incentive of this type among his reasons for participating. But board members "serve" for a number of reasons. Some board members appear to serve in order to reduce a sense of obligation or repay a debt to society or to the agency. Others seem to accept a role of community service as a given in their lives. Upper class consciousness (see Ostrander, 1980) or socialization may include this sense of responsibility to the less privileged. This "noblesse oblige" may be related to group and self-interest in maintaining order and stability in the society. Other participants, as noted above, serve, at least in part, in order to change the status quo. Still others appear to serve out of the sort of broad self-interest that recognizes that the well-being of the community affects the well-being of the individual. Finally, citizens seem to serve because their self-image or their community-image requires it of them. Reinhold Niebuhr suggested over fifty years ago: "Man's devotion to this community always means the expression of a transferred egotism as well as of altruism" (cited in Sheehy, 1981: 271).

Board members "serve," it appears, because service leads to valued secondary outcomes. This is reflected in the qustionnaire data by the fact that no board members in the study reported only "altruistic" reasons for serving. These secondary outcomes may in turn be categorized as material, social, developmental, and ideological incentives.

CONCLUSIONS AND DISCUSSION

Board members were motivated to serve by complex material, social, developmental, and ideological incentives. Board member incentives were complex and varied. Many identified incentives from three or even four of the proposed categories. In addition, according to a number of participants, the reasons they joined the board were not the same as the reasons they continued to participate.

The complexity of participant incentives appears to contribute to the stability of participant motivation. Those who participated in response to a number of different incentives were less likely to encounter conditions that reduced the value or expectation of all desired outcomes. Multiple social and developmental incentives appeared to be the most stable. Those who participated in response to a single incentive (often an employment-related incentive) were likely to end their participation when that incentive was no longer operative.

Some incentives were more fragile than others. Ideological incentives appeared to be the most fragile. It is difficult for groups to maintain consensus on ideology and few do. Board members with ideological incentives often ended their participation when they felt that other board members were unreceptive and that the board was unresponsive to their beliefs. Some incentives (like joining "for a friend") were temporary; they did not provide ongoing rewards or ongoing participation.

Some board members achieved an adequate number of incentives and some did not. There were among these board members both happy and unhappy participants. Contented board members reported benefits from serving on the board and the accomplishment of personal objectives for board membership. Discontented board members reported few benefits, the failure to achieve desired objectives, and the inability to play desired roles. Although some happy participants reported unexpected benefits, which therefore could not have served as incentives, even these unexpected outcomes increase expectations for future rewards. The degree of satisfaction expressed by board members was dependent both on the degree of attainment of one or more incentives and on the expectation of continued rewards.

Boards should, it is clear, pay attention to incentives in their efforts to recruit and retain board members. Potential incentives should be made explicit to potential members. But because incentives are unique to each individual—what one considers a reward another may consider meaningless—incentives must be matched to the individual. (A retired executive, for example, is likely to be less interested than a young professional in developing "job skills".) Incentives must be more than promised, however, they must also be delivered. Board members will continue to serve only if the incentives which motivate them are being realized or if they have developed new incentives to participate. Boards should, when possible, make every effort to insure that members achieve the material, social, developmental and ideological incentives they seek.

Few board members participated in response to incentives that were dependent on specific policy outcomes. It is often assumed that citizens participate in order to influence policy and that consumer representation is an important role and a necessary check against the power of politicians and professionals. The incentives of board members in this study, however, were rarely dependent on specific policy outcomes; and, in most cases where participants favored particular policies or programs, they were not personally affected by them. Few of the participants in this study were consumers, and even fewer reported that they participated in the role of consumer representative. Citizen participation on human service boards of directors should not be considered a process of consumer input.

There were differences among the agencies in board members' reasons for serving. Although this study focused on the incentives of individual participants, there were obvious differences among the agencies studied. These agency differences appear to be related to the characteristics of both the agency and its board. A typology of boards based the primary incentives offered (similar to Clark and Wilson's (1961) typology of organizational incentives), is suggested by the data. Some of the agencies studied, particularly those which work closely with other community agencies, had "bureaucratic boards" which offered primarily employment-related incentives. Most of the members of these boards were professionals and employees of other organizations which in some sense "did business" with the board agency. These boards tended to be fairly homogeneous in the status, income, and education of members. Recruitment was usually through professional rather than friendship networks. The meetings of bureaucratic boards were short and business-like. They were usually held during normal business hours.

Other agencies were highly ideological—a specific political, social, or economic ideology was part of the mission of the agency. These "activist boards" offered primarily ideological incentives, but developmental and social incentives were also important. Members of these boards mentioned few employment-related or "service" reasons for serving. Members of these boards were somewhat homogeneous in age, income, and education, and very homogeneous in values and beliefs. Friendship networks were important in the recruitment of board members. Members of activist boards had somewhat less experience with board participation and were less likely to vote and participate in "normal" community affairs than were members of other boards. The meetings of activist boards tended to be long, with frequent discussions of matters of principle and ideology.

Still other agencies had boards whose members served primarily in response to social and developmental incentives. These "volunteer boards" provided members with the opportunity to fulfill their "civic obligations." Within a specific volunteer board, members tended to be homogeneous in social status, but heterogeneous in age and occupation. There were large differences among these boards in the social status and board experience of members. Recruitment for volunteer boards was through friendship networks. Meetings of these boards were usually in the evening, involved at least some socializing, and tended to be somewhat ritualistic, that is, there was little disagreement among board members over the issues and actions taken.

Although "bureaucratic," "activist," and "volunteer" boards are types, these types help to explain the complex matching process that is essential for "motivated" board members.[6]

The incentive approach may be used by both practitioners and scholars. Why board members participate is a question of importance to practitioners and scholars alike. An incentive approach and the categories of incentives suggested here provide a "common language" for discussion of this question. The categories may also be used by practitioners to increase a board's awareness of the incentives the board offers and the incentives each member or potential member seeks. The categories may be used by researchers to structure future studies of boards, as well as other types of citizen participation, and to classify and compare existing data.

NOTES

Support for this research was received from the College Grants Committee, College of Human Ecology, Cornell University.
1. Trecker (1970), Zusman (Lourden and Zusman, 1975) and Conrad and Glenn (1976) all make some useful observations about the work of nonprofit boards and the motivations of board members, but Hartogs and Weber's (1974) study of boards of voluntary hospital, health, and welfare organizations is, however, one of the few empirical studies available. For a detailed review of the literature see Widmer, 1984.
2. The conceptual model includes barriers to participation and the functions and roles of participants. These parts of the model and the supporting data are beyond the scope of this paper.

3. It is important to keep in mind, however, that motivation is not the only factor determining board participation. Unlike some forms of participation (e.g. voting, attending public hearings) participants are not wholly self-selected. Both the individual and the board decide who participates.
4. The quotes in this section are from both the oral and written responses of board members.
5. The reasons were not arranged by category on the questionnaire. The letter preceding each statement indicates the original order of the reasons. There were no reasons included that represented ideological reasons. This would have required a large number of specific statements.
6. It is important to remember also that incentives are realized, not theoretically, but within a specific environment that is determined not only by the type of organization, but also by the characteristics and actions of all the members of that organization. Thus, for example, a board member who is motivated by a desire to serve the community, to achieve status, to meet new people, and to use his skills, may serve on a number of boards. Indeed, there are board members who resemble this description on almost every board studied. But the board on which a specific individual will realize these incentives must serve the community in a manner he considers appropriate, must consist of board members who can confer status on him and whom he considers "worth meeting," and must provide tasks that require his skills. Furthermore, whether this individual achieves his incentives or not, his participation on the board will affect the incentives of others. His social status, for example, may affect the social status of the board and thus the social incentives of other members; his values and beliefs may agree or conflict with those of other board members and thus affect their ideological incentives; and so on. Each member affects the incentives and roles of every other member; each member affects the manner in which the board functions; and as each member changes in response to his or her experiences both on the board and beyond, these changes also affect every other participant. The result is a dynamic state of continual adjustment and constant change.

REFERENCES

CAP
    1969   "Mobilization of Non-Poor Volunteers in Community Action," Community Action Program, Office of Economic Opportunity. OEO Guidance, 6015-1.
Clark, Peter B. and James Q. Wilson
    1961   "Incentive Systems: A Theory of Organizations." Administrative Science Quarterly. 6: 129-166.
Conrad, William R., Jr. and William E. Glenn
    1976   The Effective Voluntary Board of Directors. Chicago: Swallow Press.
Danaceau, Paul
    1975   Consumer Participation in Health Care: How it's Working. Arlington, Virginia: Human Service Institute for Children and Families, Inc.
Etzioni, Amitai
    1968   The Active Society. New York: The Free Press.
Ggaser, Barney G. and Anselm L. Strauss
    1967   The Discovery of Grounded Theory. Chicago: Aldine.
Hartogs, Nelly and Joseph Weber
    1974   Boards of Directors. Dobbs Ferry, New York: Oceana.
Herzberg, Frederick et al.
    1959   The Motivation to Work (2nd edition). New York: John Wiley and Sons.
Herzberg, Frederick
    1976   The Managerial Choice. Homewood Illinois: Dow Jones - Irvin.
Koontz Harold
    1967   The Board of Directors and Effective Management. New York: McGraw Hill.
Lauffer, Armand and Sarah Gorodizky
    1977   Volunteers. Beverly Hills: Sage
Langton, Stuart
    1978   Citizen Participation in America. Lexington, Massachusetts: Lexington.
Lourden, J. Keith and Jack Zusman
    1975   The Effective Director in Action. New York: AMACOM.
MacNair, Ray H.
    1975   "Citizen Participation as a Balanced Exchange: An Analysis and Strategy," Journal of the Community Development Society. 12 (1): 1-19
McKensie, W.M.
    1981   "Citizen Participation—What Motivates It?", Australian Journal of Social Issues. 16 (1): 67-69.

Milbrath, Lester W.
    1965   *Political Participation*. Chicago: Rand McNally.
Milbrath, Lester W. and M.L. Goel
    1977   *Political Participation* (2nd Edition). Chicago: Rand McNally.
Nadler, David A. and Edward E. Lawler
    1977   "Motivation: A Diagnostic Approach," in Richard M. Steers and Lyman W. Porter
           (1979), *Motivation and Work Behavior* (2nd. edition). New York: McGraw Hill, 216-229.
Nie, Norman H., G. Bingham Powell, Jr. and Kenneth Prewitt
    1969   "Social Structure and Political Participation: Developmental Relationships, Part I and
           II." American Political Science Review. 63: 361-378, 808-832.
Ostrander, Susan A.
    1980   "Upper-Class Women: Class Consciousness as Conduct and Meaning", in G. Wil-
           liam Domhoff (1980), *Power Structure Research*. Beverly Hills: Sage, 73-96.
Sheehy, Gail
    1981   *Pathfinders*. New York: William Morrow and Company.
Wills, David L.
    1957   *The Volunteers*. Glencoe, Illinois: The Free Press.
Smith, D.H., Jacqueline Macaulay and Associates.
    1980   *Participation in Social and Political Activities*. Washington: Jossey-Bass.
Trecker, Harleigh B.
    1970   *Citizen Boards at Work*. New York: Associated Press.
Verba, Sidney and Norman H. Nie
    1972   *Participation in America*. New York: Harper and Row.
Widmer, Candace
    1984   "An Incentive Model of Citizen Participation Applied to a Study of Human Service
           Agency Boards of Directors." Cornell University, Unpublished doctoral disseration.
Young, Robert
    1984   "An analysis of 4-H Volunteer Expectancees and Outcomes in Relation to Motivation
           and Turnover." Paper presented at the conference on Research on Volunteerism and
           Nonprofit Organizations, Association of Voluntary Action Scholars Meeting,
           Blacksburg, Virginia.

Dominant Class Culture and Legitimation: Female Volunteer Directors

Lucille Covelli

Female volunteer directors are largely drawn from affluent professional and corporate families. Their role in the reproduction of the upper class has been overlooked by studies of class culture and class legitimation. This study argues that women who take on community leadership roles (volunteer directorships in particular) are motivated to do so because of class cultural incentives: noblesse oblige, duty to community and prestige. These combine with incentives for personal achievement in ways which, at once, serve to reproduce upper class prerogatives for community leadership roles and maintain the volunteer board status quo.

The role of female volunteer directors generally, and the part played by upper class women specifically, has been overlooked by studies of class culture and class legitimation. The literature on power, class, and community and national power structures takes as its subject men who dominate the corporate sector and corporate boards (Allen, 1974; Domhoff, 1970; Higley, et al., 1979; Clement, 1975; Useem, 1978, 1979). These high profile men also take on prestigious community leadership roles. They head up large fund-raising committees, chair influential university and hospital boards, make large donations and are instrumental in garnering large donations from contacts in the corporate sector (Ross, 1952, 1953). They also provide legal, financial and other expertise, which is necessary for the formulation of organization policy and programming (Cohen, 1960; McDougall, 1976; Hartogs and Weber, 1974). Indeed volunteer board service is viewed as the testing ground of promising young executives (Ross, 1965).

With regard to upper class women, we know (from the society pages) that they organize parties, dinners and gala events; that they serve on smaller, often less prestigious boards (Babchuk et al., 1960; Ross, 1958; Moore, 1969); and that they do direct service work, for example, pushing carts around hospitals, operating thrift shops or organizing door-to-door canvasses for various annual funding drives (Burke, 1960; Gold, 1971; Frankel, 1965). Rarely do we hear about, or think to study the female volunteer who has literally made a career out of volunteer board service (Gray, 1981).

This study argues that women who take on community leadership roles are motivated to do so for the same reasons as their high profile male counterparts: first, to satisfy the demands of their dominant class culture and second, to legitimate their socially privileged positions. The purpose of this paper is to describe how women's class cultural incentives for participation—noblesse oblige, duty to community and prestige—combine with incentives for personal achievement and community leadership roles as a dominant class prerogative in the reproduction of class and the volunteer board's status quo. An analysis of women's entrance to volunteer boards, their expectations of contributing time, their sense of family tradition, commitment to a "community" and noblesse oblige, reveals the dominant class culture which prepared them for participation in voluntary sector work. In addition, female volunteers are likely to have post-secondary education and have developed expertise in decision-making, writing and speaking skills and expertise in areas of specific importance to voluntary agencies (e.g., day care, elderly care, fund raising, corrections, the arts). Thus, volunteer directorships offer women, who do not have full-time careers, an avenue for personal growth (Maxwell and Maxwell, 1971). Working with professional people at the level of policy development is an opportunity that many would not otherwise have.

The women's class membership is also an important element in their initial and subsequent membership on volunteer boards. Contact networks which supply names of potential board members, and the "selective" memberships of the Junior League, Imperial Order of Daughters of the Empire (IODE), and the women's committees of arts organizations, act to limit entrance to those from the upper class.

Less discussed but of equal importance to the personal growth and class cultural motivation for participation in voluntary organizations is the incentive for class legitimation and maintenance of the status quo. Community leadership roles in their overt helping of those in need also serve to publicize the "community spirit" of corporations and wealthy citizens. In this way the harsh profit motive of this class is softened (Domhoff, 1970), and the prerogative of the upper class to assume directorships is maintained.

This paper divides discussion of class and women's voluntary directorships into two parts. First, is a description of a sample of women who currently hold volunteer directorships, their background characteristics and class cultural incentives for participation on voluntary sector boards. Second, through an analysis of their opinions of staff and client participation on boards, I will suggest that the women do work to maintain the existing system of inequality, thereby preserving their privileged position and maintaining their class's supremacy. This they accomplish in their capacity as volunteer directors.

SAMPLE PROFILE

Sample Procedure

The sampling procedure consisted of interviewing an initial list of women who held multiple directorships in one large North American city's voluntary sector and, in subsequent interview phases, using a snowball sample technique to contact a wider group of women who had been suggested as likely respondents by the initial women interviewed. This strategy was used because the narrow focus of the research was upper class women's service on volunteer boards. The sociological literature on community leadership roles of upper class members (Clement, 1975; Domhoff, 1970; Higley, et al., 1979; Ross, 1952) documents the fact that volunteer directorships normally are given to those who can bring wider resources — in financial, legal, fund-raising and/or public relations expertise, and in contacts to others in the business community. While only a token number of women serve as directors in the corporate sector (Financial Post, 1977), there are many more women who serve on volunteer boards. These women are invited because of some use that can be made by the agency of the women's social contacts, direct service experience and fund-raising skills (Ostrander, 1976, 1980). The logical research sample was one which consisted of women who had acquired volunteer experience and who could speak to issues which are of concern to boards and generally discuss the involvement of women as volunteer directors.

A second sampling consideration was the existence of a prestige hierarchy wherein certain organizations—teaching hospitals, universities, certain social service agencies—are the domain of directors from the upper class, while other boards are dominated by individuals outside of this class. (Babchuk, et al., 1960; Moore, 1962, 1969). In order to obtain an initial (incomplete) list of women who were highly involved and prominent enough in the voluntary sector to serve on a high status board, over 100 of the largest of the city's organizations (assets) were contacted for a list of their directors between 1979 and 1981. Those women whose names appeared more than once were considered to hold multiple directorships: highly involved, experienced and in demand. Thirty-eight women made up this initial list, 33 of whom were eventually interviewed. A total of 67 interviews were eventually completed, the balance of which was obtained from suggestions offered by the first fifty women interviewed. They suggested 107 names, 24 of which appeared on the initial multiple directors list.

The Sample

At the outset, it is of interest to note the religious and ethnic background of the sample. Seventy-three percent of the women interviewed are of Anglo-English, Irish or Scottish origin, and 20% are Jewish. The sample also consists of four women from other ethnic groups: Chinese, German, Swiss and Latvian. In terms of religious affiliation, 61% were Protestant, 13% were Catholic and 20% were Jewish.

The women's age distribution is skewed toward an older age cohort: 87% (or 58) were between the ages of 50 and 79, while only 13% (9) of the women were between 35-49 years old. Of this older group of women, all had a bachelors degree and another 12 or 20% had graduate degrees: LLB, M.D., Ph.D.. Fifty-three percent of the sample also have attended private or separate schools.

Thus the interview data reflect the opinions of women who are highly involved and have had years of education and service on boards. A majority of the women first volunteered for direct service work when they were young adults, and with experience, moved to board service. By the age of 50, the women have at least 30 years of voluntary sector experience.

The occupational status of the women is important to note. Forty-two or 63% of the women are "career" volunteers, which contrasts with the 12 women who work full-time (six of whom are also corporate directors). Six of the women are currently retired and continue to participate on volunteer boards. The final seven women serve currently only as corporate directors. Thus 13 of the women interviewed have moved to the corporate sphere. For half of these women, at least part of their entry to corporate boards is the result of directorships in family enterprises. Two of the remaining six women were invited to serve as a result of volunteer director experience. The final four women are corporate directors as a direct result of their career as volunteers. Their experience includes service on at least one high status board—hospital, university, United Way or arts board—on which they have met and shown their talents to men who also serve on corporate boards.

The age and occupational distributions of this sample reflect the snowball technique which was used to contact women and their network of volunteer acquaintances. This sample also reflects the life expectations of a generation where home and family were central and where volunteer work provided the opportunity for adult company, intellectual stimulation and personal achievement. The upcoming generation of younger women will serve on boards in their own right as professionals able to provide legal and financial expertise, and contacts—combined with a family tradition of volunteering. This contrast is the subject of future research. The focus of this paper is those women who have had a wide experience in the voluntary sector, whose origins are at least the professional and corporate owner class.

The women's private school attendance suggests that their family of origin and of marriage have been at least middle class. This is verified through the occupations of the respondents' fathers and husbands. The majority of the occupations of the women's fathers involved professional and business careers. While many of their fathers were owners of their own companies, and/or were independent entrepreneurs (23 or 34%), or in upper level corporate management positions (7 or 10%), almost as many were professionals: lawyer, doctor, professor, engineer (26 or 39%). Only 11 (16%) had lower status occupations such as bookkeeper, transit operator, salesman, and carpenter.

The husband's occupations show status improvement. Only three of the husbands could be classified as having non-professional or non-corporate occupations. The sample tends to be consistent in inter-generational occupational status. Those women whose fathers were professionals or businessmen tended to marry men whose occupational status was similar.

VOLUNTEER BOARDS AND CLASS CULTURE

The majority of the women originate from at least upper middle class professional families and their family of marriage is equally high in status. It is chiefly from the ranks of this dominant class (of professionals and corporate businessmen) that men and women are drawn into volunteer directorships. They have the expertise needed by boards and the educational level to articulate policy and programming, and the social contacts to obtain funds and expertise where necessary.

What follows is a discussion of the class cultural incentives for participation in the voluntary sector articulated by the women during their interviews, and an analysis of the mechanisms for class legitimation surfacing from the women's comments. As with any small sample the analysis is a first step in a newer area of research, and necessarily raises more questions than it answers.

The women's understanding and awareness of the elements of upper class culture become immediately apparent in their comments on the 'personal' meaning of volunteer work, the unique aspects of being a volunteer director, the advantages and disadvantages of serving on multiple boards, and their initial involvement on boards. Most respondents commented that their participation was the result of a strong family tradition, a duty to community and a responsibility to return something to those who are not as privileged.

> It was a way of life in our family. It's partly an obligation just as I have to do for the family, I have to do for the community (No. 24)

> That's what life was about, to do something for the community. (No. 23)

> ... We were brought up with a sense of duty. We were all taught that because we were all fortunate we must put something back into the community. (No. 38)

> I was brought up with it. I was extremely privileged and I had to pay. It was a way of life. My father and mother and everyone was involved. (No. 25)

> You usually find that a family has a major commitment to service. You usually find that people are brought up in an atmosphere of trying to service those less fortunate than yourself. (No. 3)

Many women explained that they learned the tradition of volunteering from their families, or that it was instilled in private school. This role was acted upon through teenage volunteering and later, in direct service work through the Junior League and other women's training groups. Thirteen of the women stated that the reason for their invitation to a particular board was due to membership in the Junior League, which has the reputation of being an invitational organization, with an excellent international reputation for "turning out" trained volunteers. While the Junior League has been the premier volunteer organization for daughters of prominent Protestant families (whose membership until the mid-sixties was by invitation only), there also exist matching organizations in the Jewish and Roman Catholic communities. While it cannot be said that the Junior League excluded Catholic women (one of the Catholic respondents had League training), there was a general feeling among the Jewish respondents that it was not open to them. However, women who received training in religious-based organizations like the Catholic Women's League (CWL) and Hadassah or the National Council of Jewish Women, became presidents at the city-wide level and subsequently were recruited to serve on other boards.

During the interview, women discussed their reasons for becoming involved in the voluntary sector, their thoughts on its place in their lives and their own volunteer experience. From the outset, it became clear that a majority of the women would not otherwise have had the opportunity to participate in decision-making or policy issues if they had taken paying jobs. The following comments are suggestive of the generally held view that if the women had wanted to work, they lacked the formal qualifications to make it in business.

> If I went to get a job, they'd ask me what my qualifications are. I mix with people on boards that I wouldn't have otherwise come across. I'd probably be a filing clerk. (No. 54)

> . . . It's always changing, you're into policy changes and issues. . . . Another fact is that women who come onto agency boards do not have the training to get the jobs that they would be interested in. (No. 32)

> In the short time I've been doing board work, I've been working with a higher level of person than I would have if I had a paid job. If I have been ten years in the paid labour force I would not be at that level. (No. 33)

These comments reflect the advantages of the women's volunteer commitment. They have flexibility, which is important in raising a family, travelling or socializing with friends; and they have the opportunity to meet a wide variety of people, expand their network of friends and become involved in difficult policy issues, in a context that that is related to corporate and governmental spheres.

The women were also aware of the fact that the opportunity to serve on a board was limited to a specific few. They discussed the existence of a volunteer service network and used terms like clique and inner circle. This sample of women often became involved as a result of friendship obligations. In this regard, the women's self-reported reason for each of their directorships is instructive. Of the 417 directorships (over the past thirty years) 365 were the combined result of invitations by friends (100) and acquaintances (175), through the service network (87) and because their family had a tradition of service on a particular board (13). As an informal assessment of the importance of acquaintances and the volunteer service network as a means of "closure" to many boards, the following comments are instructive:

> You go to a board meeting and you think, "Oh my god, his sister-in-law would be perfect to do something." . . . We're always looking for bodies. But the most natural thing is if you know somebody. (No.7)

> It becomes a network system. That's really what happens. I wasn't unknown to [X organization] . . . It's very hard to take someone without knowing something about them. (No. 65)

> You learn a lot of what's going on in related organizations. It's quite incestuous too . . . and occasionally you wish to know who's going off [X board] so you can pick them up when their term is up. So there's a bit of a network out there (No. 25)

> You meet people and then when you need someone you call them; you must have a wide acquaintanceship. (No. 34)

One respondent was explicit in her assessment of the closed nature of many boards:

> I'm not unaware that it becomes a sort of, not exactly a clique, but it becomes an inner circle . . . [Y hospital board] is very heavily Anglo-Saxon. [This city] isn't that way anymore. . . . You tend to move in your own circles so you don't know a lot of people that are East Indian or anybody who would be comfortable and would feel at ease participating. (No. 8)

The final incentive for board participation is the prestige gained from invitations to serve on boards, particularly hospitals, universities and large welfare agencies. Clement (1975), Ross (1953) and Auerback (1961) have pointed out the importance of prestige for furthering a young executive's career, and the community recognition resulting from service on a socially prominent hospital or university board. For women, an invitation to a prestigious board seems to be equally important. The women work with top professionals and businessmen of the community. The women's comments reflect the importance of prestige as an incentive:

> Some get on for this. They work out, in fact, maybe even better—for their egos and a sense of accomplishment—they show the organization what they can do... I know many people who are actively seeking a spot on a hospital board. They feel they've made it in government for example and they want to make it in the voluntary sector. (No. 29)

> Being a chairman of a teaching hospital is a very prestigious job. You are selected onto these boards for your business experience, social connections and financial connections. (No. 1)

> When someone asks you to be on [X board, a prestigious child welfare agency], it's an ego boost. It makes you feel good inside. But there's no glamour. There may be a little prestige. (No. 31)

> I feel some people are on boards because having their name on them is useful and there are certain boards where they are not called upon to do anything, only to rubber stamp. Very often I see when husbands and wives are members they don't usually come together at the same time. Sometimes the husbands are there in name only because they are people of power and prestige, money. But usually where there is a husband and wife, it is the wife who will be the active one, and the husband will lend the name. (No. 46)

Thus the class culture of volunteer participation concomitantly provides incentives for participation—noblesse oblige, family tradition, prestige—and ensures that community leadership roles are retained as a prerogative of this class, through service networks and friendship obligations.

CLASS LEGITIMATION

As discussed above, respondents are aware that opportunities for participation are limited. Several women suggested that change at the board level is also slow. Two women commented that boards are often limited to certain types of people and that their programs are slow to acknowledge change in the client population. The first respondent, a self-described token ethnic on a service agency board, stated:

> The board is 100 years old and has WASP ideas. It is only now discussing what front-line workers have known for years. The agency decides to do its own study. Now, five years later, there's still no movement. (No. 13)

The second respondent, then the president of the same agency stated:

We're very aware at the agency that we're not serving our immigrant population as effectively as we should. It's mainly because we're working out of our traditional Anglo-Saxon base and the programmes just don't work. (No. 31)

It must be emphasized that while the respondents and volunteer directors generally exhibit a willingness and enthusiasm to implement changes, the class prerogative for volunteering remains intact. The idea of staff and client participation was discussed by all the respondents. Underneath the prestige of volunteer boards is the notion of exclusivity and leadership. People invited to serve, in essence, are being recognized for past or potential community leadership ability (Zald, 1970). This incentive for leadership roles is directly linked to social legitimation of their class position.

The women were questioned about their relationship with paid professionals and whether volunteer directors represent the interests of a dominant socio-economic group. Responses in each area of questioning reflect their class-bred interest in community leadership roles. The women justify their service on boards, and the existence of volunteer boards in general, by emphasizing the role played by "community" volunteers.

The two areas of their involvement as volunteer directors—with paid professionals and client directors—speak directly to the legitimacy of the women's community leadership roles. The following comments are instructive of the symbiotic yet adversarial relationship between the agency's staff and volunteer board.

The levels of knowledge are different. The staff person has a day-to-day appreciation of the problems and services. The board takes a lot longer to come to this. However, the staff are often too close to see an overall broad perspective. (No. 44)

In all these things, there is public money being spent. Whether it's money you've raised or from government, it's your money and mine. My experience with paid staff is that they're primarily interested in their own area . . . and they therefore will spend. There has to be someone to watch it. There also has to be someone in the community to get money. (No. 38)

We have so much talent on our board you couldn't pay them their fees to sit on the board. Also they don't have an axe to grind. A paid person on a board may be protecting her/his own position. A volunteer, if she sees she doesn't like something, can always leave or fire the executive director. (No. 29)

You cannot operate a fund raising agency on behalf of a sensitive social service sector out there and not understand and interpret that sector to the donor, be sensitive to their needs, their worries about policy development. . . . You may have a strong professional staff and a good deal of the leadership, the nuances of what the community needs are . . . can only [be developed] if sections of the community are involved in it. (No. 47)

The qualities required for a successful board member coalesce in the dominant class personality—a willingness to serve, contacts for fund-raising, expertise and an arm's-length perspective. The women's discussion of their role in agency money management, funding and policy development reveals the thin line between community leadership as a tradition of service and maintaining the system where they retain control of these leadership opportunities. It is therefore reasonable for the women to emphasize, as they have done, the reasons for the importance of their role on voluntary agencies. By perpetuating the need for their participation on boards, the women legitimate their rights to these roles. Indeed, the characteristics of a system which suggest inclusion of certain persons for boards service reinforce the exclusion of others.

In the interviews the women were asked to comment on the suggestion that volunteer directors represent the interests of an upper socio-economic group. The majority of their answers focused on client participation on boards. The respondents agreed that the representativeness of the community at large is insufficient. One respondent explains the attitudes of volunteer boards:

> I do think that, for a long time, that particular sector of people with the best intentions in the world, thought that they had to speak on behalf of people who could not speak for themselves, the disadvantaged, so to speak. To a certain degree, I think it still holds true. But for a long time, it was thought that those clients didn't have a voice of their own. In fact, you never asked the client. (No. 32)

This respondent articulates what Noble (1979) characterizes as class practices that preserve the existing system of class relations. While this attitude is not as prevalent today, it has not totally disappeared. For example, the women of this small sample tended to justify their class prerogative for community leadership roles by outlining why clients were not commonly found on volunteer boards. The women described board work as generally needing people with:

- Specialized skills: legal, financial, and fund-raising.
- Effective speaking and writing styles to detail policy and act as mediator in governmental funding submissions.
- Expertise in social service areas, such as day-care, child welfare and the handicapped.

In addition to the skills required in board work, the women identified personal attributes which excuse clients' inability to participate. Four respondents, in particular, articulated the problems with client participation on boards:

> It's an educational problem. You bring someone on the board who has a limited education, even if they are very bright, they're being thrown among a circle of people who speak a different language, who take for granted a lot of values and hypotheses, that these people have never been exposed to. So people from lower SES are not comfortable; they don't know what the boards are talking about half the time. (No. 32)

> An addict is not the kind of person you need on a board because . . . they have their own reality. They're not interested in whether the building is falling down. They need to be brought up through committees to see the value of that they're doing and to drop some of their narrow perspectives. (No. 52)

> We tried to have involvement from our former clients. . . . They possibly didn't have the time to spare, or the skills to express themselves and perhaps didn't have enough of the right clothes to wear. (No. 31)

> The meetings are at noon. That means people have to be non-working or work downtown and be free to take fairly long lunch hours. As soon as you get into those things, you're moving into "those" sorts of people. (No. 56)

The skills, time, point of view, education and values that the respondents suggest account for the limited use of clients on boards serve to justify the continuance of the upper class in community leadership roles. Also, the reasons given by the women for the shortcomings of client directors serve to limit their ability to participate effectively. The values and behaviors taken for granted by the upper class directors result in a situation where the client feels a need to defer to the volunteer directors. Thus the client's participation is limited in a situation where the clients must learn the rituals of board work and where they are confronted with discussions on legal and financial points about which they have little understanding. These obstacles to participation serve to unobtrusively ensure the client's inability to confront (conservative) board policies. In this way the possibility of any far reaching impact by clients on boards is effectively curtailed.

In view of the "disasters" which resulted from placing clients immediately on boards, many agencies now include clients on committees of their boards. In these committees the client learns to express her/his opinion, to adopt the expected role of a director, and to feel comfortable with people from high status positions. This tack works well for all those concerned. Clients can find their level in a small, informal group and discover whether they have the talents and interest to eventually become a client director. On the other side, boards are able to assure that potential directors have knowledge of board rituals and stances on issues. In this way the board re-socializes the client to board values, traditions and points of view as "the way things are done" on boards. This training and education has the effect of socializing new members into approved roles and of reducing behavior that is potentially disruptive to existing administrative practices.

CONCLUSION

The women interviewed are aware of and act on class-consistent incentives for taking on community leadership roles. While raised to volunteer out of family tradition and noblesse oblige, the women are not unaware of the rewards of their work: they develop expertise, expand contacts and gain prestige, and assure the continuance of community leadership roles as a dominant class prerogative and the maintenance of the voluntary sector status quo. These latter two incentives are broad class goals. Yet they surface in the respondents' comments nonetheless. By asserting the importance of an impartial perspective, expertise, contacts and community membership, the women make the case for their being the social group best suited for the job. That is, they are the natural choice to develop policy, manage agency finances and make funding submissions to the government. By doing so, they reinforce their position and obscure their interest in maintaining the voluntary sector as it is.

REFERENCES

Allen, Michael Patrick
    1974   "The Structure of Inter-Organizational Elite Co-Optation." American Sociological
                Review 39: 393-406.
Auerback, Arnold J.
    1961   "Aspirations of Power, People and Agency Goals." Social Work 6 (January): 66-73.

Babchuk, Nicholas, N.R. Marsey, and C.W. Gordon
    1960   "Men and Women in Community Agencies: A Note on Power and Prestige." Ameri-
            can Sociological Review 25: 399-403.
Burke, Mark
    1960   "Why Women Volunteer in the Hospital." Pp. 64-6 in Nathan Cohen (editor), *The
            Citizen Volunteer*. New York: Harper and Brothers.
Clement, Wallace
    1975   *The Canadian Corporate Elite*. Toronto: McClelland and Stewart.
Cohen, Nathan E.
    1960   *The Citizen Volunteer*. New York: Harper and Brothers.
Domhoff, G. William
    1970   *The Higher Circles: The Governing Class in America*. New York: Vintage Books.
    1975   "Social Clubs, Policy-Planning Groups and Corporations: A Study of Ruling Class
            Cohensiveness." Insurgent Sociologist 5: 173-184 (special issue).
Financial Post
    1977   "Women 1% of directors." 66, 14 (Sept. 5): 15.
Frankel, Ruth
    1965   *Three Cheers for Volunteers*. Toronto: Clarke, Irwin and Company.
Gold, Doris B.
    1971   "Women and Volunteerism." Pp. 384-400 in Vivian Gornick and Barbara K. Maran
            (editors), *Women in Sexist Society: Studies in Power and Powerlessness*. New York: Basic
            Books.
Gray, Charlotte
    1981   "Do Women Have a Place in the Boardrooms of the Nation?" Chatelaine 54, 4 (April):
            56-57, 89-100.
Hartogs, Nelly and Joseph Weber
    1974   *Boards of Directors. A Study of current practices in board management and board operations in
            voluntary hospital and health and welfare organizations*. New York: Oceana Publications.
Higley, John, Delsey Deacon, and Don Smart
    1979   *Elites in Australia*. London: Routledge and Keagan Paul.
Hoffman, Joan Eakin
    1980   "Problems of Access in the Study of Social Elites and Boards of Directors." Pp. 45-56
            in William B. Shaffir, Robert A. Stebbins, and Allan Turowitz (editors), *Fieldwork Ex-
            perience: Qualitative Approaches to Social Research*. St. Martin's Press.
Maxwell, Mary Percival and James D. Maxwell
    1971   "Boarding School: Social control, Space and Identity." Pp. 157-164 in D. Ian Davies
            and Kathleen Herman (editors), *Social Space: Canadian Perspectives*. Toronto: New
            Press.
McDougall, W. Jack
    1976   *The Role of the Voluntary Trustee*. London: Ontario Research and Publication Division,
            School of Business Administration, The University of Western Ontario.
Moore, Joan W.
    1962   Exclusiveness and Ethnocentrism in a Metropolitan Upper Class Agency." Pacific
            Sociological Review 5 (Spring): 16-20.
    1969   "Patterns of Women's Participation in Voluntary Associations." American Journal of
            Sociology 66: 592-598.
Noble, Joey
    1979   "'Classifying' the Poor: Toronto Charities, 1859-1880." Studies in Political Economy 2
            (Autumn): 109-128.
Ostrander, Susan A.
    1980   "Upper Class Women: The Feminine Side of Privilege." Qualitative Sociology 3, 1
            (Spring): 23-44.
    1976   Upper Class Women: A Study of Social Power. Unpublished Doctoral thesis. Case
            Western Reserve.
Ross, Aileen D.
    1952   "Organized Philanthropy in an Urban Community." Canadian Journal of Economic
            and Political Science 18 (November): 474-486.
    1953   "The Social Control of Philanthropy." American Journal of Sociology 58 (March):
            451-460.
    1958   "Control and Leadership in Women's Groups: An Analysis of Philanthropic Money
            Raising Activity." Social Forces 37 (December): 124-131.
    1965   "Philanthropic Activity and the Business Career." Pp. 20-34 in Mayer Zald (editor),
            Social Welfare Institutions. New Ycrk: Wiley and Sons.

Useem, Michael
    1978   "The Inner Group of the American Capitalist Class." Social Problems 25 (February): 224-240.
    1979   "The Social Organization of the American Business Elite and Participation of Corporate Directors in the Governance of American Institutions." American Sociological Review 44 (August): 553-572.

Zald, Mayer N.
    1970   "The Power and Functions of Boards of Directors: A Theoretical Synthesis." American Journal of Sociology 75: 97-110.

Advisory Board Performance: Managing Ambiguity and Limited Commitment in Public Television

Jone L. Pearce and Judy Rosener

Citizen advisory boards are important to non-profit and governmental organizations, yet these boards face fundamental problems of ambiguous responsibilities and limited board member commitment. In the present paper a model of these propositions is developed and tested. Board performance is operationalized as productivity and board impact, and is expected to be dependent on the development of operational objectives and a subcommittee structure, which in turn is facilitated by the financial support of management, and impeded by a large board membership. The model is tested using path analysis on a national sample of federally-mandated Community Advisory Boards to public television stations. We find that the establishment of operational objectives and subcommittees is significantly associated with productivity but only weakly with the impact of the advisory board. Board size is unassociated with board performance. The findings support the assertion that successful boards must clarify their roles and develop efficient operating structures, but suggest that the advisory board-management relationship is complex.

Virtually all organizations have boards of outsiders who pass judgment on organizational policies. These judgments may be binding on the organization or they may be purely advisory. As pervasive as these structural features are we know surprisingly little about these boards. The present study is concerned with the performance of one kind of board—the advisory board.

Advisory boards are composed of non-organizational members who meet intermittently to advise the organization's managers, with members almost always appointed or approved by these full-time managers. Advisory boards are particularly important to non-profit organizations, since they are frequently imposed on non-profits by those (especially government) providing funding. Advisory boards are assumed to provide a "public" check in return for public monies. However, uncertainty about what non-profit advisory boards can and should do is a frequent problem. There is confusion about who these boards' constituencies should be and about their roles in the organization. These confusions are exacerbated by the often limited commitment advisory board volunteers give to overcoming the barriers such uncertainty creates. Hence, board members and managers are frequently dissatisfied with advisory board performance (Sewell, Phillips and Phillips, 1979).

The number of non-profit and government advisory boards grew explosively as a result of the federal citizen participation mandates of the 1960s. Furthermore, they have been identified as one of the citizen participation techniques most likely to be used during the 1980s (Creighton, 1980). Yet advisory boards are considered a controversial form of citizen oversight by some (Lewis, Houghton and Hannah, 1978) and an outright waste of resources by others (Arnstein, 1969).

Despite several decades of debate there is limited research and no empirical tests of such views. There have been numerous studies of advisory boards and committees (e.g., *Public Administration Review* May/June and October, 1972) but few of these focus on advisory board "effectiveness," and virtually none are concerned with the relationships between those features board members can control (i.e., its own procedures) and board performance. Studies of the demographic and structural features of the communities from which members are drawn are of little direct use to board members seeking assistance.

The present study tests a model of the efficacy of board practices, such as subcommittee structure and the setting of clear objectives, in the hope of providing useful guidance to non-profit board members seeking tools for building successful boards. This problem is addressed by developing a causal model based on research on boards from the management and citizen participation literatures, and social psychological research on group decision making. This model is then tested on a sample of federally-mandated public television community advisory boards using path analytic techniques.

BOARDS IN FOR-PROFIT ORGANIZATIONS

Governing boards in for-profit organizations have received substantially more research attention than have nonprofit advisory boards. Despite the greater legal power of for-profit governing boards the processes of these two kinds of boards appear to be quite similar. They both face the dual problems of ambiguous tasks and limited member commitment.

Ambiguous responsibilities. In his excellent review of research on governing boards, Mintzberg (1983) argued that there are three important ambiguities in the role of governing boards. Mintzberg's first ambiguity concerns the question of who has the right to membership on the board. He cites a 1977 survey of the largest 500 U.S. corporations which reports that only 1.6 percent of their directors represented major outside shareholders. His second ambiguity is the uncertainty over whose interests the board or board members should represent. Representation is frequently confused; are board members supposed to represent a particular constituency, such as shareholders, or the corporation as a whole? This ambiguity in the representational roles of board members is reflected in the controversy surrounding interlocking directorates which has dominated governing board research. Interlocks, or common board memberships among organizations, are a pervasive practice (Dooley, 1969). The most common interlocks are between companies with head offices in the same commercial centers and between financial and non-financial corporations (Dooley, 1969; Levine, 1972). Do such interlocks suggest the control of corporations by financial institutions, wealthy families, or some other external constituency or do they, as Mace (1948) argued, result from the managerial use of boards for information? The debate over interlocking directorates is fueled by the ambiguity in the role of boards. Mintzberg's (1983) third ambiguity concerns the uncertainty about how governing boards actually govern or control organizations. Building on the research of Zald (1965) and Mace (1948), he concluded that part-time board members simply lack the information they need to make decisions. Mace (1948) and Zald (1969) found that boards only controlled their organizations in special cases of concentrated ownership or when the organization was dependent on the board for critical financial support such as fund raising or loans. In the absence of clear dependence on an external group using the board to control the organization, the board's responsibilities become ambiguous.

Member commitment. Not only are the responsibilities of governing boards often unclear, this problem is exacerbated by board members' part-time involvement. Those who have studied governing boards note that part-time board members have only limited information upon which to base their decisions. Mace (1948) suggested that board members usually do not ask discerning questions, because they know so little they fear looking foolish. In addition to the part-time involvement of board members their commitment to the organization is usually less than full-time executives because they are not as dependent on the organization as are full-time employees. Board members' limited involvement is reflected in their compensation; for corporate directors it is often nominal, and non-profit organizations are required by law to have an unpaid or voluntary governing board.

Given the ambiguous nature of board responsibilities and the limited commitment of most board members, in practice governing board members often look to full-time managers for guidance and direction. Mace (1948) suggested that more often than not managers select, direct, and judge board members, rather than the reverse.

ADVISORY BOARDS AND CITIZEN PARTICIPATION

The problems of responsibility, ambiguity, and management domination are even more severe for advisory boards than they are for governing boards. Advisory boards are supposed to represent organizations' clients or local community, but their members are usually selected and appointed by the organization's management rather than a specific constituency. Advisory boards exist to advise management, but what does this mean in practice? Does advise mean to make concrete recommendations, or to act as a "sounding board?" Should the board initiate proposals or react to management's proposals? In what areas should the board offer advice? Suppose the board members themselves disagree over their role?

Since the Economic Opportunity Act of 1964 mandated the use of advisory boards in local antipoverty programs, federal legislation has required citizen participation in transportation, urban planning, energy, education, and social services. Yet, as Langton (1978) notes, advisory boards are a particularly controversial form of citizen participation. Advisory board members are expected to represent the community's interests in the development of agency policies, but board members are usually selected by the agency, not by the community (see Hannah and Lewis, 1982, for a review of the political power of advisory boards). Activists who feel the citizen's role is to monitor agency performance have criticized ad-

visory boards for assisting rather than monitoring, and have questioned their
ability to represent the community (Langton, 1978; Arnstein, 1969). Further evidence of confusion about the role of citizen advisory board members is provided
by Sewell, et al. (1979).

In their review of twenty-two case studies of public participation, Sewell, et
al., (1979) concluded that agency managers and advisory board members usually
differed in their participation goals. Agency representatives saw boards as a way
to develop public acceptance for programs, increase agency performance, and
improve the agency's image. In contrast, citizens saw participation as a way to
diffuse the power of agencies and insure that those affected by agency decisions
would be able to influence policies. Therefore, it isn't surprising that Sewell, et
al., (1979) also found that the citizens and administrators used different criteria
to assess participation success: agency representatives measured success by the
extent to which the final plans were accepted by the community and whether or
not the public image of the agency had improved; alternatively, citizens measured success by the extent to which they modified agency plans. Lewis et al.
(1978) suggested that the ambiguous mandate of advisory boards means that the
administrators' expectations for their advisory boards is the most critical factor
influencing their effectiveness. They argued that the "empty agenda" of these
groups can lead to time wasted setting goals for the advisory board if there is no
clear direction from administrators. Furthermore, membership on citizen advisory boards is a voluntary, unpaid, civic activity. Many advisory board members
are likely to see their membership as one more voluntary contribution and so be
reluctant to commit substantial time to the board.

Despite these inherent problems of ambiguity and limited commitment, advisory boards can perform important functions. They provide a forum for the exchange of information between managers and interested outsiders. Potentially,
they can assist outsiders, by allowing them to influence organizational actions,
and managers, by increasing community acceptance and understanding of their
actions. Yet advisory boards cannot achieve these functions unless they overcome the inherent ambiguity of their role by developing clear operational objectives, and by finding an efficient way to use members with only a limited commitment so that members feel that they are contributing.

A CAUSAL MODEL OF ADVISORY BOARD PERFORMANCE

Given the ambiguous mandates of advisory boards and the differing expectations of important groups, it isn't surprising to discover controversy concerning
the appropriate operational definition of board "effectiveness." Lewis et al.
(1978) provide a review of various effectiveness standards and found that they
ranged from measures of "output" (number of new programs) to characteristics
of the board itself (representativeness) and members' attitudes (reduction in
board members' feelings of alienation); these authors adopted "having a significant impact on program" as perceived by the administrators as their preferred
measure. Similarly, Kamienecki and Clarke (1982) defined effectiveness as the
"value of the board's advice as perceived by managers." Since the present paper
focuses on the internal operations and management of advisory boards, a mea-

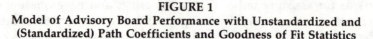

FIGURE 1
Model of Advisory Board Performance with Unstandardized and
(Standardized) Path Coefficients and Goodness of Fit Statistics

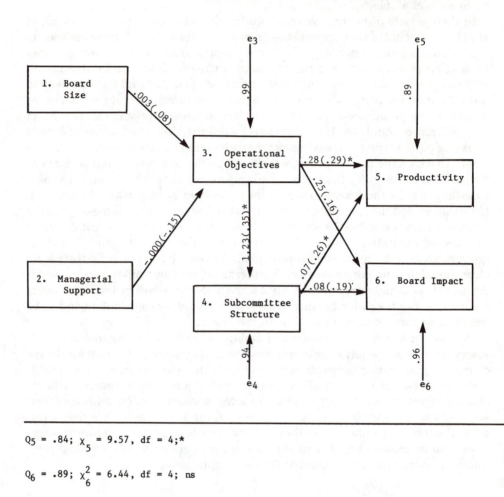

$Q_5 = .84$; $\chi_5 = 9.57$, df = 4;*

$Q_6 = .89$; $\chi_6^2 = 6.44$, df = 4; ns

*p < .05

sure of board effectiveness called "performance" composed of measures of both productivity and organizational impact is adopted.

It is proposed that high performing advisory boards must have both clear operational objectives and a subcommittee structure. Further, the establishment of operational objectives is hypothesized to be impeded by a large board membership and facilitated by a strong management commitment to a high performing board. This model of advisory board performance is diagrammed in the Figure.

Objectives. The presence of concrete objectives allows board members to organize and direct their efforts, thus overcoming the inherent ambiguity of their
responsibilities. The very process of establishing objectives forces board members to make their various expectations explicit and gives the board a focus.
Lewis, et al. (1978) argued that advisory boards have vague mandates and spend
much time deciding what they are supposed to do; we suggest that the more
time they spend clarifying their objectives the more likely they are to be productive and have a significant organizational impact.

This is consistent with the social psychological research on group decision
making performance. Hackman and Morris (1979) proposed that group decision
making performance is improved when groups spend relatively more time discussing task strategy. Hackman, Brousseau and Weiss (1976) found support for
this proposal using a laboratory task that required coordination and sharing
among subjects.

Structure. High performing advisory boards are expected to be more likely to
adopt some form of internal division of labor, that is, subcommittees. As noted
above, part-time advisory board members face a broad array of issues and information. A subcommittee structure facilitates the focusing of attention in a
manner that helps compensate for the limited commitment that part-time volunteers give to board membership.

Both operational objectives and subcommittee structure are expected to lead
directly to better advisory board performance. But what is the causal relationship
between objectives and subcommittees? The development of operational objectives should lead a board to establish subcommittees. The formation of subcommittees implies implicit, if not explicit, objectives, since each subcommittee
would be expected to investigate whether or not it is prepared to offer advice on
the topics covered by its subcommittee. Therefore, as the Figure indicates, operational objectives are assumed to antedate the formation of subcommittees.

Size. Large boards are hypothesized to find it more difficult to agree on operational objectives than are small boards. The greater the number of members the
greater potential variety in their expectations and goals for the advisory board,
and so size is expected to be inversely associated with the establishment of operational objectives. With greater diversity more time is required to discuss and
clarify operational objectives, time that part-time volunteers may be unwilling or
unable to commit.

This idea has found support in laboratory research on decision making
groups. Large groups seem less able to fully use all of the available member resources (see Hare, 1962, or Steiner, 1972, for reviews). The larger the group the
more limited the opportunities for individual participation (Indik, 1965), and the
greater the conformity pressures (Gerard, Wilhelmy and Conolley, 1968).

Managerial Support. Although advisory boards may be imposed on organizations, full-time managers still retain a great deal of control over them. Above it
was noted that managers frequently control the governing boards which are
their legal superiors. With an advisory board, managers retain all of the advantages of full-time commitment and information, as well as the power to decide
who shall serve. Further, advisory board members (more than governing board
members) are dependent on management for guidance, since they are assumed
to want to give advice that will be used by managers and are dependent on these

managers for resources. Lewis, et al. (1978) found that the more effective advisory boards had the assistance (but not dominance) of professional staff. Thus, advisory board members are expected to be receptive to managers' suggestions on operational objectives, and a positive relationship between managerial support and the establishment of operational objectives is proposed.

METHOD

Sample and Procedure

The Telecommunications Financing Act of 1978 required all public broadcasting stations, as a condition of receiving federal funds, to establish Community Advisory Boards by May of 1979 to provide taxpayer oversight. Each station was required to make "good faith efforts to assure that the composition of its advisory board reasonably reflects the diverse needs and interests of the communities served" and that "the board shall be permitted to review programming goals established by the station, service provided by the station, and the significant policy decisions rendered by the station (Public Law 95-567, Section 307)." Survey instruments were mailed to all 167 public television stations listed in the *1980 Directory of Information Sources for Public Television* in April 1981, two years after the stations were required to have their advisory boards in place. Each station received a questionnaire to be completed by the station manager. A followup letter to non-responding station managers was mailed by May. Feedback summarizing the findings was mailed to responding stations in October, 1981. We received 59 usable manager responses, a 35% response rate. Despite this disappointing response rate, analyses indicated that the responses were representative of geographical regions, and large and small stations in the population, but there was a relative oversampling of community licensed stations (39% of responding managers) and undersampling of television stations operated by states, cities, and educational institutions.

Measures

Two indicators of advisory boad performance are available. Board "Productivity" is indicated by a dichotomous variable from the questionnaire item "Has your CAB produced any written documents?" with a "yes" response scored as "1" and a "no" response as "O." The variable representing "Board Impact" is the number of board-initiated changes using responses to the questionnaire item "Have there been any changes in the station as a result of the CAB?" with choices including "No changes, policy changes, programming changes, public access and outreach changes, financial management changes, operations or organizational changes" summed to get an estimate of the range of the advisory boards' impacts.

Each of these indicators of advisory board performance is limited; yet they appear to be quite distinct, measuring independent dimensions of board performance (see the Table). Productivity does not indicate what was written, but is used because written reports take more effort and deliberation than verbal reports. They are also more likely to command management attention because they are available to outside groups. For example, the first written report of the KCET (Los Angeles) advisory board received coverage in *Variety* and *The Los Angeles Times* (January 25, 1980), and the management of KCET subsequently published a public response to each of the advisory board's recommendations and implemented many of them. Board Impact ignores the relative importance of each change, but a simple count of the number of areas in which change has been initiated should have a rough correspondence to overall influence.

The variable "Board Size" was taken from responses to the question "How many board members were originally appointed? "Managerial Support" is the managers' estimation of the dollar cost (including staff time) of their advisory boards during the prior twelve months. "Operational Objectives" is represented by the dichotomous responses to the question "Does your CAB have specific written responsibilities other than those identified in the Telecommunications Act?" scored "yes" = "1" and "no" = "O." "Subcommittee Structure" is indicated by the number of subcommittees used by the advisory board; the questionnaire item is "We have subcommittees with the following responsibilities:" summed for number listed. This variable is surprisingly independent of Board Size (r = .10, n.s.). The means, standard deviations, and intercorrelations among the variables appear in the Table.

RESULTS

The proposed model is tested using path analytic techniques (c.f., Duncan, 1975; Pedhazur, 1982).[1] These techniques allow the testing of a set of hypothesized relationships among variables. In path analysis a set of relationships (paths) is proposed (like those appearing in the Figure). These hypothesized relationships (the over-identified model) are compared with the "null" or just-identified model (all variables are significantly related to all other variables). Support for the proposed model is ascertained in two steps: first, are all of the paths that are hypothesized to be significant, in fact significantly greater than zero? And second, does the proposed model "fit the data" better than the "null model"? The unstandardized path coefficients appearing in the Figure are the "beta" weights from the regression equations, the standardized coefficients can, for convenience, be interpreted like correlation coefficients (i.e., O=no relationship, 1=perfect relationship). The standardized and unstandardized path coefficients are presented in the Figure and the original and reproduced correlation coefficients appear in the Table.

Managerial Support

The proposed model receives only limited support. Board Size and managerial support are independent of the Operational Objectives. However, Operational Objectives are significantly associated with Subcommittee Structure, and both have a positive association with one performance indicator—Productivity. The other performance indicator, Board Impact, is weakly associated with both Operational Objectives and Subcommittee Structure, but their separate path coefficients did not reach statistical significance. The proposed, over-identified model

TABLE 1
Original and Reproduced Correlations, Means and Standard Deviations for Model

VARIABLES	1	2	3	4	5	6
1. Board Size	--	.12	.06	.10	-.14	.16
2. Managerial Support	np	--	-.14	.21	.36*	.28*
3. Operational Objectives[a]	.06	-.14	--	.35*	.38*	.22*
4. Subcommittee Structure	.02	-.05	np	--	.36*	.24*
5. Productivity[a]	.04	-.05	.38	.36	--	.18
6. Board Impact	.00	-.01	.23	.25	np	--
$\overline{X}$	17.86	4,009	.34	1.09	.32	.97
s.d.	13.09	10,972	.48	1.71	.47	.77

Original correlations in upper half of matrix

[a]dichotomous variables

np = not predicted

n = 59;

*p<.05

is compared with the just-identified model (i.e., all paths among all variables hypothesized to be significant) with a null hypothesis that the proposed model fits the data. The relevant statistics are reported in the Figure. We are not able to reject the null hypothesis.[2] Since a Q_5 of .84 and a Q_6 of .89 are only moderately close to 1, the proposed causal model appearing in the Figure is a moderately good fit.

DISCUSSION

The proposed model obtained limited support. Attempts to reduce the negative effects of ambiguity and limited commitment through the establishment of operational objectives and subcommittee structures were strongly associated with advisory board productivity, but unassociated with the impact of the board. The exogenous variables of board size and managerial support for the board were, contrary to expectations, unrelated to the establishment of objectives. Although, board size was unrelated to any of the other variables, the Table suggests that managerial support has a direct association (significant correlation coefficient) with the performance indicators, rather than the indirect path hypothesized. Therefore, the present test suggests that the establishment of operational objectives and a subcommittee structure leads to greater board productivity, and managerial support is directly associated with both board productivity and impact. The limitations of the present study, the differential impact of objectives and structure on performance, and the direct relationship between managerial support and performance merit discussion.

This study is limited in several ways. First the data are limited to survey responses from the station managers alone. Their views may be different from those of board members, and there is always the potential problem of methods bias (all responses taken from the same self-report instrument tend to be positively correlated). Several of the variables are only limited representations of their concepts (for example, the financial costs of the board would be expected to be only imperfectly associated with managerial support). Finally, the sample size of 59 was disappointingly small. Although this study is a very limited one indeed, it is important to note that it is the first to systematically test hypotheses about the effects of board procedures on board performance. As such it has lead to some interesting findings.

The fact that operational objectives and subcommittee structures lead to board productivity but *not* to board impact could indicate that other, nonmodeled variables may be more important in influencing board impact. It may be that task clarification and an efficient internal structure are more strongly associated with "quantity/output" variables like productivity than quality indicators such as impact. After all, for a board to have a large impact it must not only establish clear priorities and efficiently organize its activities (be productive) but it must pick important and meaningful priorities. That is, clear goals and structure are probably necessary but not sufficient for board impact; whereas productivity probably has a stronger and more exclusive dependence on clear objectives and structure.

Management support of advisory boards was not associated with the establishment of operational objectives. However, its significant direct correlation with both productivity and board impact is suggestive. In developing the model it was assumed that managers would take the lead in initiating and directing boards toward their own (managerial) operational objectives. It may be, however, as Lewis, et al. (1978) found, that as representatives of specific constituencies or the local community, the board felt uncomfortable allowing managers to establish their priorities. After all, advisory boards, unlike governing boards, are designed to institutionalize oversight or a kind of "opposition." Our informal observations indicated that board members were quite sensitive to management domination. It could be that managers influence, not through control of the boards' operational objectives ("setting the agenda"), but through their support of board activities after the objectives have been set. If managers see that their boards are becoming helpful they can provide staff support and documents, if not, they will probably find that they are too busy to support their advisory boards.

These results also suggest the importance of empirical verification. Both the management literature on governing boards and the citizen participation literature provide useful insights drawn from case studies. However, we could locate no empirical tests of the causal statements in either body of writings. In the present test, we found support for the expected relationship between operational objectives and subcommittee structures and one measure of performance—productivity—but not for the other—board impact. The results of tests such as these help to remind us that empirical research is necessary precisely because it can lead to a more complex and complete understanding of the role of advisory boards in non-profit organizations.

In conclusion, this study suggests that, to be productive, advisory boards need to overcome the ambiguity of their responsibilities and the limitations of member part-time commitment through developing clear objectives and an efficient subcommittee structure. What we do not know is why some boards are unwilling or unable to establish objectives and subcommittee structures. Are they unable to agree on objectives because their individual goals are divergent? Do the participants actually want an active and effective board, or are they content to merely have their names associated with a worthy cause? The present study does indicate that advisory boards wishing to be productive are more likely to be successful if they devote time to resolving the ambiguous nature of their role and the limited commitment of their members through the development of operational objectives and a subcommittee structure.

NOTES

Research supported in part by the Faculty Research Fund of the Graduate School of Management. Special thanks to Bill Stevenson; and to Jane Kaupphan, Betsy Youd Amador, Diane De Moulin and Georgi Wright for research assistance.
1. Productivity is a binary dependent variable, and several writers have suggested that this creates special problems with non-normal error terms, non-constant error variance, and constraints on response function. However, the present analysis was conducted based on Neter and Wasserman (1974, p. 323) who suggest that "the method of least squares still provides estimators which, under quite general conditions, are asymptotically normal."
2. A cautious approach prevents a conclusion that the proposed causal model does fit the data. Jöreskog (1974) suggests that the X^2's should be interpreted with caution, since they are influenced by sample size and in cases such as the present, in which the sample size is relatively small it could lead to retention of the null hypothesis even when the model is not a good fit. The more useful statistic is the nonsample dependent Q, consisting of the ratio of unexplained variance in the over-identified model to the unexplained variance in the just-identified model. Values of 1 would indicate perfect fits (Pedhazur, 1982).

REFERENCES

Arnstein, S.R.
   1969   "A Ladder of Citizen Participation." Journal of American Institution of Planners, 35: 216-224.
Creighton, L.
   1980   The Future of Citizen Participation; Results of an Abbreviated Delphi. First Global Conference on the Future, Toronto, Canada, July 22, 1980.
Cronin, T. and Thomas, N.
   1971   "Federal Advisory Processes: Advise and Discontent." Science (February).
Dooley, P.C.
   1969   "The Interlocking Directorate." The American Economic Review, 59: 314-323.
Duncan, O.D.
   1975   Introduction to Structural Equation Models. New York: Academic Press.
Gerard, H.B., Wilhelmy, R.A. and Conolley, E.S.
   1968   "Conformity and Group Size," Journal of Personality and Social Psychology, 8: 79-82.

Hackman, J.R. and Morris, C.G.
    1979   "Group Tasks, Group Interaction Process and Group Performance Effectiveness: A Review and Proposed Integration." In L. Berkowitz (Ed.) *Advances in Experimental Social Psychology*, (Vol. 12), New York: Academic Press.

Hackman, J.R., Brousseau, K., and Weiss, J.A.
    1976   "The Interaction of Task Design and Group Performance Strategies in Determining Group Effectiveness." Organizational Behavior and Human Performance, 16: 350-365.

Hannah, S.B. and Lewis, H.S.
    1982   "Internal Control of Locally Initiated Citizen Advisory Committees: A Case Study." Journal of Voluntary Action Research, 11: 39-52.

Hare, A.P.
    1962   *Handbook of Small Group Research*. New York: Free Press.

Indik, B.P.
    1965   "Organization Size and Member Participation: Some Empirical Tests of Alternatives." Human Relations, 18: 339-350.

Jöreskog, K.G.
    1974   "Analyzing Psychological Data by Structural Analysis of Covariance Matrices." In D.H. Krantz, R.C. Atkinson, D. Luce, and P. Suppes (Eds.), *Contemporary Development in Mathematical Psychology* (Vol. 2), San Francisco: Freeman.

Kamienecki, S. and Clarke, M.
    1982   "Organization Theory, Evaluation Research and the Effectiveness of Citizen Advisory Bodies." International Journal of Public Administration, 4: 81-98.

Langton, S.
    1978   *Citizen Participation in America: Essays on the State of the Art*. Lexington, Mass.: Heath.

Levine, J.H.
    1972   "The Sphere of Influence." American Sociological Review, 37: 14-27.

Lewis, H., Houghton, D. and Hannah, S.
    1978   "The Effectiveness of Local Citizen Advisory Bodies: Expectations and Realities." Delivered at the 1978 ASPA Conference, Phoenix, Arizona, April 10-12.

Mace, M.L.
    1948   *The Board of Directors in Small Corporations*. Cambridge, Mass.: Harvard Business School Research Division.

Mintzberg, H.
    1983   *Power in and Around Organizations*. Englewood Cliffs, N.J.: Prentice-Hall.

Neter, Jr. and Wasserman, W.
    1974   *Applied Linear Statistical Models*. Homewood, Ill.: Irwin.

Pedhazur, E.J.
    1982   *Multiple Regression in Behavioral Research*. 2nd ed., New York: Holt, Rinehart and Winston.

Sewell, W.R., Phillips, D. and Phillips, S.D.
    1979   "Models for the Evaluation of Public Participation Programmes." Natural Resources Journal, 19: 337-358.

Steiner, I.D.
    1972   *Group Process and Productivity*. New York: Academic Press.

Zald, M.N.
    1965   "Who Shall Rule? A Political Analysis of Succession in a Large Welfare Organization." Pacific Sociological Review, 8: 52-60.
    1969   "The Power and Functions of Boards of Directors: A Theoretical Synthesis." American Journal of Sociology, 75: 97-111.

Board-Staff Relations and Perceived Effectiveness in Nonprofit Organizations

Robert D. Herman and F. Peter Tulipana

Boards of directors perform both internal and external functions. After reviewing research on the external function, this paper reports the results of an empirical study of the internal role. Based upon responses from 142 people in seven private nonprofit organizations the study finds that: (1) participants experience less actual influence than they think they should have; (2) board members' influence is positively related to the frequency of board meetings and the extent to which board members feel informed of their duties, though neither is very strong; (3) ratings of organizational effectiveness are positively related to board member ratings of staff educational sufficiency and the extent to which board members feel informed of their duties; and (4) at the organizational level of analysis, organizational effectiveness is strongly related to the amount of total influence in the organization though this result seems to be based mostly on the strong relation between the influence of the executive director and effectiveness, as effectiveness is unrelated to board influence and positively related to the difference in influence between the executive director and the board.

How important are boards of directors in private, nonprofit organizations? The rhetorical consensus hold that a "good board" is crucial, both in its contribution to internal (planning and control) but especially in its contribution to external (fund-raising and community linkages) effectiveness. What is a "good board" and what does it do? The practicing professional literature frequently defines the attributes of the good board in demographic and skills terms (e.g., Hummel, 1980; Flanagan, 1981). Though the virtues of diversity and community representativeness are often lauded, the "good board" usually includes a number of the community's corporate, professional and social elite. Thus, the "good board" very much resembles the "power board" described by Wilensky and Lebeaux (1958).

Both theory and research support the contention that board composition has important consequences for external effectiveness. The open systems and organization-environment perspectives emphasize the uncertainties that environments pose for organizations and conceive of organizations as adaptive systems that attempt, in various ways, to cope with the uncertainties confronting them.

"Power boards," those featuring a significant number of prestigious and well-connected members, are commonly assumed to provide nonprofit organizations with the knowledge, skills and influence to more effectively cope with environments than less powerful baords. Though there is a great deal of anecdotal evidence in support of this hypothesis, two comparative, empirical studies, while basically supportive of the proposition, suggest that the relation between board power and environmental effectiveness may be more complicated than suspected. Pfeffer's (1973) study of hospitals found a strong relationship between dependence on local, private donations and the relative ranking the chief administrator gave to fund-raising as a board function and as a criterion for selecting board members. In hospitals affiliated with religious institutions and thus less dependent on local, private donations, fund-raising was less highly ranked, while knowledge of hospital administration was more highly preferred. Furthermore, Pfeffer found that three measures of effectiveness (i.e., percentage increase in beds, percentage increase in budget and number of programs, services and pieces of equipment added in the period from 1965 to 1970) were related to high ranking of selecting board members on basis of community influence and political connections and low ranking of knowledge of hospital administration as a selection criterion. These results support the hypothesis that nonprofit organizations that are highly dependent on local giving use board composition as a strategic tool and that power boards enhance a nonprofit organization's ability to attract financial resources.

Provan's (1980) study of human service agencies also found significant positive relationships between measures of board size and power (prestige, linkages in the form of the number of agency board members also on the United Way board) and absolute level of both United Way and other funding. Interestingly, Provan found no relationships between power (or size) and percentage increase in United Way or other funding (except for a *negative* relationship between linkages and percentage increase in United Way funding). This result seems to contradict Pfeffer's (1973) findings. We believe the studies are reconcilable.

Few hospitals are affiliated with United Way and perhaps being a United Way agency reduces some financial uncertainty, leading board members to put little effort into fund-raising. Additionally, we believe that board power is probably much more important in securing admission to the United Way and an agency's initial allocation than in affecting subsequent allocations. Subsequent allocations may be based on "objective" criteria (power may be important in defining criteria) and be consistent with the budgeting practices known as incrementalism.[1] If United Way membership reduces an uncertainty that boards are often called on to cope with and if United Way allocations are basically incremental, then it is not surprising that power board is unrelated to changes in funding. In any case, the empirical evidence supports the contentions that the composition of nonprofit boards varies with the environment and that power boards affect resource acquisition.

In addition to their external role boards also have internal functions. In carrying out their internal functions boards are highly dependent on the organization's full-time staff, especially the executive director (or other chief administrative officer). Thus, the quality of board-staff relations is frequently seen as fundamental in affecting the internal effectiveness of the board. Can board-staff relations be conceptualized and measured? What accounts for different patterns of relations and do different patterns lead to differences in organizational effectiveness? This paper presents the results of an exploratory study that provides some initial answers to those questions.

MEASURES AND METHODS

Board-staff relations are multi-faceted and could be characterized on many dimensions (e.g., frequency, status differentials, trust, and communication patterns). A dimension very frequently discussed is *influence*. Organizations, of whatever type, are arenas in which individuals and coalitions attempt to affect decisions, the definitions of the occasions for a decision, the allocation of resources, and so on. Influence (or power, control) is frequently conceived as strictly a distributional phenomenon. Whatever influence the board has might have been the executive director's.

An important series of studies by Tannenbaum and his associates (e.g., Tannenbaum, 1956, 1961) has demonstrated that influence within organizations varies not only in distribution, but also in *total amount*. Two organizations may have the same distributional profiles but one may have much more influence exercised at all levels. The "control graph" technique developed by Tannenbaum has been used in research on many types of organizations including voluntary organizations. Tannenbaum (1961) examined the relation between the distribution of influence, the total amount of influence, and a measure of organizational effectiveness (rating by national headquarters personnel) in a sample of 112 local Leagues of Women Voters. As hypothesized he found that Leagues with more egalitarian distributions of and more total influence were more effective.

Pearce (1983) recently used the Tannenbaum technique to test hypotheses drawn from Etzioni's (1961) compliance typology of organizations. Pearce compared the perceived influence of leaders in purely voluntary (unpaid) organizations with that of leaders in employing (paid staff) organizations as well as the perceived influence of "rank-and-file" members in each type. She found, contrary to Etzioni's theory, that leaders in organizations with no paid staff are more influential than leaders in organizations with paid staff. The high influence of leaders in voluntary organizations is attributed to their willingness, and the unwillingness of rank-and-file members, to take on time consuming responsibilities. Pearce also found, again contrary to the hypothesis derived from Etzioni's theory, no significant difference between the influence of rank-and-file members in both types of organization.

The basic method of measuring control developed by Tannenbaum is to ask a person completing a questionnaire to indicate "how much influence do you have" in what happens in that organization. The response alternatives are: (1) little or no influence; (2) some influence; (3) quite a bit of influence; (4) a great deal of influence; and (5) a very great deal of influence. In addition to the question on actual influence, respondents are often asked to indicate their preferred or ideal amount of influence. In this study we asked respondents to indicate their actual personal influence and ideal personal influence, using the five traditional response alternatives. We also asked each respondent (whether board member, executive director, or other employee) to rate, using the five alternatives, how much influence the (1) board of directors, (2) executive director, (3) senior staff and (4) other staff have on program planning and development, major financial decisions, the budget, daily operation, personnel, policy and procedures, and minor financial decisions.

The other major concept we are examining—organizational effectiveness—has long troubled theorists and researchers. As Petersen (1982) has noted, theoretical conceptions of effectiveness have evolved from an initial view of one, official goal through multiple, operative goals to the systems resource approach. Indeed, some authors (e.g., Hannan and Freeman, 1977) assert that effectiveness cannot be a scientific concept. Though effectiveness is a difficult concept to fully capture (perhaps especially for nonprofit organizations), we believe that most people believe, and act upon their beliefs, that nonprofit organizations differ in effectiveness. It is a concept we cannot ignore.

If measuring effectiveness in business organizations is difficult, it is even more difficult in nonprofit organizations where surplus has a much different meaning than profit. While recognizing its limits, we have used a common measure of effectiveness—member ratings. We asked all categories of respondents "How effective compared to other private, nonprofit organizations in this area, has your agency been?" using a 1 (very ineffective) to 10 (very effective) scale. Additionally, in a separate questionnaire section sent only to board members, we asked: "How effective has your agency been in achieving its goals, in terms of your own expectations?" using the same scale.

This research is based upon the willingness of agency board members and staff to complete questionnaires. It is not based upon any sort of random or probability sample. Several organizations, through their executive directors, were approached and asked to cooperate. Two organizations asked to participate declined to do so. Organizations asked to participate are mainstream human service organizations. A total of 142 individuals, from seven organizations, completed questionnaires. Both individual and organizational level data will be analyzed and reported.

RESULTS

Individual Level

Of the total 142 respondents, 96 are board members, 7 executive directors, and 39 other staff (5 senior or supervisory staff and 34 employees without supervisory responsibilities). As a group the respondents believe that board-staff relations are very good. Using a 1 (low end) to 10 (high end) scale, the mean rating given board-staff relations is 7.6 and 76% of the respondents rated board-staff relations as 7 or better.

Respondents, overall, when asked how much influence they actually have, have indicated (1) a fair amount ($\bar{x}$ = 2.47), about halfway between (2) some influence and (3) quite a bit of influence. However, they generally believe they should have more ($\bar{x}$ = 2.69). The difference between the actual and ideal influence is statistically significant (correlated t test, t = 4.69; $p < .001$; df = 130).[2]

Respondents believed that influence varied with issues (see Table 1). The board is perceived as much the most influential in major financial decisions, the executive director as most influential in program planning, and the board and executive director as relatively equal in influence regarding the budget.

TABLE 1
Perceived Influence of Board, Executive Director,
Senior Staff, and Other Staff by Issue (Averages)*

Issue	Board	Ex. Dir	Senior Staff	Other Staff
Major financial decisions	4.37	3.97	2.48	1.73
Program planning	3.2	4.18	3.44	2.68
Budget	4.08	4.11	2.65	1.75
Daily Operation	2.46	4.45	3.55	3.00
Personnel	2.85	4.4	2.96	2.06
Policy & procedures	3.63	4.17	2.97	2.31
Minor financial decisons	2.69	4.36	2.78	2.08

*Averages are based on all respondents. Larger numbers represent greater influence. 1 = "little or no influence." 5 = "a very great deal of influence." N's vary for each cell, board and executive director averages are based upon 130–135 responses, while senior staff and other staff averages are based on smaller n's (90–115) as many board members reported they were unknowledgeable of staff influence.

Respondents believe their agencies to be quite effective. The average value of responses to the question of "How effective compared to other private, non-profit organizations in this area, has your agency been?" was 8 with standard deviation of 1.96 ($n = 119$). The average of board members' responses to the effectiveness question in relation to their expectations was slightly lower—7.87 with standard deviation of 1.67 ($n = 90$). The correlation between the two estimates of organizational effectiveness for board members only is $r = .74$, suggesting that however board members conceive effectiveness that both questions tap that conception in similar ways.

We asked the board member respondents for basic demographic information. As expected board members are by and large drawn from the higher socioeconomic segments of the community. Seventy-five percent of the board members have college degrees, with 37 percent holding advanced degrees. Seventy-six percent have incomes of $25,000 or more and 37 percent or more than $50,000.

TABLE 2
Regression Analysis of Board Members' Feelings of Influence

Independent Variable	B	Standard Error B	F	Adjusted R^2
Frequency of board meetings	-.430	.175	5.89*	.085
Informed of board duties	.110	.062	3.26**	.115

*probability of F with 2,68 df < .01
**probability of F with 2,68 df < .05

Nearly all the employed board members work in white-collar occupations, 11 percent identified themselves as attorneys, 10 percent as corporate executives with smaller numbers of accountants, physicians, teachers, business owners and bankers. Interestingly, the single largest category is housewife/homemaker with 17 percent. The 15 who so identified themselves were concentrated in two agencies that serve girls and young women, 13 serving on those boards. The great majority of board members were recruited to their board by other board members (71%), though 16 percent were recruited by the executive director. Given the emphasis on boards as fund-raising bodies we were a little surprised to discover that 42 percent had not been involved in a fund-raising campaign. Similarly, when we asked all respondents if they contributed to their agency we were surprised to find that 43 percent contributed only through the United Way and 11 percent did not contribute in any fashion. Thirty-eight percent contributed to their organization in addition to their United Way contribution and nine percent contributed to their agency instead of to United Way. When we asked board members "How well are you informed as to your duties and responsibilities as a board member?" we found that they generally felt quite well informed, averaging 8.3 (where a rating of 10 was labeled "extremely well informed"). Similarly, when asked "Is the educational level of staff members in this agency sufficient to perform the tasks of the agency?" board members indicated that staff education is very sufficient with an average of 8.6 (where 10 is "highly sufficient").

Our first step in examining the relation between feeling of actual influence and effectiveness was to determine if the operationalizations of those concepts resulted in distinguishable variables. In other words did respondents perceive their influence and organizational effectiveness as highly correlated, those with high feelings of influence believing the organization quite effective, while those with lower feelings of influence rated organizational effectiveness lower? The zero-order correlation between perceived actual influence and organizational effectiveness based on comparison to other organizations is $r = .13$ ($n = 109$). Though this value for a sample of 109 reaches what is often considered an acceptable level of statistical significance ($p = .094$, one-tailed test), its magnitude suggests that respondents have distinguished the concepts. The zero-order correlation of perceived actual influence and the organizational effectiveness measure based on expectations is $r = .05$ ($n = 81$, $p = .34$, one-tailed test). This value is based only on board member responses and lends further credence to the contention that respondents, especially board members, conceive personal influence and organizational effectiveness independently.

Though we are interested in the determinants and consequences of perceived influence on the part of executive directors and other staff, this research concentrates on boards. To explore what variables affect feelings of influence on the part of board members we used a "step-wise" multiple regression analysis, entering frequency of board meetings, income, education, frequency of attending board meetings, and the extent to which board members feel informed of board duties as independent variables (see Table 2).

The most important variable in predicting board member influence is the frequency of board meetings. Those members whose boards meet monthly rather than quarterly or annually have slightly greater feelings of influence (the regression coefficient is negative because frequency was coded with small numbers

TABLE 3
Regression Analyses of Organizational Effectiveness

I. Effectiveness measure based on comparison

Independent Variable	B	Standard Error B	F	Adjusted R^2
Staff educational sufficiency	.66	.11	34.97*	.41
Informed of board duties	.26	.12	4.86**	.45

II. Effectiveness measure based on expectations

Independent Variable	B	Standard Error B	F	Adjusted R^2
Staff educational sufficiency	.52	.10	27.67***	.36
Informed of board duties	.39	.11	13.73***	.47

*probability of F with 2,58 df < .0001
**probability of F with 2,58 df < .02
***probability of F with 2,58 df < .0005

representing greater frequency). This variable "explains" about 8.5 percent of the variation is influence. The only other variable whose F value reached significance, the extent to which board members feel informed of their duties, explains an additional 3 percent of the variation in influence. That these two independent variables affect influence seems fairly obvious. Nonetheless we believe it is important to test the obvious, and there clearly remain many other variables that affect board member influence.

We are also interested in exploring the determinants of board effectiveness. Since we have two measures of organizational effectiveness, and though they are fairly high correlated ($r = .74$), we used each as the dependent variable in a step-wise multiple regression analysis where the independent variables were frequency of board meetings, personal influence, education, income, informed of board duties, and staff educational sufficiency rating. The two regressions result in very similar conclusions (see Table 3). Though the regression coefficients and the proportions of variance explained by each independent variable differ somewhat in the two analyses, the same two variables, in the same order, with very similar R^2 values result. What is surprising is the importance of staff educational sufficiency, accounting in both equations for more than 35 percent of the variation in effectiveness ratings. We suspect that responses to that question represent board member assessments of staff competence. At any rate, that variable seems to be tapping more than we expected. Due to the ambiguity of that variable we ran the same regression analyses again, excluding staff educational sufficiency from the independent variable list (see Table 4). These analyses confirm the impact of being informed of board duties and suggest that none of the other independent variables importantly affect effectiveness ratings (the income variable is very marginal, both in significance and amount of variation explained).

Organizational Level

Though we have a very small sample of organizations we believe an exploration of the relationships between both total influence and the distribution of influence and effectiveness ratings is warranted. Total influence (TI) is operationalized as follows. The respondent ratings of board influence in each of the seven issues are averaged, and the respondent ratings of the executive director's influence in each of the seven issues is also averaged, and the two averages totaled. The measure is based upon the responses of all those surveyed in a given organization. The measure ideally should include ratings of senior staff and other staff influence as well. Because a variable but usually large proportion of board members in each organization did not respond to these items, pleading ignorance, we believe that the influence measure at those levels is more likely to be subject to substantial error. We could have based estimates of staff influence solely on their and the executive directors' responses, but either no or very few (1-4) staff completed questionnaires in four of the organizations. We are reluctant to rely upon few responses for the estimates of staff influence. Thus, "total influence" is actually the combined influence of the board and the executive director. Since we have excluded estimates of staff influence, our measure of the distribution of influence is simply the difference between the average of the board influence ratings in the seven areas and the average of the executive director's influence in those areas (DIF).

Following Tannenbaum (1961) we expected that (1) perceived effectiveness (EFF) would be positively correlated with total influence and (2) negatively correlated with the difference in the influence scores of the board and the executive director, in which the more effective the organization the smaller the difference in influence. As Table 5 shows, there is substantial support for the first hypothe-

TABLE 4
Regression Analysis of Organizational Effectiveness
(Excluding "Staff Educational Sufficiency")

I. Effectiveness measure based on comparison

Independent Variable	B	Standard Error B	F	Adjusted R^2
Informed of board duties	.52	.14	13.31*	.14
Income	.40	.23	2.95**	.16

II. Effectiveness measure based on expectations

Independent Variable	B	Standard Error B	F	Adjusted R^2
Informed of board duties	.55	.12	21.0***	.24

*probability of F with 2,58 df < .001
**probability of F with 2,58 df < .10
***probability of F with 2,58 df < .0005

TABLE 5

Correlations Among Effectiveness and Influence Measures*

	EFF(Comparison)	EFF(Expectations)	TI
TI	.849	.555	
DIF	.549	.534	.243
Board Influence	.045	−.133	.428
Ex. Dir. Infl.	.846	.682	.698
EFF (Expectations)	.868		

*n = 7 in each cell; r values greater than .55 are significant at .10 level (1-tailed) and r values greater than .65 are significant at .05 level (1-tailed).

sis but none for the second. In fact, there is a positive correlation between the extent of difference in influence and effectiveness ratings.

Indeed, while total influence is clearly related to effectiveness, it is a composite based on the influence on the board and of the executive director. Of those two, influence of executive director is much more strongly related to effectiveness. This pattern of correlations (EFF positively correlated with DIF, strongly positive correlated with influence of the executive director, and uncorrelated with board influence) suggests that the strong relation between total influence and effectiveness mostly reflects the relation between high influence on the part of the executive director and high ratings of effectiveness. Regrettably the very small sample size and the fact that TI is a composite measure that must be highly correlated with its components (board influence and executive director influence) prevents any multivariate analyses that might disentangle the relations of the influence variables with effectiveness. Though it would be unwise to treat these results as anything more than suggestive given the small sample size, the nature of the sample (all human service agencies with fairly stable funding environments), and the nature of the measures (influence and effectiveness based on participant's perceptions), the results *do* suggest that more effective nonprofit organizations may be those with "strong" executive directors, and that the influence of the board is not very important. Certainly, this hypothesis deserves further comparative investigation.

SUMMARY AND CONCLUSIONS

The research reported in this paper has focused on the internal position of nonprofit organization boards of directors, and on relations between boards and executive directors. It has found the following:

1. Participants in nonprofit organizations experience less actual influence than they think they should have.
2. Board members influence is positively related to the frequency of board meetings and the extent to which board members feel informed of their duties, though neither factor "explains" much variation in board member influence.

FIGURE 1
Fundamental Position and Relations of Director, Board, and Coalition

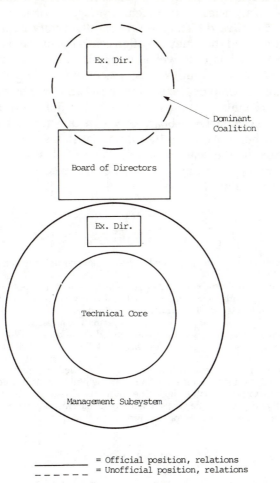

_____ = Official position, relations
_ _ _ _ _ = Unofficial position, relations

3. Ratings of organizational effectiveness are positively related to board member ratings of staff educational sufficiency and the extent to which board members feel informed of their duties.
4. At the organizational level of analysis, organizational effectiveness is strongly related to total influence in the organization—though this result seems to be based
   mostly on the strong relation between the influence of the executive director and
   organizational effectiveness, as effectiveness is unrelated to board influence and
   positively related to the difference in executive director and board influence.

   In conjunction with the few empirical studies of the board role in external effectiveness, this research suggests that boards are a paradoxical "part" of the
nonprofit organization. Boards are not part of an organization's technical core.
Both by tradition and strategy the technical core is buffered from the board.
Boards may often not even be part of the organization's management subsys-
tem. Rather, the board is a device used by the organization's dominant coalition
to co-opt and otherwise "manage" the organization's environment. A nonprofit

organization's dominant coalition must almost always include some of its board members, but it is also likely to include representatives of major funders, regulatory and licensing agencies, and sometimes regional or national bodies in the same domain. Executive directors are frequently a very important part of the dominant coalition, and thus they are often centrally involved in decisions about who to include on the board, as well as in training new board members and setting expectations. While executive directors are ordinarily part of the dominant coalition they are also employees, who are hired and fired by the board. it is this "duality" that accounts for much of the subtle interpersonal and political dynamics that often characterize board-executive directors' relations. Sometimes this duality is further exacerbated by substantial status differences between the executive director and the board members. Figure 1 illustrates our interpretation of the fundamental position and relations of the executive director, the board and the dominant coalition.

NOTES

This article is a revision of a paper presented at the Conference on Nonprofit Leadership and Management, Boston, 1983.
1. There is a large literature on the general concept of incrementalism in policy making and its application to budgeting. "Budgeting is incremental, not comprehensive. The beginning of wisdom about an agency budget is that it is almost never actively reviewed as a whole every year in the sense of reconsidering the value of all existing programs as compared to all possible alternatives. Instead, it is based on last year's budget with special attention given to a narrow range of increases or decreases," according to Wildavsky (1964:82) in a seminal study of governmental budgeting.
2. Though we do not have a random sample from a specified population, we have frequently utilized tests of statistical significance. Such tests are helpful to some, including us, in evaluating magnitudes of differences or relationships. The entire study is *not* conceived to be a rigorous theory-building (or theory-testing) one. Thus, the use of significance tests should not be taken as evidence for or against the verification of any hypothesis.

REFERENCES

Etzioni, A.
    1961   *A Comparative Analysis of Complex Organizations*. Glencoe, Illinois: Free Press.
Flanagan, J.
    1981   *The Successful Volunteer Organization*. Chicago: Contemporary Books
Hannan, M.T. and J. Freeman
    1977   "Obstacles to Comparative Study." Pp. 106-131 in P.S. Goodman and J.M. Pennings (eds.), *New Perspectives on Organizational Effectiveness*. San Francisco: Jossey-Bass.
Hummel, J.
    1980   *Stating and Running a Nonprofit Organizations*. Minneapolis: University of Minnesota Press.
Pearce, J.L.
    1983   "Comparing Volunteers and Employees in a Test of Etzioni's Compliance Typology." Journal of Voluntary Action Research 12, no. 2: 22-30.
Petersen, J.
    1982   "Structuring Voluntary Associations for Effectiveness." Paper presented at 1982 national convention of the Association of Voluntary Scholars.
Pfeffer, J.
    1973   "Size, Composition and Function of Hospital Boards of Directors: A Study of Organization-Environment Linkage." Administrative Science Quarterly 18: 349-64.
Provan, K.
    1980   "Board Power and Organizational Effectiveness Among Human Service Agencies." Academy of Management Journal 23: 221-36.

Tannenbaum, A.
    1956   "Control Structure and Union Functions." American Journal of Sociology 61: 536-45.
    1961   "Control and Effectiveness in a Voluntary Organization." American Journal of Sociology 67: 33-46.
Wildavsky, Aaron
    1964   *Politics of the Budgetary Process*. Boston: Little, Brown.
Wilensky, H. and C. Lebeaux
    1958   *Industrial Society and Social Welfare*. New York: Russell Sage Foundation.

The Implication of Board Member Composition for Fund-Raising Success

Donald L. Plambeck

United Ways are local community-based fund raising and planning organizations that exist in most cities in the United States and Canada. The effectiveness of these organizations in fund raising for community agency services, varies from community to community. This variation occurs even when the fund raising practices utilized by the organizations are similar. This article reports the results of a study that examined United Way organizations seeking to identify variables related to the governing boards that were unique to the organizations that achieved high fund raising results. The study sample consisted of four United Ways located in the mid-west. The results of the study indicated that certain board leadership variables were present in successful United Ways that were not present, or present to a lesser degree in less successful United Ways. These variables included attendance at board meetings, composition of the board, and length of residence in the community. Although the sample was limited to United Way organization the results of the study can have significance for any type of community-based nonprofit organization.

There are an estimated 2,100 United Way organizations in the United States. These organizations are locally organized, independent and incorporated as tax-exempt, 501(c)(3), charitable organizations, governed by a board of volunteers. Their purposes are to: (1) raise money in the local community from individuals and organizations and (2) allocate these funds to various local, nongovernmental, social service agencies. United Way organizations are established in order to respond to the social and human needs of a community. Through a United Way, citizens determine priority needs of the community and raise money to fund agencies or programs that offer services to respond to those needs.

Thirty-two million people—about one out of every three people employed in the U.S.—contribute to United Way each year. Contributions to United Ways result in financial support for about 37,000 agencies and service groups providing human services. (U.W.A., 1982).

Raising money has never been considered an easy job. The problem is compounded because a community is seldom, if ever, able to raise all the money that its human services and health care agencies need. Additionally, economic, political, and social conditions change and create new or expanded demands for funds. One traditional approach to fund raising, used by local United Way organizations and other nonprofit community agencies, has been to recruit as many prominent community leaders as possible to become members of the board of directors. The principle underlying this practice is that an organizations's success is related to the community power represented on the board of directors and that the more powerful or influential the board members are, the more successful the organization will be in raising funds to carry out its mission or program.

In 1966, the national association of United Ways made two recommendations: the members of the local boards should be chosen with extreme care, since they had the responsibility of raising funds for many agencies; and, while the board must represent the community, nothing should prevent the organization from choosing the best and strongest community leaders as board members (UCFCA, 1966). Another organization, the National Association of Hearing and Speech Agencies (1969) recommended to its members that board members should be sought from the top leaders available from the power structure of the community. These leaders according to NAHSA, are the men and women who are the financial, corporate, social, and thought leaders, and a Hearing and Speech Agency should not settle for less than these types of people on the board.

This paper presents the results of a study of the fund-raising effectiveness of four local United Way organizations; the results indicate that this longstanding practice of creating a board comprised predominately of powerful community leaders may not be a sound organizational practice (Plambeck, 1984). The research indicates that a United Way's efforts to achieve significantly increased fund raising could be hampered when the board of directors is comprised of too many long-time community leaders. The research also supports the statement by Lee (1974:16) that "A board of directors does not exist because all organizations must have one, or because a certain list of names makes an organization look good. A board has an absolutely essential role to play, and nothing can substitute for it determining the success of a nonprofit organization. The board is the pivotal point upon which the attainment of an organization's goal turns. It is the board that determines what an organization's goals will be, and when and how they will be refined to meet the changing needs of society over time."

STUDY METHOD AND RESULTS

The study examined the structure and operational practices of four large metropolitan United Way organizations located in the midwest. Two of the cities had raised significantly larger amounts of money in the annual fund drives over a three year period (1979, 1980, 1981) than the two other similar-sized United Ways. The four organizations studied had similar economic and demographic conditions. The study was based on *ex post facto* case studies utilizing structured interviews, annual reports, board minutes, and other written documents. The study indicated that there were certain variables present in the successful United Ways that were not present, or present to lesser degree in the unsuccessful United Ways. One of issues studied was the make-up of the board of directors and included the following variables:

TABLE 1
Summary of Leadership Values

| | Average Goal Increase (1) | THE GOVERNING BOARD | | | | | |
		Number of Board Members (2)	Average Board Meeting Attendance (3)	% Male Board Members (4)	% White Board Members (5)	Average Age of Board Members (6)	% of Board Members With 20 + Years Residence (7)
Successful Case 1	13%	61	70%	67%	84%	48	62%
Successful Case 2	12%	52	60%	79%	87%	50.6	63%
Unsuccessful Case 1	6.2%	60	45%	87%	80%	53	90%
Unsuccessful Case 2	7.2%	58	40%	83%	91%	55	79%

Sources: Column 1, 2,: Annual Reports of Case United Ways.
           Column 3, 4, 5, 6, 7: Interviews with Board and Staff.

1. The number of members that comprise the board of directors.
2. The ethnic and sexual composition of the board, consisting of the number of male and white members.
3. The average age of board members and the average length of time board members had resided in the community.
4. The average attendance of total board membership at board meetings.

While it was not possible to distinguish successful from unsuccessful cases based on the variable of racial composition of the board, as reflected by the percent of white board members, or by the size of the board, the results of the study, as indicated in Table 1, did indicate that the successful cases differed from unsuccessful cases in a number of ways. Successful United Ways had boards of directors with higher attendance at board meetings; a smaller percentage of male board members; a lower average age of board members; and shorter periods of residence in the community.

The two successful cities (those which raised significantly more money) also had established higher percentage fund-raising goals each year than the two unsuccessful United Ways. The unsuccessful communities set much smaller goals each year that were more easily attainable. These two communities felt that it was more important to succeed in reaching a minimal goal than to risk the possible failure of not reaching a higher level goal. The establishment of goals that were significantly higher than the previous year's results indicated the willingness of the volunteers in the successful communities to assume greater responsibility and a higher risk of failure. The establishing of higher goals also meant that the community leaders who comprised the top volunteers in the fund raising drive became more active in the campaign and assumed more individual responsibility for results.

The successful cases utilized community priority needs studies in the goal-setting process. The purpose of using priority studies on fund raising was to set the fund-raising goal more in line with the human service problems and needs of the community. This awareness of community needs by board members appeared to increase their willingness to risk establishing higher fund-raising goals.

That the successful United Ways had boards composed of higher percentage of younger and newer community leaders may be reflective of communities that were not as conservative in their approaches to community affairs. The presence of newer leaders may provide the opportunity to examine traditional approaches to fund raising and management of the United Ways. Such an examination of previous methods of operation is necessary for any organization to maintain its ability to be more open and responsive to the changing needs of the community. Further, the presence of a wider range of non-male members would indicate that the boards could look at issues and decisions with a broader community perspective.

The successful United Ways utilized more of a strategic rather than a tactical approach to fund raising. While all four of the cases used similar fund raising methods during the annual campaign, the successful cases worked with longer time frames for campaign planning and staffing. The volunteers that chaired the annual campaign were recruited two or three years prior to the campaign. The fund-raising campaign was directly affected by early identification of leadership in that it allowed long-range planning of the campaign as well as providing one or two opportunities for a volunteer to observe or become involved with a campaign before assuming the responsibility of chairmanship.

In contrast, when a campaign chairman was recruited for the current year's fund drive, there was a tendency to run the campaign by simply repeating the previous year's efforts. This short-term recruitment also reduced the opportunity to plan new fund-raising methods or programs. The willingness of community leaders to commit themselves to assuming the chairmanship of the annual campaign several years in advance of the campaign also may have reflected the community's view of the role or importance of the United Way.

Successful United Ways had, as strategy, the development of a wider range of contacts and collaboration with other community and government organizations concerned with human and social programs. These successful organizations consciously expanded contacts and involvement in the community in order to assume a broader community posture and strengthen their role in the community as the primary community volunteer organization. This stronger image helped in the ability to recruit new volunteers who move into the community. Additionally, the image of the United Way and its role in the community affected the support that corporations provided in conducting fund-raising campaigns within their organizations. When the United Way was recognized and accepted by the community, the fund raising campaign was accepted as a major community responsibility.

IMPLICATIONS OF RESULTS

Because the policies and programs of any community-based organization are influenced by the composition of the board of directors, one could hypothesize from this study that nonprofit organizations with younger and less conservative boards will establish policies that are less conservative and have members who commit to programs with greater elements of risk. This hypothesis runs counter to the traditional assumption that the more established board members a United Way has, the more successful the fund-raising results will be. United Ways may want to examine the make-up of present boards to incorporate board members that will support goals that require greater effort and represent greater risk.

If a nonprofit organization feels it needs to be active and risktaking to be successful, it would perhaps be best served by a board with a limited number of established community leaders and a broader community representation. However, if an agency is comfortable with its role and position in the community, it would function best by building or maintaining a board consisting of the recognized leaders in the community.

Twenty years ago, Lippincott and Hannestad (1964: 88) stated, "The most important element in agency structure is the membership and activity of its board of directors. No other aspect of a voluntary agency is a more certain indicator of the state of its health or more crucial to that health. If one were limited to a single question on the status of an agency, it would be well to ask for attendance by name of members at meetings of the board and executive committee held during the last three years. If the answer shows the average to be less than the indicated

50% of the four meetings per year, and if those attending are always the same members, then one may be sure that something is wrong with the agency."

The members of the board are responsible for the determination of the policies and strategy of the organization. Swanson (1978) describes the board as the "determinative team," responsible for the formulation and determination of policy and seeing to it that the policies are carried out by staff.

Swanson (1978) points out the problems of recruitment of established individuals as board directors: "There is a tendency for agencies to pursue the bigger names in the community and big names are frequently spread far too thin to be of any more than occasional use to a community service organization. If occasional service meets a specific need, all well and good, but good organization is usually better served by qualified and experienced people, albeit people with lesser community reputations.

It is far better for the long haul to have a solid organization made up of capable team players than to build one's hopes upon having a community star at the helm. This is not to belittle those to whom the accolade 'community star' applies, as these are very often men and women who leave a large legacy of good works behind to the community wherein they live and work. However, it is also true that such stars quite often do their thing in a highly individualized manner and then move on to repeat performances elsewhere—leaving behind an organization bereft of leadership."

Haller (1972: 163-164), in providing guiding elements to nonprofits regarding the selection of board members, stated, "New views and energy can only come from new faces. People who are in the same position or environment for too long often lose their ability to probe and find solutions to new problems. They tend also to prevent others from trying to look at old problems or traditional methods in new ways. ('Oh, we tried that before,' or 'you have some good ideas there but...'). The organization of change requires new views of new people."

In this study, fund raising success was used as the success criteria. Further research needs to be done to help identify other criteria that measure effectiveness and success that could be applied to a variety of nonprofit organizations. Since the study was limited to four cases and utilized the case method of analysis it was not possible to predict fund raising success of a United Way organization based on this research. To predict fund raising success a much larger sample of United Way organizations should be utilized in order to permit the use of statistical methods. However, the evidence of the patterns of variables in successful United Way organizations, when compared to less successful organizations, points out the desirability of conducting further research based on larger samples of organizations and utilizing more powerful statistical methods. Additional research questions this study leads to include:

1. What other organizational variables are affected by the age, sex and longevity characteristics of board members?
2. How does board composition influence the job expectations and the performance evaluation of the executive director?
3. Can a board composition model be constructed for board member recruitment in order to influence the effectiveness of the organization?

REFERENCES

Haller, Leon
    1982   *Financial Resource Management for Nonprofit Organizations* Englewood Cliffs, New Jersey: Prentice-Hall Inc.
Lee, James C.
    1974   *Do or Die: Survival For Nonprofits* Washington, D.C.: Taft Productions, Inc.
Lippincott, Earle and Aannestad, Elling
    1964   "Management of Voluntary Agencies." Harvard Business Review (November-December): 87-98.
National Association of Hearing & Speech Agencies
    1969   *Fundraising Programs Community Voluntary Agencies* Washington, D.C.: NAHSA.
Plambeck, Donald L.
    1984   "Voluntary Organizations in Transition: A Case Study of United Way Organization in Four Communities" (Doctoral dissertation, Virginia Tech).
Swanson, Andrew
    1978   *The Determinative Team.* Hicksville, N.Y.: Exposition Press.
United Community Funds and Councils of America
    1966   *Organizating A United Fund.* New York: UCFCA.
United Way of America
    1982   *Fact Sheet, Questions and Answers about United Way* Alexandria, Va.: UWA

Conjoint Directorship: Clarifying Management Roles Between the Board of Directors and the Executive Director

Robert F. Leduc and Stephen R. Block

There are a number of management roles that must be played if a nonprofit organization is to be successful. Drawing on the work of Mintzberg, ten managerial roles in nonprofit organizations are reviewed and prescriptions about the appropriate allocation of each role between board and staff are advanced. Throughout, it is stressed that recognition of the skills of the executive director and the responsibilities of the board of directors is critical for appropriately assigning the various functions. Finally, teamwork should be the ultimate goal of the board and staff in order to move the organization toward fulfilling its mission.

In any organization, there are a number of management roles that must be played if the organization is to be successful. In business organizations, for example, the board of directors empowers a management staff, comprised of a chief executive officer and a top management team to run the operation in the interest of earning money for the shareholders of the corporation. Toward this end, the management team is assigned the authority and autonomy to make and implement their own program plans and operational decisions. Meanwhile, the board's role is shaped by its own culture, history and the canons of the corporation (Mueller, 1982).

Management roles in the nonprofit sphere are somewhat different. In nonprofit organizations, the board is the legally constituted leadership body and shares actively in fulfilling the mission of the organization (Connors, 1980). Although the nonprofit board usually delegates the day to day management tasks to the executive director, many of the most important management roles and program functions are shared among the board, the executive director, and support staff. These shared management areas include planning, budgeting, marketing and fund raising.

Nonprofit organizations generally maintain fuzzy lines of management responsibility. In fact, the ambiguity of assigned responsibility in nonprofit organizations often leads to staff and/or board concerns about the parameters of tasks assigned to both paid and unpaid personnel. Furthermore, serious tension in the nonprofit organization is a common outcome when volunteers and staff are unclear about the boundaries of their assignments. In fact, various writers (Conrad & Glenn, 1979) have addressed the phenomenon of "dynamic tension" in the nonprofit organization and suggest that there are benefits in struggling for perfect role clarification.

Unlike the concept of dynamic tension which relies on a tug and pull approach to clarify management role responsibility, the authors favor another view of shared management. In this article, it is suggested that board/staff relations can, from its outset, reflect a positive *team* approach. One might call this approach "conjoint directorship," the goal of which is to maximize the management capacity of the organization while simultaneously fulfilling the board's legal responsibility to control its mission and allow the executive director the range of management prerogatives necessary for proper operations. The premise of "conjoint directorship" is based on the idea that important management roles can be thoughtfully and intentionally ascribed to board members or staff. This approach builds on the theoretical management framework advanced by Henry Mintzberg. In *The Nature of Managerial Work*, Mintzberg (1973) examined the cluster of managerial roles and developed a model which describes responsibilities and a set of activities that is expected of an individual in a management position. Here we explicitly apply his model to the nonprofit arena.

The goal of this article is to review Mintzberg's ten managerial roles and demonstrate their applicability to nonprofit organizations. Through this application we will see how role identification in the nonprofit organization is possible, and how the division of management functions can be a consciously stated process rather than an unguided behavioral course. The outcome of this exercise is a better understanding of the role difference between board members and staff members which, in the end, will help advance the mission of the organization (see Table 1).

MINTZBERG'S INTERPERSONAL ROLES

The Figurehead

A figurehead is a person who is put in charge or identified as the leader of the organization or occasionally the head of a special project for the organization. While this position is often symbolic in nature and does not carry the power for independent decision-making, the person who serves in this status role is immediately identified with the organization. This special identification can be an influential tool as well as a valuable asset for gaining entree into meetings and ceremonial civic events. In fact, the figurehead often emerges when the organization is expected to be represented at public functions and community activities. Generally, the dominant personality in the organization will evolve into this position.

Although this role can be played by board or staff members, the role is almost always served by the executive director. In some situations, a board member (typically the board president), one of the organization's founders, or an organizational volunteer of longstanding may assume this position. Some organizations build the image of the organization around their executive director. In this case, the figurehead is a paid staff member who can bring continuity to the organization as volunteer members come and go. Furthermore, the organization may consider more than one figurehead to share the duties, responsibilities and

TABLE 1
Summary of 10 Roles for Managing Nonprofit Organizations[a]

ROLE	DESCRIPTION	PRINCIPAL RESPONSIBILITY
Interpersonal		
Figurehead	Symbolic head; obliged to perform a number of routine duties of a legal/social nature	Executive Director
Leader	Responsible for motivation and activation of subordinates	Executive Director Board President
Liaison	Maintains self-developed network of outside contacts and informers	Executive Director Board Members
Informational		
Monitor	Seeks and receives information to understand organization and its environment	Executive Director Board Secretary
Disseminator	Transmits information received and interprets information	Executive Director Board President
Spokesperson	Transmits information outsiders; serves as "the voice" of the organization	Executive Director
Decisional		
Entrepreneur	Initiates improvement projects and searches for opportunities	Executive Director
Disturbance Handler	Responsible for trouble-shooting and planning for crisis intervention	Executive Director
Resource Allocator	Allocates the organization's financial and human resources	Executive Director Treasurer
Negotiator	Negotiates/mediates internal and external disputes	Executive Director Board President Board Members

a. Headings and role descriptions are adapted from Henry Mintzberg, The Nature of Managerial Work (New York: Harper & Row, 1973); principal responsibilities have been added.

the prestige of the figurehead role. However, if more than one is selected, it is a good idea to partialize or carve out specific aspects of the organization or issues for them to represent. For example, someone can be identified with the organization as a whole, while someone else is seen as the organization's expert in child issues, housing issues, or health care, etc.

It is a good practice for the Nominations Committee to choose individuals with leadership qualities who can eventually serve in the figurehead role. Finally, the figurehead position should generally not be assigned to an individual who is already identified with another voluntary cause.

The Leader

Mintzberg defines the organizational leader as one who is responsible for the motivation of subordinates and for staffing the organization. Since it is virtually impossible for anyone but a fulltime employee to keep up with the daily staffing demands of a medium size or larger organization, this role is most likely to be played by the executive director. On the other hand, motivation within an organization is a more complex issue. Anyone can generate the motivational force in the organization. In this case, motivation is an outcome of vision and charisma, and people other than the executive director can provide this quality. Although others may have the ability to demonstrate this force, they may not have the time and positional power that is inherent in the executive director's station.

The concept of "leader" can also be considered from another perspective, especially as it relates to policy decisions. In this area, the board must take primary responsibility. While the board's role may largely be delegated, it is critical that it maintain an overview and final authority. In fact, the board must be involved in establishing the parameters of the organization's mission, markets, and services, in addition to participating in efforts to raise financial resources.

In the truest sense, the board and the executive director must work in partnership to lead the organization. A useful distinction to make here is that the board's decisions are the longer term ones (with the advice of the executive director), while the executive director must make the short term decisions (hopefully with the advice and counsel of one or more members of the board). In addition, boards may delegate much of their responsibility to an executive director, but the board must assume a willingness to change the chief of staff when that person is not consistently accomplishing the duties of the job. To underscore the point, it must be emphasized that the board holds the ultimate leadership responsibility for hiring, and if necessary, firing the executive director.

The Liaison

The liaison role calls on the organization to maintain an outside network of people who can keep the organization informed as well as provide the occasional favor (e.g., when an outside source informs the executive director or a board member of a grant opportunity or a proposed piece of legislation that might affect the organization's clientele). Usually, the executive director will evolve as the principal functionary in this area because of the time demands, attention and visibility that is necessary to cultivate a meaningful network. Nevertheless, it is possible through their own personal business and community contacts for board members to share in this responsibility. The only potential for conflict in this situation is when different sources provide contradictory information. In this instance, rather than try to persuade everyone that their "inside" information is correct, it will be important for both the board member and the executive director to direct the conflict outside of the organization by returning, diplomatically, to their original informants for clarification.

Mintzberg's Interpersonal Roles: An Overview

In all three roles—figurehead, leader, and liaison—the emphasis is on the interpersonal management activities of the organization. A most important skill is an ability to interact with people in a manner that will promote their voluntary support of the organization and its goals. The role is what Wilson (1976) referred to as "an enabler of human resources." In order to accomplish this end, it is necessary for the organizational leadership to be visible, accessible, and responsive. Naturally, the executive director has the time and, hopefully, the interest, to assume the interpersonal role effort. However, the organization would be far better off if it recognized that one or more of the board members can also participate in a noncompetitive way, by actively engaging in one of the interpersonal functions, especially when the organization must interact with key stakeholders, such as funders, volunteers, and other community leaders. Indeed, the three interpersonal roles can reinforce the teamwork concept.

MINTZBERG'S INFORMATIONAL ROLES

The Monitor

Because an organization is deluged with information of both an internal and external nature, it is necessary that all information funnel into one nerve center. Again, time pressures plus an intimate understanding of the organization and its surrounding environment virtually demand that this monitoring role be assigned to the executive director. Furthermore, the executive director might delegate monitoring tasks to staff, but in the end they should be required to brief the director fully to assure knowledge of the nature and content of information that has been received or exported.

Also, the board, through the office of the secretary, is responsible for certain monitoring functions. Specifically, the board has oversight of legal and informational documents such as the articles of incorporation, tax determination letters, and by-laws.

The Disseminator

In this informational role, the disseminator is the individual who transmits the mass of information received by the organization from outsiders or insiders. This is a very important role because the function demands a great deal of integration and interpretation of information. Consequently, the position allows the translator to "tell the story" as it is perceived. Naturally, the disseminator would yield influence and direction by how the facts are perceived or the organizational world interpreted, or even by variations in self-image (Bales, 1970; Boyatiz, 1982). In practice, this role is primarily performed by the executive director. In turn, the Chair of the board assumes this role when reporting to the board of directors.

The Spokesman

The spokesman is the voice of the organization, the person who transmits information to outsiders about the activities, issues and positions of the organization. The format, content, and seriousness of the message is the key for determining the organizational spokesman (Stech, 1983). The range of functions for the spokesman may vary from sending news releases to debating public officials on radio or television. While the board may hold the legal responsibility for informing the public about its mission, purpose and activities, this role is likely to be delegated to the executive director who has the time to fulfill this function and was often hired for excellent verbal and writing skills.

Mintzberg's Informational Roles: An Overview

The informational roles assigned to the monitor, disseminator, and spokesman are critical for moving information through the organization. How the information is sent and the content of the message will reveal meaning about the organization's stated and unstated positions, in addition to providing clues about the leadership's strengths and weaknesses (Watzlawick, et. al, 1967). Therefore, the most insightful and skilled management individual should assume the informational roles. These competencies should be identified in the executive director who has the time and rank to accomplish these important tasks.

While the executive director is the most appropriate person to control the flow of organizational information, the board must understand that the ability to control information places the executive director in a very powerful as well as vulnerable position. Intentionally or unintentionally, the executive director can influence the policy decision capability of the board by either stressing or withholding certain information.

Being aware of the executive director's potential power to filter certain information, the chairperson of the board must ask the executive director for as much information as seems necessary for the board to responsibly govern the organization. Finally, board members should also feel comfortable to make inquiries to the executive director or request information which they believe will enhance their individual voluntary or governance role.

MINTZBERG'S DECISIONAL ROLES

The Entrepreneur

In the role of entrepreneur, the goal is to search the organization's environment for opportunities to improve both its standing in the community, through "improvement projects," and its financial resource base. While it is probably true that nonprofit organizations are not as enterprising as most people feel they should be, it is categorically true that nonprofit organizations are not as entrepreneurial as they could be (Crimmins, 1983). Indeed, the search for resources continues to focus on gifts from foundations, corporations and the affluent friends of board members (Koch, 1979).

In many respects, the individual who is able to raise the bulk of the financial resources, or ascertain a place for the organization in an important community endeavor, will be acknowledged as "the entrepreneur." In this role, the individual may also be viewed as spokesman, figurehead and leader.

While members of the board can play a significant role in the development of resources, it is usually the executive director who can devote the time necessary to this important activity. Finally, to be successful at entrepreneurship, the organization must adopt a willingness to examine creative alternatives to raising revenues and investing funds (Brandt, 1982).

Disturbance Handler

The role of the disturbance handler is that of a "trouble shooter." Through this role, the organization can take corrective action when faced with important, unexpected disturbances. In this case, the disturbance handler will facilitate an emergency staff meeting, or board/executive committee meeting to discuss the problem facing the organization. At the meeting, the disturbance handler keeps the group on target in order to develop a strategy or plan for resolving the crisis. The legal responsibilities of the board demand that it address organizational problems, but the execution of the plan may be delegated to the executive director and staff. While the executive director or the board president are the likely individuals to assume the disturbance handler role, it is not uncommon for a committee chairperson, or other board officer to be thrust into this position.

Resource Allocator

Since competent financial management is imperative to the survival of any nonprofit organization (Connors and Callaghan, 1982), the role of resource allocator is a most important one. The individual who is assigned this role is responsible for alloting the organization's finances or other assets for the purpose of moving the organization forward toward meeting its program plans and mission. This role has been legally defined as one which every board member must sustain, but it has particular import for the treasurer (Leduc, 1980). In fact, the duties of the treasurer are so significant, it is critical that this officer be motivated, strong, and attentive to the whole financial picture of the organization (Leduc, 1980). The importance attached to this function necessitates that this officer rely on the day to day financial management skills of the executive director and the bookkeeper. Furthermore, the board and the treasurer must depend on the budget plans and recommendations from the one individual who is most intimately acquainted with the operations of the organization, i.e., the executive director.

Finally, the executive director should have some independent authority to change budget line items and allocate resources, up to an agreed upon level, without waiting for the next board/executive committee meeting. Besides enhancing decision-making capacity, this flexibility in resource allocation authority permits the executive director to maintain greater continuity of operations.

The Negotiator

The activity of negotiation is "a basic means of getting what you want from others. It is a back and forth communication designed to reach an agreement when you and the other side have some interests that are shared and others that are opposed" (Fisher and Ury, 1983: xi). In the nonprofit organization, the negotiator bargains with the organization's significant stakeholders, such as funders, volunteers, and community groups. Furthermore, Gordon (1977) suggests that a leader with proven negotiation skills will increase the likelihood of effective management meetings, and the establishment of acceptable policies.

The negotiator role is usually played by the executive director, but can be assumed by the president or other members of the board. In some instances, it may also be necessary to contract with a consultant or attorney to assist the organization in negotiations of a critical nature.

Mintizberg's Decisional Role: An Overview

The four decisional roles—entrepreneur, disturbance handler, resource allocator, and negotiator—require more board involvement than do the informational and interpersonal roles. The activity that threads the four decisional roles together is "strategy" development. Whether the focus is on designing cash producing projects, alleviating a crisis, determining cash outlay, or settling disputes, the board must be involved in the planning process or, at the very least, it must sanction the plan of the executive director. Indeed, decisional roles are partnership opportunities which provide a chance for coordinating the views of both the board and the staff. As with the informational and interpersonal role sets, the board may delegate key managerial activities to the executive director without diminishing their legal responsibility to make or approve final decisions.

CONJOINT DIRECTORSHIP: RECOMMENDATIONS FOR APPLICATION

The framework offered in this article outlines roles that must be played by the board and/or executive director of a midsize or larger nonprofit organization. Throughout, it was implied that organizational success is a measure of both the careful assignment of managerial roles and respect for the participants' abilities. Mintzberg's model was adapted to the nonprofit arena in order to identify the key management roles. In addition, the model offers guidance in determining which organizational character would be best suited to handling each of the roles. The nonprofit organization will perform more effectively and with less confusion if the members of the organization assess the competency and time commitments of its personnel and volunteer body, and fit the right person to each of the important operational roles.

Although members of an organization can find several ways to integrate the conjoint directorship model into their organization, we favor the method in which the board of directors, the executive director and key management staff participate, at least annually, in a planning/reevaluation retreat. This type of retreat has the capability of enhancing team building providing that the agenda focuses on goal-setting, problem-solving, and developing collaborative efforts (Dyer, 1977). In addition, the retreat should permit the participants an opportunity to renew their organizational commitments as well as clarify expectations of each other. Also, when planning a retreat, we recommend a balance in the schedule between business items and social activity in order to facilitate relationship-building.

One of the more important goals of the business agenda will be the development of a "job description" which details the role assignment, tasks, and functions of the volunteers and the executive director. By utilizing the managerial descriptions found in this paper, the participants can establish job descriptions which not only outline the key responsibilities of essential positions, but also define the limits of both the volunteers' and the executive director's role.

In some cases, the organization will already have existing job descriptions and new ones will not have to be written. In this situation, the board and staff should still review the existent job descriptions. By following this process the board and staff will have an opportunity to reaffirm current policy and be reminded of the responsibilities which they may or may not have effectively assumed. Of course, during the review of extant job descriptions, modifications also should be made which reflect changes in the organization's goals or fiscal capacity to achieve them. Finally, besides detailing the role of the board members and the executive director, the retreat participants should also outline their expectations of committees, describe major organizational projects, and set appropriate deadlines for evaluating organizational achievements.

Following the retreat, a comprehensive written summary of the events should be sent to the board and management staff. Included in these "minutes" should be a copy of the agreed upon job descriptions and assignments. By distributing the products of the retreat, the idea that the meeting was successful will be reinforced, and the newly stated commitments and expectations of the board members will have moved from the informal retreat setting back to the formal organizational environment. Furthermore, copies of the job descriptions and revised organizational goals should be sent to the nominations committee in order to assist them in their search for appropriate board members.

CONCLUSION

Throughout this essay the emphasis on the qualities and expectations of the executive director has not been exaggerated. The executive director should be capable in a variety of managerial roles and should support those competencies with talented personnel. On the other hand, the board is legally responsible for the organization and should exert its influence, like the corporate board, with a sense of ownership.

The objectives of the staff and the board should be a shared vision and determination to advance the organization's mission and goals. In order to accomplish this objective, the organizational participants will need to pool their skills and choose their assignments carefully. Indeed, teamwork is not only possible, it is in the best interest of the organization and its goals.

REFERENCES

Bales, R.F.
    1970   *Personality and Interpersonal Behavior*. New York: Holt, Rhinehart, & Winston.
Boyatiz, R.E.
    1982   *The Competent Manager: A Model for Effective Performance*. New York: John Wiley & Sons.
Brandt, S.C.
    1982   *Entrepreneuring*. Reading, Mass.: Addison-Wesley.
Connors, T.D. (Ed.)
    1980   *The Nonprofit Organization Handbook*. New York: McGraw Hill.
Connors, T.D. and C.T. Callaghan (Eds.)
    1982   *Financial Management for Nonprofit Organizations*. New York: AMACOM.
Conrad, W.R. and W.R. Glenn
    1976   *The Effective Voluntary Board of Directors*. Chicago: Swallow Press.
Crimmins, J.C. and M. Keil
    1983   *Enterprise In The Nonprofit Sector*. Washington, D.C.: Partners For Livable Places.
Dyer, W.G.
    1977   *Team Building: Issues and Alternatives*. Reading, Massachusetts: Addison-Wesley.
Fisher, R. and W.Ury
    1983   *Getting To Yes*. New York: Penguin.
Gordon, T.
    1977   *Leader Effectiveness Training*. Toronto: Bantam Books.
Koch, F.
    1979   *The New Corporate Philanthropy*. New York: Plenam Press.
Leduc, R.F.
    1980   "Financial Management and Budgeting." In Connors, T., ed., *The Nonprofit Organization Handbook*. New York: McGraw Hill.
Louden, J.K.
    1982   *The Director*. New York: AMACOM.
Mintzberg, H.
    1973   *The Nature of Managerial Work*. New York: Harper & Row.
Mueller, R.K.
    1982   *Board Score*. Lexington, Mass.: Lexington Books.
Stech, E.L.
    1983   *Leadership Communication*. Chicago: Nelson-Hall.
Watzlawick, P., J.H. Beaven, and D.D. Jackson
    1967   *Pragmatics of Human Communication*. New York: W.W. Norton & Company.
Wilson, M.
    1976   *The Effective Management of Volunteer Programs*. Boulder, Co.: Volunteer Management Association.

Managing Expectations: What Effective Board Members Ought to Expect from Nonprofit Organizations

Terry W. McAdam and David L. Gies

Expectations are one key component of the glue which holds an organization to-gether. When expectations are not explicitly developed and clearly communicated, effective relations between board and staff are not likely. This article prescribes the basic expectations an effective board member should have, especially regarding key organizational factors such as: administration and management information, fiscal information, and human resource management. Fifteen specific questions are de-scribed which will provide board members and the executive staff with one useful set of tools to insure effective communication of expectations.

This article discusses the widespread condition existing in many nonprofit or-ganizations (NPOs) in which board members are not given and do not develop clear expectations of their roles and responsibilities (or the role of the staff in helping the board carry out its functions). The article identifies board members themselves as primarily responsible for this condition and suggests why clarity of expectation is important, yet sometimes difficult to achieve. Next, it discusses insuring against organization dysfunction. Then, the article presents a series of questions which can serve as useful board tools with illustrations of their appli-cation in clarifying board roles and responsibilities. The result of such applica-tion should be a strengthened NPO performance.

The authors conclude that a nonprofit organization board member will be both more constructive and more effective in helping guide the NPO in carrying out its mission by posing and reviewing the answers to these questions. Moreover, the NPO's staff will be more efficient, effective, satisfied in their work, and clear about their roles and responsibilities in the process.

WHY CLEAR EXPECTATIONS ARE IMPORTANT

The nonprofit sector, though somewhat hidden from much of society's view (or at least not readily identifiable by many persons as a separate segment), rep-resents approximately 5% of the Gross National Product and "one-third of the employment in the nation's rapidly growing service sector" according to Sala-mon and Abramson (1982: 222). These statistics demonstrate the magnitude and value of resources being coordinated and controlled by the nonprofit sector. The responsbility to be clear about board leadership and effective in the conduct of this leadership has never before been more critical. Clear expectations regarding the board's role is important because it represents a significant contribution to meeting the needs of American people.

Lack of clarity about mission, role, function and responsibility deprives the organization one of the key elements of sound leadership—i.e., a knowledgeable, wise and purposeful board of directors. Current environmental conditions surrounding nonprofit organizations demand knowledgeable leadership by board members. President Reagan has advocated "giving the government back to the people through voluntarism" (1981). This approach of returning the provision of social goods to private nongovernmental programs will require greater capacity of voluntary boards to lead effectively. In the face of this new national emphasis on voluntary leadership, nonprofit organizations are demonstrating a mix of both strong and weak leadership.

Ineffective voluntary boards are the result of many factors, including limited communication and understanding of mission. Mission changes with environment. The environment is always changing. This situation of change (at varying rates) requires constant vigilance on the part of the Board of Directors, Chief Executive Officer, and staff in order to adjust the organization to its always-new environment. Lack of attention to the organization's environmental position causes unnecessary stress, resulting in organizational dysfunction.

INSURING AGAINST THE RISK OF ORGANIZATIONAL DYSFUNCTION

State legislation and the Internal Revenue Service require a board of directors to incorporate and document the purpose of the organization before tax-exempt status can be granted. But there are disturbing trends in the insurance industry which support the notion that many voluntary boards may be facing an increasing risk of being judged to be dysfunctional. The authors recently investigated several of these trends for this paper. Today's trends reflect a shift of responsibility from the public sector to the nonprofit sector and an increase in legal actions against voluntary leadership. According to our national source there have been significant changes in the insurance industry's coverage of nonprofit board liability. Minimum annual premium increases for this type of insurance have been in the 25% to 40% range. Increases are expected to go much higher in the near term.

There have also been significant increases in the "writing" of such insurance policies over the past several years. "It is safe to say that writings increase yearly anywhere from 35% to 75% or higher."[1] At this rate the demand for board malpractice and/or liability insurance will more than triple in three years making 1988 a critical and possibly desperate period in which voluntary board membership may be inhibited due to personal financial exposure. Granted, there are to date few cases where individuals have suffered as a result of a litigation in the nonprofit sector. But the trends indicate insurance companies are providing for increased defense costs and further increases are anticipated. In 1984 there were 15 major insurance companies offering nonprofit organization liability coverage. Currently this number is down to five or fewer companies. Moreover, the subject of leadership risk and its relationship to the insurance industry deserves further study.

Despite such disturbing news many people continue to accept the responsibility to serve on boards and attempt to meet community needs. Individual motives for voluntary service are numerous. We asked people who risk service on a nonprofit board why they bother. Their responses are listed in rank order as follows:

- To influence the institutional practices of an organization which is providing a social good.
- To express a commitment to the community.
- To affect public policy.
- To achieve some personal recognition.

Another important reasons is that people care vary much. Brian O'Connell describes the personal meaning of volunteering in the context of community service, that "caring and service are giving and volunteering" (O'Connell, 1985: 3). Yet the caring doesn't always lead to effective institutional action. Often this is because the players are not clear about their roles and responsibilities—they need to clarify and manage well their expectations.

In the nonprofit organization, many board members lose their effectiveness as organizational actors. It is as if the economic conditions, organizational/management issues and solutions they confront in the for-profit or government sectors where they are employed are not transferred when these same people are analyzing nonprofit organization management issues. Administrative procedures and controls in a nonprofit organization are often different when compared to for profit or government organizations. Perspectives are different because the motivation of volunteers and many times the staff are different. For example, board members in nonprofits are not paid for their contributions. Compare this voluntary action to shareholders in the for profit sector in which individuals participate to enhance their financial positions. Nonprofit "shareholders" or volunteer board members participate in order to affect public policy or one of the other reasons listed earlier.

Not only are the dynamics and participatory incentives different between sectors in our society, the relatively lower level of resources, defined as senior staff time, available for managing the board of director relationships impairs nonprofit organizations (Conrad and Glenn, 1983: xv). More often than not, many members of nonprofit organization boards are uninformed and taken for granted. The Chief Executive Officer spends time with only one or two key figures and leaves the other voluntary members ignorant due to an inadequate management information system and process for disseminating and modifying the information to be provided.

Ignorance can be deadly! The thinking nonprofit organization board member must take initiative to ensure he/she understands what is going on. Nonprofit organizations can benefit significantly from new voices or consciences. The reader could become such a voice for constructive change and benefit significantly from increased accountability.

The next section offers a few questions/tools which might help clarify the board member's role and, thus, enable more effective institutional behavior to take place. Consider these questions as specific tools to help your nonprofit organization's staff to stay out in front of the organization's mission, resources, key problems and opportunities, remembering that it is the overall health and performance of the organization for which the board of directors has accepted both responsibility and liability.

WHAT ARE THE RIGHT QUESTIONS?

There are at least 15 questions a thinking board member should consider asking during the first year of service on a nonprofit organization's board. The timing of asking these questions, of course, depends on the size of the organization, the state of organizational development, and the level of sophistication and management capacity of the staff. Board members can also select from among this ideal list those questions which they believe will generate the most constructive activity for the organization. The questions are divided into three groupings: (1) administrative and management information, (2) fiscal information, (3) human resource planning.

The balance of this article will review these three groups of questions providing selected situational examples of activities which lead to poor communication between the board of directors and administrative staff and describe actions and or tools which can help clarify roles and authority, thus strengthening the management capacity of all parties.

Questions about Administrative Information

The first question is a strategic one, aimed at making sure board members are on the same wavelength with one another and the staff regarding the nonprofit organization's basic mission and purpose. This key question is: Are the mission and objectives of the organization specifically stated in writing?

- Are operational objectives connected to a comprehensible and clearly-stated mission statement? After attending a few meetings, can board members describe in brief and succinct terms what the organization is all about? Would most of them say pretty much the same thing? If not, are there any actions planned to forge the consensus necessary to release the organizational power that can stem from a unanimity of purpose?
- Were the objectives discussed and approved by the Board?
- Are objectives measurable at least to some degree? (Has anyone ever tried?)
- Are objectives reviewed annually?
- Do these objectives (and the mission upon which they rest) make sense to you as a lay person in today's environment?

Understanding these strategic mission/purpose questions is essential to successfully reaching the organizational goals. If confusion reigns, there can be many useful sign posts to be found in the mandates for the organization (if it was stimulated by government action) or by the minutes of the incorporators.

For example, handicapped consumers of rehabilitation services were empowerd under the Rehabilitation Act, Title VII, Part B, to develop nonprofit organizations specifically for the purpose of providing independent living rehabilitation services. The nonprofit independent living rehabilitation system began in

1979 and in a very short period of time has grown into a major source of service delivery and advocacy power. This group of agencies came into their own effectively through clear conceptualization of today's environment and a concise review of program performance by informed board members. In many cases the board members were inexperienced in trusteeship and governance principles initially, but many were quick to ask the right questions and set forth an orderly process to answering those questions most relevant to helping the nonprofit organization achieve its goals.

The second administrative question focuses on board member responsibilities and accountability: Are there written policies regarding board member responsibilities and accountability? For example:

- Is there a board orientation meeting ... or written background and briefing materials provided to new board members?
- Is overall board responsibility for the organization's business affairs under applicable State laws clear?
- Is there a stated attendance requirement for board meetings?
- Are committee and subcommittee structure, membership and responsibilities clearly spelled out?
- Does the board approve retention of outside auditors and legal counsel? Is the process for these actions clearly spelled out?
- Are the legal liabilities which board members may face discussed? What, if any, provisions are taken to reduce risk for board members and insure against remaining risks?
- Are fund-raising responsibilities made clear? Is there an explicit financial target for the board as a whole? As individuals? Are specific fund raising tools or training provided (e.g., sample letters, fund raising, training sessions and the like).
- Is tenure of board terms with specific dates of expiration for each member specified in writing?
- Are the number of terms before retirement or temporary separation from board stated?
- Are nomination procedure in the hands of the board subcommittee? How is this subcommittee appointed? Do its members rotate?
- Is *individual* independence on the Board encouraged and/or protected? The environment at board meetings should be supportive to minority opinions. All alternatives and opinions should be heard to avoid reaching a compromise at the least common denominator.

The Pacific Crest Outward Bound School (PCOBS) in Portland, Oregon has recently done a good job of outlining many of the items in this question group via a recently-developed "Board Book" which contains, *in writing*, the answers to a number of these questions. By sending a copy to all board members (especially new ones), a foundation is being laid upon which good individual board member practices can be built. A portion of the PCOBS Board book table of contents is attached as Appendix 1.

The third administrative question is: Are the levels of authority between board and staff and among staff (where appropriate) clear?

One of the best examples of a straightforward-approach to this question was executed by a YMCA based in a major Eastern city. They used a simple written chart which spelled out the action and then the organizational level which could authorize the action. Table 1 gives a partial illustration of the approach.

TABLE 1
Authorized Personnel Actions by Authority

Nature of Action	Level in Organization			
	Dept. Mgr.	Div. Mgr.	CEO	Board
Employ New Person	Up to $20K	Up to $30K	All over $30K	Approve Annual Personnel Budget
Increase Wage	All in dept.	All in div.	All	Approve Budget
Purchase of Services or Significant Capital Items	All up to $X	Up to $Y	Up to $Z	All over $Z

The fourth group of administrative questions is aimed at the efficacy of the organizations communication with the balance of its environment, the key question being: Does the organization communicate effectively its purpose and methods to its appropriate constituencies?

- Do board members endorse and approve the basic elements and/or underpinnings of the organizations message? Said another way, has the board signed off on a basic communication strategy? Does anything about it exist (and been reviewed) in writing?
- Do board members ever participate meaningfully in delivering the message? Has the reader been briefed regarding how?
- Are there concrete measures taken periodically about communication effectiveness?
- Does the communication ever have a constructive influence on public policy? How?

A good example of boards communicating effectively with their constituencies can be found in the independent living rehabilitation movement. While legislative activity by staff members of nonprofit organizations receiving public funds is discouraged to some degree (within given guidelines), board members can constructively influence public policy. The positive political energy generated by the nonprofit sector is largely the result of board members effectively communicating important public issues to community leaders—if in fact, they themselves are not the recognized community leaders volunteering services on a board of directors. Fundamentally, constructive influence on public policy by the voluntary sector is critical to our democratic process.

The fifth group of administrative questions looks at basic organizational performance issues, starting with this key question: Does the board periodically reassess the agency's overall performance and its continued need to exist? For example:

- Does staff ever spend time with board members and vice-versa to get to know one another? This informal time provides a more useful and less threatening environment in which performance appraisal and constructive change can take place.
- Do board members ever meet clients of the agency? If not, why not?
- Is there a program to ensure board members visit the field (see the agency in action) periodically?
- Is it clear to the board what the direct benefits of the program are to the community? Are these written down and periodically reassessed by the board?
- Is there any self-evaluation process?

The Greater New York Fund (the United Way giving organization in New York City) has developed a very useful NPO self-assessment process including a written guide (1984).

An effective board member should also want to know the answer to the sixth administrative question: Does the board balance its (and perhaps the organization's) entrepreneurial zeal with adequate and concrete fiduciary responsibility?

Upon examining the continued need to exist, new ventures and problems to address are often discovered. During times of constricting budgets there is powerful temptation to diversify programming areas in search of revenue generating projects. This can be desirable, but thinking board members must balance their fiduciary obligations. Here are a few tools to help (more will also be outlined in the second section on fiscal questions):

- Do the organization's by-laws allow for programmatic diversification? Have members been given and studied carefully these by-laws?
- Is expansion into related or semi-related areas in the best interest of the organization's mission and current goals?
- Is the nonprofit organization moving into the profit sector, thereby using its nonprofit status to unfair advantage? A "little" encroachment may be useful . . . but you need to get the borders crisply drawn.

The U.S. Small Business Administration's publication "Unfair Competition by Nonprofit Organizations with Small Business: An Issue for the 1980's" (Small Business Administration, 1983) raises several interesting policy issues the reader may wish to help his/her board address. Board members should ask very pointed and to-be-concretely-answered questions about (1) the financial impact of new ventures, (2) the staff skills required, and (3) the impact of new ventures in the minds of the organization's various publics. Directors should weigh the anticipated "public good" and any projected impact on commercial activity very carefully and should ask the following question: Is there a vigorous administrative improvement effort under way? For example, has the board and/or staff looked at:

- Cost control (did the last budget review identify any particularly troublesome areas . . . and has staff reported on progress, in writing)?
- Cost reduction efforts (are they described to the board, and are results specified)?
- Adequate cost reimbursement from outside sources and/or fee schedules?
- Aggressive programs to secure new sources of income (what Directors are specifically involved in these activities, and are any Directors providing leadership in this regard)?
- Cost/program sharing with similar agencies?

For example, a group of summer camp owning NPO located in and around New York City joined together several years ago to identify and implement joint cost saving activities such as pooled camper transportation, shared maintenance and shared specialty instructors. In addition they conducted joint inter- agency activities to increase each agency's earned and unearned income. Initially called the Camp Management Project, it now functions as the Association for Recreation Management.[2]

Finally, an effective Board member should ensure he/she has the top line information needed upon which to make timely and sound decisions. Hence, this key question: Is the management information provided to Board members timely and useful?

- Are most major problems identified and discussed before the "total crisis" stage?
- Do board members ever see written reports of agency progress vs. objectives?
- Do board members sign off on written major program plans before they are executed? (It is easier and cheaper to prevent mistakes than to correct them afterwards.)
- Do board members understand the basic sources and uses of the agency's financial and human resources? (See Appendix 2 for an illustrative list of top-line reports which may help structure discussions with senior staff executives.)
- Is it relatively easy for Directors to secure information from the staff when it is requested?
- Is the information presented to the board clear; and are quantitative reports understandable, reasonable to interpret and properly labeled, footnoted and sourced?

Questions About Fiscal Information

The first area for consideration regarding fiscal information is the NPO's communications with regulatory bodies, contributors and the public. The key question is: Do the nonprofit organization's financial statements accurately and completely state the agency's financial status? What assurances does the board have?

- Are all publicly required reported filed on time? Is there a written list of them and their due dates?
- Which reports should be shared with key donors? All donors? The general public? Other key constituencies?
- Is the FICA account really paid up?
- Is there an audit subcommittee?
- Are the staff and Board bonded? Is the insurance at a sufficient level?
- If the agency operated at a deficit last year, how was the deficit financed? Has there been any discussion, substantively, about whether it was worth it?

The second area has to do with longer term questions, the key question being: Is there a long-term financial resource plan?

- What are the program and financial plans for the short, medium and long term? Did the board specifically approve a written plan?
- Has the board initiated any specific longer-range development programs? Has there ever been an objective review of the long-range mission of the organization? Did anyone from the board participate in any way (i.e., sign off on the work plan, participate in a staff briefing)?
- If concrete plans and/or programs exist, how is progress toward them reviewed and reported to the board?

Failure to plan in a longer time frame (as well as a shorter one) can result in both missed opportunities (e.g., not accommodating a large demographic shift such as an influx of a particular ethnic group with different service needs or tastes) or missing the opportunity to prevent a major problem (e.g., not recognizing a rapidly widening gap between fees charged/reimbursements received and costs).

Next, in the financial area, the effective board member should ask: Do the budgetary and actual expenditure procedures reflect fairly well the financial capacity of the agency to conduct its affairs? Is a budget developed, with management's assistance, even leadership, which reconciles realistically the organization's financial resources with its programs? What will prevent the agency from "running away" financially?

Finally, looking at financial control can also be very important. The key question: Is there a periodic board review of the key financial control mechanism by the finance or audit committee of the board?

- Does the finance committee also function as the audit committee? Are both sets of responsibilities clearly identified and executed?
- Is there a periodic review of the key financial control mechanisms? By whom?
- Is the board satisfied with activities being executed to safeguard the NPO's assets?

Note that this last review can be as simple as ensuring that two parties handle checks to a much more complex review of the adequacy of the organization's accounting and auditing practices.

Human Resource Management

One of the most valuable resources within the nonprofit sector are the people who work within the sector. Sound and sensitive human resource management is critical to effective organizational performance. And, it often is an area in which attention to it is forfeited for the immediate attention to some other crisis. In fact, problems with staff relationships and the management of personnel are one of the most litigated areas of nonprofit organization management, consuming considerable board time and concern. "Equal Opportunity Employment" and requirements for "Affirmative Employment" are issues nonprofits support, but NPOs are not immune from legal action of employees. The board must monitor the actions of the executive director and senior staff in their management of personnel. The following question may stimulate some constructive dialogue between the board and management—a healthy and perhaps preventative interchange: Is there an adequate human resource development program for the agency staff?

- Is there an annual performance review for the executive director?
- Are his/her performance expectations spelled out clearly in writing in advance?
- Is the director's performance reviewed in writing by the chairman?
- Is there an adequate senior executive compensation plan . . . and is any of his/her compensation tied to clearly articulated performance standards?
- Has the executive director implemented sound personnel practices? Are these ever monitored by board members?

- Are there specific personnel training plans connected to the mission of the organization's objectives? For each person?
- Are written performance reviews conducted for all staff at least annually?
- Do written job descriptions exist?
- Has the board acted on compensation and expense guidelines?
- Are fringe benefits simply and fully explained in writing?
- Is the termination procedure clear?
- Is there a plan or at least periodic discussion regarding executive succession for all senior positions? Most good managers are known for having at least one replacement "in the wings."

Both the Ford Foundation and the New York Community Trust (New York City's Community Foundation) have made considerable progress in developing concrete tools in the human resource development area specifically applied to program officers in Foundations. Personnel evaluation forms identify many of the key skills and behavior traits necessary to be a good foundation program person (copies are available by mail).

Second, you need to observe the answer to this question: Does the board recruit new members with fresh ideas and perspectives?

We all know organizations which become rigid and uncompromising, some nearly comatose, by the lack of fresh ideas brought in by new staff or board members. Probing "why" they come into this position may have a very constructive long term impact on the board.

Finally, does the Board member understand how the enterprise is organized? Specifically: Does the Board understand and approve of the NPO's overall organizational structure without becoming enmeshed in individual decision on staffing or substructure?

This is difficult but important. It is important for thinking board members to be knowledgeable about internal staff relationships and the effect of past organizational structure decisions on program efficiency. Caring organizations generally reward past good individual performance with job security. Over time, the organizational patterns change and promotional decisions or decisions to keep someone who should have been terminated can be detrimental. Board members should be in tune with internal culture, history, and past decisions in order to provide for balance, equity and sound personnel management.

CONCLUSION

The articulation and answering of these basic questions is no guarantee to NPO effectiveness. But, the mere process of the query, like the Hawthorne effect, is likely to stimulate improved institutional behavior. Moreover, since a number of these questions are rooted in "reasonable" managerial/public administration theory, they should, unto themselves, strengthen the process. Finally, as board members, as in life, learning is essential to leadership. John F. Kennedy said it best: "Leadership and learning are indispensable to each other."

APPENDIX 1

Pacific Crest Outward Bound School: Selections From The Table of Contents

I. Board of Trustees.
    A. Memo to New Board Members from Executive Director of the School.
    B. Board List (Names, Addresses, Telephone Numbers).
    C. Mailing List (Board and Staff).
    D. Telephone Listing (Board and Staff).
    E. Board by Class and Term.
II. By-Laws and Mission Statement.
III. Board Responsibilities and Key Dates to Remember.
IV. Committees.
    A. Committee Members.
    B. Description of Committee Functions.
    C. Development Fund-Raising Teams.
V. History and Philosophy.
VI. Statement of Key Operations Principles of the School.
VII. Frequently Asked Questions & Answers.
VIII. Administrative Staff Job Descriptions.
IX. Budget.
X. Summary of Financial Highlights.

APPENDIX 2

Sample Summary of Top-Line Board Reports

Report Name:	Suggested Frequency:
1. Trial balance sheet.	1. Semi-Annually.
2. Statement of income and expense.	2. Quarterly.
3. Budget variance report.	3. Quarterly.
4. Formal performance review of executive director.	4. Annually.
5. Fund-raising progress report.	5. Quarterly.
6. Programmatic performance vs. objectives.	6. Annually.
7. Minutes of board meetings.	7. After every meeting.
8. Follow-up reports on topics raised at board meetings.	8. Periodically.
9. Investment reports.	9. Annually.

NOTES

1. Data describing current trends in the insurance industry were provided by one of the top five underwriters in the country. Because of the demand for this type of coverage, the underwriter requested anonymity. While insurance companies are in the business of providing protection our source did not want to encourage or bring attention to one particular product.

    As nonprofit organizations and voluntary boards become more dominant, leadership risk factors, historical costs, and frequency or probability of litigation will be projected. As better NPO statistics are available, new supply will equal the sector's growing demand.
2. For further information, contact John Cimarosa, North River Company, 22 Oak Street, Westport, CT 06880 (212) 477-2244.

REFERENCES

Conrad, William R., Jr. and William E. Glenn
    1983   *The Effective Voluntary Board of Directors*. Athens, OH: Ohio University Press.
Greater New York Fund
    1984   *Self-Evaluation for Human Service Agencies*. New York Fund (99 Park Avenue, 10016).
O'Connell, Brian
    1985   *The Board Member's Book*. New York: The Foundation Center.
Reagan, Ronald
    1981   "Message to Congress."
Salamon, Lester M. and Alan J. Abramson
    1982   "The Nonprofit Sector." In John L. Palmer and Isabel V. Sawhill, eds., *The Reagan Experiment*. Washington, D.C.: Urban Institute Press.
U.S. Small Business Administration
    1983   Unfair Competition by Nonprofit Organizations with Small Business: An Issue for the 1980's." Washington, D.C.: Small Business Administration.

Community Agency Boards of Directors: Viability and Vestigiality, Substance and Symbol

Justin Fink

INTRODUCTION

While scholars continue to debate the specific standards appropriate for the behavior of nonprofit boards of directors (Blickendorfer and Janey, 1986), the general legal expectations of nonprofit board membership are widely known.

> The corporation form (as we have come to know it) was created as a means of accomplishing 'desirable' ends that were beyond the capabilities of individuals. Boards of directors were created and recognized in law in order to insure continuity in the management of organizations and to fix a locus of responsibility for the control of 'independent' organizations. Boards are charged with the proper use of resources in pursuit of organizational goals. Directors are not personally responsible for organizational losses, but they are responsible for prudent action in behalf of the 'owners' (whomever they might be) ... Prudent action includes appointing and perpetuating effective management of the organization and overseeing the work of such management. This control function is inward looking; the board operates as the agent of the corporation at the request of the owners (members) to oversee organizational activity. (Zald, 1974: p. 173.)

As fiduciaries, directors have the explicit responsibility of guiding and overseeing an organization's affairs in order to safeguard the interests of the public which has granted it special status and privileges. (For additional discussion of the legal role of nonprofit boards, see also Oleck, Howard L. 1974: Chapters 22–3; Conrad, William R. Jr. and Glenn, William E., 1983: esp. Chapters 3, 4, 7, and 8; O'Connell, Brian, 1985: Chapter 4; and Connors, Tracy, 1980a: pp. 2, 35–63.)

The broader functions of nonprofit directors are also reflected in materials disseminated by such large institutional supporters of voluntarism as the National Charities Information Bureau (NCIB) and United Way's National Academy of Voluntarism. The training manuals of these and most other sources accept as an article of faith the basic role of trustees of voluntary organizations in setting mission, determining policies and program priorities, raising resources, and providing oversight. Most writers are in agreement that, in today's voluntary human service or cultural organizations, the role of the board is to set the broad outlines of policy pertaining to program and management. Connors (1980), particularly, has been in the forefront of recognizing the impact on boards of the shift toward greater representativeness and expertise on one hand, and increasing staff professionalism on the other. In this new climate especially, the role of directors is a broader, more leadership–oriented one. As has been put forth in the literature of the National Charities Information Bureau, "A good board inspires and it leads."

Implicitly, the role of boards in voluntary organization leadership has been viewed as a function of the commitment of participants to shared benefits or to the beneficent results of organizational activity. The organizational basis of voluntary leadership however, is rarely, if ever examined. So tied up with our self–image as a culture are the virtues of voluntary organization participation, that we take as a given the primacy of volunteer leadership in guiding and sustaining voluntary organization life. And yet too often in practice, experience suggests that the Board is not really carrying out its responsibilities.

In fact, seldom is the role of boards examined within the context of formal organization theory and research. Little work of depth has been done to date, and most studies have been cast in a decidedly nontheoretical light. What little formal research of quality that has been carried out on voluntary agency boards has reflected concern with levels of and motives for participation, levels of board skill and knowledge, and community representatives among other factors. (See for example, Hartogs, and Weber, 1974: pp. 74–5.)

In the popular or applied literature the favored perspectives mainly entail leadership, knowledgability, expertise and what might be called the "moral" imperative. When the efficacy of governance—that is policymaking and oversight—is called into question, it is often assumed that its shortcomings are owed to a lack of adequate leadership, understanding or expertise on the part of directors, or perhaps insufficient personal commitment due to individual failings. More intensive and discriminating recruitment would help to turn things around. Board training, better leadership preparation, better communication or better systems of organizing and carrying out the work are often called for.

This seems rational enough, given the likelihood that the complexities of the modern voluntary organization are not always willingly or quickly assimilated by lay volunteers, no matter how much they support designated charitable purposes. However, being inundated with orientations, organizational charts, manuals, goals and objectives, budgets and the like can be disappointingly counterproductive. If volunteer activity is at least partly a function of available leisure time, then it must successfully compete with a variety of less demanding alternatives lest it become too much like work. As Max Lerner (1983: pp. 88–9) has written: "Keeping up with the club work has become one of the new imperatives of middle–class life. What makes it worse for a small group is that the range of leadership is a constricted one, and the most difficult tasks fall upon a few. America has been overorganized and association–saturated."

Perhaps more to the point, though, would be a consideration of several concepts grounded in one hundred years or so of scholarly work on formal organizations. That is, can it be assumed a priori that the ineffectiveness of some voluntary organization governance is always a result of shortcomings in individual performance such as insufficient leadership, information or expertise, or even personal commitment? Could there be other factors inherent in the nature or structure of some kinds of organizations themselves which might be operative? Are our common assumptions about the proper exercise of role and authority in voluntary organizations appropriate given the realities they face?

This chapter is devoted to examining these questions as well as the wisdom of our common assumptions. In doing so it will draw on organizational theory and upon case data gathered during a five–year study of boards of community service agencies. The theoretical issues raised will be explored in light of the "natural history" of some of these cases. Some hypotheses will be developed and tentative conclusions offered, as well as some implications of all of the above for policy and practice. First however, a conceptual framework will be offered utilizing the thinking of a couple of the leading, contemporary organizational theorists.

LINKS BETWEEN ROLE AND AUTHORITY, RESOURCES AND GOALS: A FRAMEWORK FOR LOOKING AT THE BEHAVIOR OF VOLUNTARY BOARDS

One writer, Charles Perrow, has devoted substantial scholarly attention to voluntary organizations. As such he is one of the few serious students of organizational behavior to try to place the voluntary organization within the larger context of formal organization theory and research. As a theorist Perrow is unabashedly wedded to the "structuralist" point of view. (For the best introduction to his thinking see Perrow, 1970b, esp. Chapter 1.) In his view, answers to the most significant questions about organizational behavior i.e., questions concerning "the enduring patterns of behavior that give it its form and structure," are to be found not in examination of attitudes, "people problems" or "leadership problems," but in looking at the roles people play and the organizational structures in which they operate. The nature of goals, derivation of resources and impact of environmental factors are all seen to be central variables which condition organizational life and success.

In an important essay entitled "Members As Resources In Voluntary Organizations" Perrow begins to place voluntary organizations within this larger context. His approach suggests that many aspects of organizational behavior can best be understood by examining the nature of organizational roles and authority. In line with many other of the best contemporary organizational theorists, he leavens this concern for the formal and informal structure of roles and authority—essentially a perspective derived from Weber—with an "open–system" sensitivity to environmental factors, especially the derivation of organizational resources as a conditioner of internal organizational life.

Others have held to a similar theoretical perspective. Zald, for example, recognizes the importance of resource control upon relations between voluntary organization boards and executives: "In the relationships among boards (as collectivities), individual board members and executives, each party brings to bear 'resources.' These resources may be based in legal rights, in monetary control, in knowledge, or even in force of personality and tradition ... It is the balance of resources for specific situations and decisions that determines the attribution of relative power in the encounter between boards and executives." (Zald, 1974: p. 173.)

In looking at voluntary organizations, Perrow embellishes this perspective with a couple of additional, key features. His input–output model focuses on the fact that "most of the resources are contributed by members and most of the output is consumed by them." Further, he is concerned with the relationship between the derivation of resources and their application to the varied purposes to which organizational energies are devoted. Establishing social legitimacy, rewarding supporters, insuring organizational maintenance, and attaining a variety of sub–goals secondary to the officially designated ends of participation or service—all are activities which are typical of organizational life and which demand some extent of resources to sustain. The last group, which he refers to as "derived goals," are distinguished from "societal, output, investor, system and product goals" and are often the object of analysis in studies of goal displacement (Perrow, 1970a: pp. 107–8).

Significantly, Perrow views the central, bread and butter voluntary action concern for the encroachment of oligarchy upon democratic participation as a relatively insignificant issue of organizational behavior per se. The primary conceptual and empirical questions for him pertain to "the conditions under which those who contribute resources have control over the uses of those resources *which are relevant to them*" [italics the author's]. In Perrow's view, then, the balance of power to condition organizational character and life is tied to the degree to which organizational players' contribution, acquisition and consumption of resources relate to any organization's central purposes and goals.

If Perrow is correct, then the preoccupation of so many of the popular writers in the nonprofit field with the authority of boards presumes a close proximity of trustees to the securing and deployment (or consumption) of organizational resources, be they comprised of either money, people or material goods. That is, board material from NCIB, United Ways, writers such as O'Connell, Conrad and Glenn, and to a lesser degree, Connors, all seem to accept a priori the link between the legal primacy of officially designated leaders—the trustees—and their actual role in conditioning the main attraction of central purposes, as opposed to the sideshow of derived goals. If this holds true, then one would expect the active participation of nonprofit directors to be both evident in and essential to organizational maintenance. On the other hand, if this assumption is false, then we might well expect to see voluntary organizations within which the role of trustees is in fact secondary or nominal, or perhaps even counterproductive or irrelevant at the extreme.

BACKGROUND ON A FIVE–YEAR STUDY OF COMMUNITY AGENCY BOARDS

Some authors have suggested that the role of boards of directors evolves to accommodate the changing demands of organizational life over time. (See for example Zald, pp. 180–3; and Mathiasen, 1983.) Zald has stated that "examination of the functioning of a board over long periods of time would reveal an ebb and flow of board functions, importance, and power during different phases of organizational development and activity." Undoubtedly, much is to be learned from observing changes in non–profit boards over an extended period of time. Presumably a look at such things as board composition, and especially the functional variation in board roles—and changes therein over a significant period of time—would serve to reveal the underlying nature of community agency change and adaptation. In particular, detailed observations on the actual behavior of real boards and their agencies provide a basis for comparison with their idealized roles as portrayed in the popular, prescriptive and training literature.

In 1981 a five–year, descriptive study was initiated which looked at the evolution of board structure, roles and behavior within twenty community based, not–for–profit organizations serving low–income communities with a variety of programs. Part of a more comprehensive set of case data examining many other aspects of community agency life and evolution during a period of shifting policies and funding arrangements, this phase of the research sought to detail some of the characteristics and roles played by trustees in one particular class of voluntary organization: the small to medium sized agency which had originated during the 1960s and 70s to provide advocacy and fill gaps in the service system for a primarily low–income constituency. By combining the multitude of data sources characteristic of the case method with a comparative organizational approach, it was hoped that new insights might be gained about the fundamental nature of the relationship between organizational structure, organizational behavior and adaptation to changing and often stressful conditions.

The primary research strategy entailed the use of qualitative methods, with an orientation toward naturalistic inquiry (Lincoln and Guba, 1985). The agencies studied comprised a sample of opportunity or "convenience sample" accessed through a state–supported nonprofit management assistance program. To briefly describe them, all agencies studied were community based, not–for–profit corporations under Pennsylvania Commonwealth law, and each carried exemption from federal corporate taxation under Section 501 (c) (3) of the Internal Revenue Code. Three–fourths—fifteen of the twenty—had been started through what might be termed "collective action" at the community level, or had been originated on behalf of low–income groups by other institutions. The remainder had been initiated chiefly through the efforts of a founding executive director. According to legal requirements and in point of fact, each organization had a volunteer board of directors. As a final, unifying characteristic, each agency designated low–income persons as its primary client population.

In 1981 total agency budgets ranged from about $65,000 to $3.5 million. Many of the agencies had originated under funding from the Community Services Administration, Title XX or CETA. By 1981 some had become United Way members or had secured a variety of other public, private or church–related support. While a few collected modest fees when the study began, none had budgets where self–generated income accounted for more than about 5% of total income.

Data were collected in two phases. During 1981–82, two to five days were spent on–site at each agency conducting extensive interviews with agency board and staff, reviewing a wide range of agency documents, and observing programmatic, administrative and board activities. Interviews were guided by, but not restricted to, a list of questions pertaining to knowledge of and involvement with board roles, responsibilities and functions. Throughout the first phase of the study, every attempt was made to verify data through multiple indicators from interviews, document analysis and observation.

In Winter, 1986, sixty to ninety minute follow–up interviews were conducted by telephone. In this instance agency executive directors served as key informants. Again using a guided interview geared to elucidating many areas of agency life, the author queried informants about developments in the agency and its board since the first contacts. As a follow–up to previous findings, questions were asked concerning changes in the make–up, knowledge and involvement of board members in a variety of agency activities, such as policymaking, oversight, fundraising, volunteer work with clients, and so on.

Data collected were reduced into summary reports and arrayed in tabular form for comparative analysis. This report utilizes some of those findings, but especially more in–depth, case data to provide more detailed descriptive material illustrative of comparative findings.

FINDINGS ON THE COMPOSITION, ROLES AND FUNCTIONS OF
COMMUNITY AGENCY BOARDS OF DIRECTORS 1981–86

The 1981–82 examination of agency articles of incorporation and by–laws revealed a few basic facts concerning the purposes, ages and origins of organizations in the sample. Of the organizations examined, sixteen demonstrated clarity of mission and could show at least some programmatic goals derived from that mission. Each agency was noted to have a discernible program identity, although it would later become apparent that the working out of mission into programs was not always clear cut or unproblematic. In terms of stated purposes, the sample agencies could be said to be fairly representative of community based organizations developed during that period to serve low–income populations (see Table 1).

Service recipient characteristics, as well as actual program and service types, were quite diversified. Old, young, male and female, and a variety of racial groupings were represented in the composition of boards, staff and clientele. Clients included children, families, women and the elderly. Programs offered entailed the categories of adult basic education; children and youth services; day care and early childhood education; drug and alcohol prevention and treatment; emergency food, clothing and shelter; crime prevention; employment and training; energy assistance; housing and community development; information and referral; rape crisis intervention and women's special services; recreation; social casework and counseling; services for the elderly; transportation and others.

At the outset the age of agencies in the sample ranged from just under one year to seventeen years, but the average was about eight and one–half. Fully half of the organizations had originated between the years 1971 and 1977 (see Table 2). Among these was a concentration of women's centers, day care centers and Hispanic organizations, with two of the three community action agencies having begun somewhat earlier during the War on Poverty. As a whole, the sample organizations could be taken to reflect the growth of nonprofit activity during the middle 1960s up to the beginning of the 1980s which has been noted by researchers such as Rosenbaum and Smith (1982) and Weitzman and Hodgkinson (1986).

For those organizations studied a number of changes were to come about during the years of this investigation, 1981–86, which coincided with implementation of the Omnibus Budget Reconciliation Act of 1981 and other Reagan Administration initiatives. These were to include changes in programs and services, budgets and funding streams, and in some cases even clients and basic mission.

TABLE 1
Summary of Agency's Designated Purposes

Agency Purposes	# Agencies
Bilingual advocacy & services	6
Women's advocacy & services	4
Early childhood education	3
Employment & training	2
Drug & alcohol treatment	1
Anti–poverty programs	3
Multi–service	1
Total	20

TABLE 2
Summary of Agency's Year of Origin

Years Created*	# Agencies
1978—1980	3
1974—1977	6
1971—1973	4
1968—1970	4
1964—1967	3
Total	20

* Six agencies had begun as delegate agencies or subsidiaries of established organizations. In these cases, the actual year of origin was counted, rather than the year when an agency had become independently incorporated.

Of the original twenty organizations studied, eighteen had survived through the end of 1985. Their budgets originally ranged from about $65,000 to $3.5 million. By 1986 that range was from about $121,000 to over $4 million. Somewhat unexpectedly, only three of the surviving eighteen had total budgets smaller than in 1981–82. The other fifteen experienced budgetary growth averaging about 100 percent, and this during a time of extensive cuts in Federal funding and comparatively low inflation.

A Shift in Board Composition

During the mid–1960s through the early 1970s, the civil rights and women's movements had focused attention upon the exclusion of racial and sexual minorities from community decision–making structures. The changes brought on by this had been reinforced by such public policy mandates as the maximum feasible participation clause contained in the Economic Opportunity Act of 1964 and its successors, and "affirmative action" in hiring and recruitment for participants in all sorts of occupational, educational, and service delivery contexts. Complementary to participation was the notion of self–determination through community control of community institutions. This was in the spirit of both the 60s and the resurgence of the so–called "neighborhoods movement" of the 1970s. (N.B. For one of the best studies on this see Kramer, 1969). To a large extent, the exclusion of disenfranchised groups had provided much of the impetus for the development of new, community based organizations, including those which are the focus of the present research.

Thus, it might be expected that the composition of agency boards would reflect the concerns for participation and self–determination by the inclusion of grassroots persons. The militant or ideological context in which a number of the agencies had begun would seem to demand that this be the case. At the outset, this generally was true. Many board representatives who were interviewed in 1981–82 were of low–income background or minority status and had been involved with either civil rights, community activism or advocacy. Many saw their board involvement as an extension of those activities.

For most organizations in the sample, the emphasis upon grassroots representation on governing boards of directors would later prove to be problematic. In some cases, the earlier emphasis upon indigenous, community leadership, activism and/or ideology would actually become something of a liability, and by 1986 virtually all of the boards studied would experience a shift in their make–up. For eleven out of twenty, this shift proved to be very extensive indeed. Instead of looking to those who could, through a combination of political commitment and personal qualities, rouse the people and fight the system, boards would look to those who could lend their own credentials, contacts or expertise to boost agency credibility in the eyes of funders. By 1986, only a half–dozen agencies would have any present or former clients on their boards, whereas in 1981–82 nearly all had had some client representation amongst board members. One might say that the majority of boards had become middle class and somewhat professionalized in terms of the vocations represented among members.

Although the study was not intended to fully assess motives for board participation, some changes in motives for serving on boards were evident, along with changes in the backgrounds and qualifications of directors. Beginning with Kramer (1969) research had documented the fact that the motives for grassroots participation in the community action movement had included neighborhood politics, the chance for a new form of enfranchisement of the poor or empowerment for indivduals, and job opportunities among other things. The veracity of Kramer's observations was still apparent at the outset of the study. But the decidedly middle class profile of community agency boards in 1986 was accompanied by a somewhat different and mixed set of motives, according to follow–up interviews with agency executives. Among these were the fulfillment of a sense of civic duty, the desire to be involved in a community service activity with which the individual identified personally, and the personal rewards of sociability through participation. Of these, the first two were most prevalent and the latter appeared the least important.

As mentioned earlier, merely a half–dozen agencies had clients or client representatives on their boards of directors, and three of those, the community action programs (or "CAP's") were required to do so by regulation. As mentioned above, a few board members, increasingly few, were persons who had themselves come from a disadvantaged background or had overcome adverse personal experiences. Some of them saw volunteering through board work as a means of "repayment." As one Hispanic agency executive put it, "A few of my board members started out as clients here, and now they're working, they're professional, and they're on the board. They're doing their share and giving something back to the Hispanic community." By far, though, motives for serving on boards as reported by agency managers in 1986 were intrinsic; that is, not overtly tied to actual needs or benefits received by directors themselves as a result of their participation. It might be said that they were active as third parties on behalf of a client constituency to which they seldom anymore belonged. It could be said that many board members were participating as a result of what they saw to be the value and importance of the programs in which their organizations were engaged. By 1986, this orientation leaned far more heavily upon the rectification of constituent problems or injustice through the delivery of services than the advocacy of a more abstract cause or set of political values. With few exceptions it was complemented by a shift away from those who demonstrated a heavy, personal and political investment in the outcome of their activity as directors.

No matter what the underlying motives of board members might be, the paramount concern expressed by executive directors regarding board composition was for diversification including the addition of persons with credentials, contacts and expertise. This was a far cry from earlier days when grassroots activists vied for position and power on boards as a means to empowerment. As such, these shifts might be seen as a reflection of the objectification or depersonalization of individual involvement in the life of the organization.

Board Relevant Knowledge

In order to try to determine the extent to which board members were aware of and understood their ideal roles, both individual and group interviews were conducted. While the number of board representatives questioned from each organization ranged from two to thirteen members per agency, the average number was about five. Whenever possible, which was in most cases, these included officers or members of executive committees. (N.B.: In the Hispanic agencies, where language might have posed a barrier, a bilingual/bicultural interviewer thoroughly trained in interview techniques conducted the sessions.)

Based upon a range of questions posed in interviews, the boards of directors represented were informally classified as being more or less knowledgable of their prescribed functions as trustees. While this informal classification tended to obscure the variation of knowledgability within particular boards, it did serve to give a general picture for the purpose of comparison across the sample.

Of the twenty boards of directors in agencies which constituted the original study sample in 1981–82, only three could be said to be fully knowledgable of their role and responsibilities based upon accepted standards. Of the others, ten had only a limited understanding, seven were not knowledgable in any true sense, and the last did not yield data sufficient to pass judgement. That is, based upon the combination of interview and other data, it was determined that only 15 percent of boards in the sample exhibited more than a minimal understanding of the extent of their exposure to risk as keepers of the public trust, the nature of policymaking and oversight, and/ or a grasp of information, policies and issues particular to the organization they served. The remainder did not. Indicative of this lack of knowledge was the fact that, at the time, only three agencies conducted any structured board orientation, just one had compiled a board operations manual, and none of the agency boards had had exposure to any training workshops for directors of nonprofit organizations.

By 1986 substantial change was evident in this regard. Although the follow–up surveys did not permit re–interviewing board representatives, it did include the posing of a number of pertinent questions to executive directors serving as key informants. In thirteen of eighteen surviving agencies, executives had remained since the earlier data collection, while two of the others had some prior familiarity with the organization and its board. According to their responses, nine of the ten which had shown limited knowledge were better versed at follow–up, and six of the seven without any understanding of their proper role had also improved. While this could be attributable to recruitment of persons more knowledgable from the outset, it is also worth noting that at least ten organizations had undergone some type of formalized board training, nearly all had developed a written orientation package and process for new members, and about a half–dozen had board operations manuals. Clearly, board members in 1986 were at least better exposed to the formal role and responsibilities of governing boards, if not actual guidelines for their participation in the running of their specific agencies. As one community action agency executive reflected:

All of them now have a picture of what their responsibilities are. I would not say all of them dispatch those responsibilities effectively. Some operate very effectively during Board meetings and I would have to say that in between, the program doesn't come to mind. Others are sensitive on an ongoing basis, always are available, not only ready to be called upon, but indeed are calling and contacting us and sharing things between Board meetings.

Thus, what was observed within this admittedly nonrandom but diversified sample of community service agencies was a trend toward agency boards that were reported to be more middle class and professionalized, better informed as to their ideal roles, but also seemingly motivated more for intrinsic reasons or for political idealism than as a result of their own personal struggle or direct involvement in social conditions they wanted to see changed.

The Evolution of Board Roles

The examination of changes in the actual functioning of trustees in the sample would go much further toward delineating the board role within organizations experiencing the turmoil so prevalent within the nonprofit sector during the early 1980s. As discussed earlier, knowledge of accepted roles, responsibilities and functions of nonprofit organization trustees is commonly seen to constitute a basis for effective fiduciary behavior. At the outset of the study, however, the lack of relevant knowledge on the part of many trustees was not the only aspect of governance that was problematic for the agencies studied. In 1981–82, only in nine of the organizations studied did boards evidence sufficient commitment to their agencies to actively participate in at least some aspects of governance with regularity. In nine others there were constant problems with attendance at meetings, getting quorum, formulating policies, carrying out oversight, conducting planning and other functions critical to the fulfillment of the fiduciary role and to the ongoing life of community service agencies. Only five agencies had any written rule concerning attendance, the violation of which could result in dismissal from board membership. It was apparent, too, that in those that did, there was often reluctance to enforce that rule for fear that the board ranks might well become too thin. This was true even in the largest and most outwardly successful of agencies. The result in a number of agencies was instability of board membership, a sort of ongoing fluctuation of the board list. The difficulty of recruitment was often exacerbated by a high degree of attrition between elections.

Further, in 1981–82 only about half of the board studied actually had any actively functioning committee structure through which to do their work. Seldom did committees have either a clear sense of purpose, clear mandate, assignment of specific tasks or effective leadership. Most agencies had at least some nominal committees established through a provision on the by–laws or by informal tradition. Not surprisingly, committee reports in most agencies were infrequent. When made, they were usually done in a verbal, as opposed to written presentation.

Often, boards showed a distinctly informal approach to governance overall. This was evident in their lack of adherence to parliamentary procedure, anecdotal board minutes, the absence of motions reflecting conduct of official business, failure to formulate or adhere to any formal lines of communication, and at best, a spontaneous or detached approach to problem solving. While there were some exceptions, the pattern was remarkably consistent. Major exceptions occurred mainly in the three day care organizations studied, a phenomenon worth noting.

During the initial phase of the study in 1981–82, it was observed that all but one of the organizations examined had formally adopted an arrangement which designated a governing board and an agency executive director. Under this type of structure, which was often reflected in by–laws, a board would in theory be responsible for formulating policy and carrying out oversight. Authority for agency management would be delegated to a hired individual. This division of labor could be contrasted with that of other voluntary organizations, such as many membership organizations with administrative boards which were consistently implicated in day–to–day decisionmaking, management, and program activity. Typically, the organizational chart might appear as in Table 3 below. In this hierarchical arrangement of authority, the agency executive director was responsible to the board, but all other staff and volunteers would be subordinate to either him or her.

In fact, the extent to which that model of authority was operationalized in daily practice varied considerably. In at least five of the organizations there was either a lack of clarity on the board's role, or a lack of agreement around the extent of authority vested in the executive versus the board. On the surface, this lack of consensus seemed to center mainly around issues of hiring and firing, or board involve-

TABLE 3
Example of Hierarchical Division of Labor & Authority in a Community Service Agency

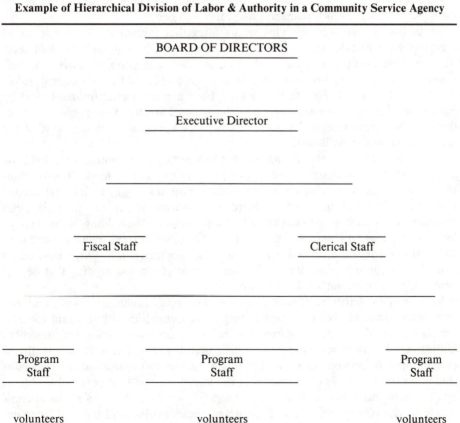

BOARD OF DIRECTORS

Executive Director

Fiscal Staff   Clerical Staff

Program   Program   Program
Staff   Staff   Staff

volunteers   volunteers   volunteers

ment in day–to–day programmatic affairs. In several cases there was apparently a solid tradition of misunderstanding established over a period of years in this regard, and this could sometimes be traced to the vague or equivocal designation of authority in agency by–laws.

Role conflict at new life treatment center: how one board's confusion led to agency defunding—A graphic example of this was observed in the New Life Treatment Center, a pseudonym for the residential treatment program for substance abusers located in a small town in the anthracite region of Northeastern Pennsylvania. The agency had been started in 1977. At the time of the initial site visit and interviews in 1981, four of the original incorporators retained their Board membership, with three being officers. As an unwritten rule, Board membership from the start tended to be dominated by those who were also recovering. This served to effectively discourage participation by many—though not all—others in the community who might contribute to the agency's governance and continued development. (N.B.: This was probably tied to adherence to some of the philosophy of the Synanon movement which was influential in so many treatment programs throughout the country during that time, and which stresses personal responsibility for one's abuse of drugs and/or alcohol. It also fits quite well with the emphasis upon the control of community institutions by the client constituency which conditioned the development of so many community organizations with different programs.) One of the original trustees had become the agency's first Executive Director, and later, he was succeeded by his wife. Two other agency managers had come and gone.

Those Board members interviewed, six altogether including officers, displayed great interest in and dedication to the purposes of New Life. Although they had never had any orientation or training in the responsibilities of nonprofit directors, their interest in maintaining the program's quality was evidenced by the frequent, informal visits of some of them to the facility. They met on a monthly basis, and by agreement, their agenda was prepared by the agency Director. A core group of members which constituted the Executive Committee appeared to make most of the major decisions for the Board.

A review of minutes of meetings for the preceeding year, though, revealed little attention to policy, oversight, planning or program evaluation, fundraising or community relations issues. Mostly anecdotal, the minutes suggested internal agency conflict and the involvement of the Board in day–to–day affairs. Two potential areas of conflict of interest were noted initially. These included the holding of the agency's lease by one Board member, and the presence of another trustee's spouse on staff with the trustee voting on decisions pertaining to her compensation. When confronted with these, only one of the Board members voiced concern, confiding that he was contemplating resigning for this and other reasons.

Most trustees' verbal acknowledgement of their role as fiduciaries was somewhat perfunctory. Instead, they displayed a marked preoccupation with program content. Nearly all agreed that their responsibility was to insure that "things run smoothly." Unfortunately, this was the exception rather than the rule. The level and quality of communication between Board and staff was uneven and unregulated. Repeatedly, staff and even clients would circumvent the Executive and take personal problems and issues to individual trustees, thus abrogating any semblance of chain of command or supervisory procedure. Sometimes, their involvement entailed interventions in treatment issues, wherein they were consulted by clinical staff. In sum, when the agency operated without difficulty, the manager was allowed full authority. More often when a problem arose, though, several on the board would strip the executive of authority through ad hoc actions. Finally, authority for hiring and firing of staff other than the Executive Director alternated between the Board and the agency manager.

Despite this there were substantial areas of the agency's operations that appeared to be quite well run. A division of labor between Executive Director and Clinical Director had been worked out so that, in most cases, each handled administrative or treatment issues respectively. The financial management system met standard requirements for procedure, records and controls up to the level of the Board's own involvement. Program record keeping and reporting was in order. Personnel administration also conformed to accepted practices and procedures.

Still, the prevailing atmosphere in the agency was one of great tension. It is safe to say that trustees who were at least aware of the existence of personnel policies and other guidelines for program management failed to follow them. There was, though, something more fundamentally wrong. Closer examination of the basic structure of the organization revealed a built-in source of ambiguity and conflict and which seemed to underlie most of the problems described above. A portion of the by-laws of the New Life Treatment Center—Article III, Section 5 which outlined the duties of the agency executive—was sufficiently equivocal to have engendered conflicting interpretations and constant role confusion over a period of four years. The qualifying clause "with the advice and consent of the Board" had provided justification for involvement of individual Board members in virtually any matters they wished, and the frequent contravention of decisions by the manager. In instances where this became exacerbated, the result was a marked inability to retain any agency manager for any significant length of time. This was to be borne out in the succession of five managers over the course of four years.

An interim follow-up carried out by the researcher in 1983 revealed that, in fact, the organization had folded. Discussions with the agency's former program officer at its primary funding source, the County's Drug and Alcohol Commission, were revealing. She commented that the agency's demise constituted a serious problem, for there were no other facilities in the area which could provide needed services. She did not hesitate to lay blame on the now defunct Board of Directors. Most significantly of all, she was quick to firmly dispel lack of money as an issue: "It's too bad the Board couldn't get it together. They just could not keep any of their [Executive] Directors, and they had a couple who were okay. The last one did a lot to improve things, but they couldn't leave her alone . . . We really needed that agency. It wasn't a problem of dollars. We had the money committed from the state. Because of the Board—those same people all along—it just wasn't a viable agency. . . ."

In the case of New Life then, the agency manager had been able to heighten the level of professionalism almost in spite of the Board. The Board itself, though, had failed to recognize or adhere to its proper role, and ambiguity within the agency's formal structure had reinforced this. In this case then, the Board was a liability. Its confusion about role and misguided actions actually hindered the ability of the organization to get the resources it needed to carry out its mission.

From leading to following board: the evolution of roles at College Point Women's Center—In another instance of board-staff conflict, an agency which had been founded upon the values of feminism and egalitarian participation in governance within a collective structure was forced by internal and external demands to change, and was able to do so successfully over a period of years. This, the one organization in the study sample that had failed to organize along bureaucratic lines was a women's center, here referred to as "College Point Women's Center."

College Point had been set up as a collectively run organization. When first encountered in 1981, the Center was experiencing much difficulty in becoming a contractually funded agency in terms of meeting grant management obligations, monitoring and reporting on programs, and in dealing with funders, vendors and the landlord. Considerable dissension was also evident around the board's ad hoc actions pertaining to administrative affairs and personnel matters.

A review of the Center's by-laws revealed that they called for the Board to be an operational or "administrative" board, even though since the outset, it had chosen to engage a paid administrator. Examinaton of the job description of the Executive Director showed that this half-time position was mainly focussed upon public relations and promoting the image of the Center within the local community. Their was little mention of any responsibility for development of new programs, fundraising or supervision of volunteer and paid staff. Further, by-laws called for the elected Treasurer to "pay bills," despite the fact that the job description of the Grants Manager gave that position "responsibility for fiscal management of all grants." In fact, it was clear during the time spent on-site that it was this individual who really had been responsible for sustaining grant support. She in turn was being seriously hamstrung by the inability of the Board to reach consensus on a variety of administrative matter that they had chosen to retain direct supervision. Rather than exemplifying sisterhood and solidarity, life of the Center was marked by factionalisim, repeated power struggles and growing acrimony. Most critically of all, perhaps, severe cuts were threatened in the Center's primary source of support, Title XX funds for services to low-income groups. In 1981, there were no contingency plans for handling that.

By 1986, the shift to a functional division of labor and clearly distinct lines of authority was complete. An Executive Director with management authority fully delegated to her had finally been hired in 1983. At the time of the follow-up, three full-time and two part-time staff were led by the present Executive Director. She reflected upon what she perceived to have brought about the move:

> I think there had to be some changes just based on the reality of running a nonprofit organization and its certainly true that there is a hierarchy here ... I think as we've gotten more closely tied in with funding sources that are demanding more in terms of reporting and more sophistication in terms of submitting proposals and that sort of thing, I think that recognition has pretty much been forced on everybody. . . .

Most telling, however, was her portrayal of the revised role and authority of the Board, and especially how the agency had attempted to accommodate change within their own framework of feminist values:

> One word that came up in some meetings is that the Board is responsible for oversight of all the programs. There was a lot of discussion about that because, given our commitment to egalitarian feminist ideals, that word kind of got thrown out. Nevertheless, what replaced that is just the Board's responsibility to provide some insight from the outside to really look at what we're doing and the programs, to offer suggestions and try to be more objective in looking at what were doing than we can be as staff people. Really, I think there's been increased recognition that the staff is here and should be the ones who are

responsible for the day–to–day operations and the Board doesn't need to get involved with that. This, I think, took up a lot of their time in past years, rather than their looking at some of the larger issues and being a forum for the kind of philosophical discussions about the kind directions we want to go in. . . . I think that with the full–time Director, who really had a lot of nonprofit experience, that certainly helped a lot in making the shift.

As Director, I make some decisions that need to get made on a day–to–day basis and there's really no need to consult with other people. Not with the major decisions. For instances, if it's a philosophical question: 'Should we do this or not? What direction do we want to go in for the future?' For example, we're hoping to expand our shelter facility and that's a decision that's really a joint decision through discussions with the Board. I meet regularly with the Executive Committee and also the staff. Those kinds of things are really mutual decisions. Again, I think that on a day–to–day basis, I make a lot of decisions that I am given the freedom to make. . . .

Under this arrangement of functional authority, the organization had managed to weather the threat to its survival which had been posed in 1982 by Title XX reductions by restructuring its budget and finding alternative sources. Further, since then it had substantially increased its programs, budget, facilities and its ability to serve its constituency. It was evident, too, that agency life was by far more harmonious and that the Center had established its credibility with funders, including the state, United Way and other donors. To some extent the ability of the Board to relinquish control and accept an experienced professional administrator had been the critical factor, much as the failure of New Life to do so had precipitated its demise.

Policymaking: Mysterious, Misunderstood or Misappropriated?

Despite indications that boards were more middle class, more professionalized and better exposed to their responsibilities in the abstract through orientation, training or written board manuals, the difficulty of operationalizing that ideal role was still apparent in 1986. Reports indicated that policymaking remained illusive. Most boards continued to be unsure of what policy was and what issues were important to be addressed. Even in an agency which had the appearance of effectiveness reflected in a stable or growing base of programs and services, the board was not necessarily focused upon providing the prescribed guidance. In 1986 the executive director of one, a highly successful day care consortium, recounted her frustration with a lack of policy support from her Board which was not that different from what she had expressed in 1981:

We're struggling with some of the same kinds of things on policy issues, (but) I'm feeling that they're just really laid back and not participating or taking an active role. But in other things that I consider really not even my job, somewhere below my job, day–to–day kinds of routine things, I find enormous interest on what I really don't feel are significant policy matters . . . There are a couple of parents who have children who are in the centers, so I think that that sometimes gets in the way of objectivity and their ability to see the broader issues.

Another agency, one that primarily served farmworkers and their families, had successfully weathered severe financial crises and achieved a measure of stability and even growth. The relatively low level of active involvement of the Board as described by the agency executive reflected the prevailing situation in most organizations studied:

> I think our Board members take a certain pride in being on the Board. We are seen as a liberal, advocate–type agency and people who are on our Board are concerned about social issues. As an example, at a (recent) Board meeting one of the Board members brought up the issue of the young boys that are in the mushroom camps now, under sixteen, and they set up a date for a special meeting and invited some people involved in this issue to come. We had a terrific turnout, yet this was an informal meeting, not a regular Board meeting. What happens is that they get so bogged down with the boring routine of the Board meetings, the minutes, the approving of contracts, financial statements, budgets, all that kind of stuff. They know their responsibility but this kind of stuff turns them off. If you're going to really deal with issues like conditions in the mushroom camps, or something like that or there's one particular social issue, then there's a terrific interest . . . A lot of Board members are aware of what we do on a day–to–day basis. They come in and they see this place full of people and all the different programs. This is what turns them on . . .

> All of our Board members are active at least on an informal basis with the agency. I think that our Board meetings probably suffer more. We still have trouble maintaining a quorum. We've had to reduce the size of the quorum just so we could operate . . . This is a very busy board . . . I'm the one that manages the agency. They really don't get into policy. I do report to them, make sure they are aware of what's going on with the different programs . . . They are not involved in fundraising at all . . . I think the technical nature is what turns them off. If it's something glitzy or sexy then they'll get involved.

At the time of follow–up some board members were said to display behavior which more approached the idealized view in terms of consistent involvement and attention to policy issues. This was especially true in the day care agencies. Most directors in these cases were parents of children enrolled in the program, so their commitment could be seen to have been based upon strong personal interests. In fact, so strong was the commitment to remain involved that it sometimes caused dissension reminiscent of earlier years. An experience of this kind which occurred in one of the day care agencies was recounted by its former Executive Director as it related to the issue of board rotation:

> We really needed to develop more of a structure in terms of how long people would remain on the Board because some people were on for a very long period of time. There was an investment in the Board and I think it was a community investment. People were involved in that program because it was a grass roots program. They helped begin and structure that program, and so it was very difficult for them to leave the Board. At times there was a feeling, I think, of ownership, although it was a private non–profit organization. It was very difficult for other people on the Board to ask them to leave because they were instrumental in the beginning and in the development of the program. One of the suggestions was to develop a policy and to have the Board really look at terms, and that was done. It's a very painful process for people, but it was done.

In the former agency manager's view, the investment or "psychic equity" that some held in the organization not only conditioned its present, but also guaranteed its future. At the least, they would become sufficiently involved in times of transition or crisis to make certain that progress continued. Still, in this organization the Board relied almost totally upon the manager to develop programs and secure funding. Almost exclusively due to her efforts, the agency realized significant expansion between 1981 and 1986. Ultimately, their failure to assume some of this burden would cause her departure from the agency.

It became clear then that in the majority of instances, the true role of trustees was, at best, oriented to providing advice and consent to the agency executive who really carried out policymaking and oversight. Indicative of the increasing complexity of agency development and management and the growth of professionalization described so widely in the literature, (Connors, p. 39; Reisch & Wenocur, 1981; Milofsky, 1982) the majority of agency managers readily admitted their true, functional status vis-a-vis most decisionmaking and reporting. In relation to decision making the following somewhat ambivalent comments from one of them describes what Mathiasen (1983) has labelled the "following board," a predominent phenomenon in three quarters of the sample in 1986.

> What's happened is that all that kind of stuff lays at my doorstep now, and I don't have time to do it all well. The lines of authority aren't murky. What we've tried to do is get the Board more involved in some of the—not daily, hands-on stuff—but sort of general reporting and accountability function, and that hasn't worked very well . . . I make them make the decisions. In all honesty, it's probably my decision that they're endorsing . . . Things get voted on and they get voted on usually after some discussion. I try to make it very clear what the alternatives are.

It was observed that some executive directors—who often played the major role in board recruitment—were able to inspire enthisiasm and loyalty through their own interpersonal skills and attractiveness. Regarding board/staff relations, the primary challenge of agency maintenance, according to several agency managers, was maintaining a satisfactory flow of information to trustees, and facilitating at least the perception of participation in governance. It was important for most managers to work to engage their boards around ratification of their policy recommendations:

> The Board gives me support in carrying out the stated goals and objectives of the Board. Now that's a two-way process. I must, through the Board structure, keep them well apprised and informed of what's going on, and I must also make recommendations to assist their decision making process. Being able to be very clear in their direction and communications to me makes it easier for me to function. I'm not saying that I couldn't do a lot of things without it, but it's like walking on thin ice. I never know how safe my actions are unless I know very clearly they are supported by the Board. So I need that reassurance psychologically. I need that reassurance technically. I need that reassurance legally, and they supply all those things . . . Unfortunately, they usually are dealing with corrective kinds of things, as opposed to projective things where they look into the future and say these are some of the things we're going to need. But when problems come up, they deal with them very effectively.

Still, there was little variation in the pattern of policy emanating from managers themselves, as opposed to the other way around.

The Proprietary Role of the Nonprofit Executive

Why would this be so? Practically speaking, executive directors saw themselves as being in a better position to make informed decisions in the best interests of their agencies. Most importantly, agency managers were by and large responsible for the development of programs and funding. (N.B.: The concept of the entrepreneurial non–profit manager is explored in–depth by Dennis Young (1983) in his excellent study *If Not For Profit, For What?*.) Often they were called upon to react very quickly to grant and funding opportunities with little time for discussion or consensus building.

Interestingly, a number of agencies that had done very well in sustaining and even expanding their programs despite years of sustained financial pressure seemed to have done so with comparatively little tangible help from trustees. In point of fact, the actions of boards seldom appeared to have much bearing upon whether or not agencies were able to get the funds they needed. By far, more creedence was placed on the credentials and appearance of the board to the public and funders. In this respect, the role of many boards seemed to be a symbolic one which was evident in their portrayal in grant proposal materials and in the few key personal appearances they would make before funding review committees or program contract monitors. Successful agency executives learned to be adroit at conveying the proper image of board governance to the right sources at the right moment through verbal and written contacts.

The evidence confirming the ability of agency managers to develop and carry out programs was compelling. Mainly success seemed to depend upon the skill of the individual at dealing with the grants process and putting together a viable annual budget that could be sustained over a period of years. Over and over again the challenge of agency maintenance came down to making a quick and skillful response to general or specified grant opportunities or some type of external threat to funding which could alter an agency budget for years to come.

An excellent and not atypical example of this involved a women's agency which will be referred to here as Women's Services, Inc. WSI had been formed in 1972 in a large eastern city to serve the needs of women undergoing a variety of life changes, including separation and divorce, workforce re–entry, middle years reorientation, and so forth. WSI had begun as a collective and had undergone some of the same kinds of structural evolution as had College Point Women's Center described earlier. Its transition, though, had been considerably less traumatic for board and staff, and it had entered into a period of rapid expansion, adding employment and several other programs. Having flourished for several years during the mid–1970s, it had tumbled from a half–million dollar budget under CETA and had re–grouped to gain a new measure of stability in the early 1980s but never really recaptured its former fiscal glory. In 1985, the executive director got wind through personal contacts that the city's Office of Drug and Alcohol Programs was anxious to utilize unexpended Federal funds to launch a women's alcohol treatment program which was supposed to have been operative for some time. Although the agency had never before dealt with substance abuse, it did have experience with a crisis hotline. As the Executive recalled:

> From time to time Board members and staff have said we should be in that area, too, you know, looking at specialized services. We had all of about ten days to soul search, but we probably had only three (days) to make the decision to go for it. It was not done with a lot of research and investigation. There was a sense of 'Yes!' It was like a snap feeling of appropriateness and both the Board and staff liked it . . .

> There was competition. We wrote a proposal that got rated by everyone on their committee. One of the key ingredients was that a new counselor had come onto our staff a year

ago who had drug and alcohol expertise. When I went to her and said 'This is an opportunity,' she blossomed unbelievably. She and I dropped everything. I would not have done it without her. We could not have handled it internally without her expertise.

Now the most cynical on our Board said 'There goes long range planning .. They annualized us at about $120,000.

This sort of ability to respond in a swift, flexible and competent manner left little or no time for extensive policy deliberations on the part of agency Board members. At best, they were able to ratify the executive's feelings in time for her to act. Undoubtedly, this organization which had begun ten years earlier as a women's collective, would have had great difficulty in pursuing the opportunity if they had had to adhere to the kind of process of consensus building which had characterized their earlier days.

Agency Accountability as Part of the Professional Role

The case described above was intended to highlight the fact that it has been primarily agency executives and not their boards which have identified and responded to opportunities for agency growth and development. Likewise, it has been primarily the role of professional staff to respond to the levels of accountability imposed by government and increasingly, private funders such as United Way. During the course of this study many improvements in agency programmatic and fiscal recordkeeping and controls, personnel management, etc. were seen to have emanated from the demands of funders. In numerous instances purchase of service contracts ("grant" is now most often a misnomer in the non–profit lexicon) are predicated upon an agency's management credibility which is vested in the image of its staff and board, but especially staff. Further, purchase of service agreements with Federal, state or local government are typically accompanied by a litany of rules, procedures, policies and practices which comprise more or less explicit guidelines for recipients. It has been this and not agency board policymaking or oversight that has heightened the level of managerial sophistication and professionalism in community service organizations over the years. This was reflected in the comments of yet another agency manager whose programs included adult basic education and job readiness/job placement services:

"You have evaluation every year. You have to meet the guidelines all the time . . . The County comes here once a year and they go through our files. The (state) will come here every year and go through our files and our fiscal management; much more accountability than some years ago. The sad part is that everyone is asking for accountability but no one is paying for overhead and administration! Everybody's paying for program!"

The evidence is that, when government contracts would end that had brought with them new and more complex requirements for agency management and accountability, many of the newly installed policies and procedures tended to continue. While certain governmental agencies (most Federal offices and state and local authorities in the fields of drug and alcohol, day care, employment training and housing) are notorious for red tape, overregulation and a bean counter mentality, the strictures they impose are often desirable nonprofit management practices. In some instances they enable an agency to establish the level of credibility necessary to secure new sources of support; in effect, to project a more competent image and to compete more favorably in increasingly tight nonprofit service markets. To a large extent, boards of directors are effectively excluded from the substance of this type of accountability, although their appearance of involvement may often be critical.

Thus, what emerged from this study was a picture of some of the most well-developed and programmatically active agencies looking less like a vehicle for conventional, voluntaristic community involvement and more like something cast in the image of one hardworking, paid individual. Even if agency executives technically hold no equity or official fiduciary role, most of those studied were seen to assume an unmistakably proprietary role in their organizations day after day. To a great degree and from a functional perspective, they faced the attendant risks and constant financial uncertainties in isolation, and often made policy decisions in the breach.

Further, it was primarily the agency executive who was observed to be the vehicle for agency accountability, often responding to the demands of the funding environment. As one commented, "Business has to go on . . . you just can't sit at the table and twiddle your thumbs and not let things happen."

DISCUSSION: INCENTIVES, FORMALIZATION AND THE
ROLE AND FUNCTIONS OF BOARD MEMBERS

Voluntary associations and organizations have been most consistently characterized by the involvement of individuals freely coming together independently of the state to bring about some kind of mutual benefit or to accomplish commonly held goals (Sills, 1968: 362–3). Manser and Cass (1976: 42) have defined voluntarism in a slightly different way as:

> those activities and agencies arising out of a spontaneous, private (as contrasted with governmental) effort to promote or advance some aspect of the common good, as this good is perceived by the persons participation in it. These people are *volunteers* [sic]— persons who, motivated by varying degrees of altruism and self–interest, choose to give their time and talents freely.

A definition such as this is broad enough to accommodate the ever widening variety of individual and shared motives underlying voluntary activity. Neither does it contradict the assertions of writers who have recognized the limitations of the traditional reliance upon religious beliefs or "altruism" as an explanation for voluntary contributions or involvement (Smith, D.H., 1981; Van Til, 1985; and Widmer, 1985 and in this volume). Today, it is generally accepted that motives are multiple, complex, and mixed, and that personal incentives—albeit non–pecuniary ones—are admissible as reasons for individual involvement in voluntary organization activity.

This thinking is also in line with the tenor of research and writing derived from writers such as Clark and Wilson (Clark & Wilson, 1961; and Blau and Scott, 1962: 42 ff). It stresses incentives and benefits as a means for analyzing organizational behavior. The incentive or benefits based perspective has its roots in the work of early cultural anthropologists such as Marcel Mauss (1954) who observed the prevalence and patterns of gift giving in primitive societies, and who helped to established reciprocity as a nearly universal characteristic in all societies. Taken forward by later social theories such as Homans (1958), Gouldner (1960), Blau (1964) and others, this basic premise of mutuality in giving has been developed into a theory of social exchange wherein what is exchanged between people or groups need not be tangible, but may in fact be partially comprised of sociability, personal gratification, power or other intangibles.

Much currency is to be placed in the "psychic" rewards and gratifications which accrue to those who serve the needs of others through voluntary efforts. Whether organized simply to result in the gratification of individuals through their own direct involvement ("expressive" ends), or to promote a particular charitable objective or bring about a change in social conditions ("instrumental" ends), *shared* personal incentives are seen to form the foundation of formalized, collective voluntary action. Viewing it from a political perspective, Tocqueville labelled this "self–interest rightly understood," since those working together to achieve shared goals were serving their own needs at the same time. This individual basis for mutuality of interest and effort he recognized as embodying the particular genius of American society and institutions, and especially its voluntary associations formed for every conceivable purpose. O'Connell (1981, p. xiii) has paraphrased the application of this idea to the voluntary sector:

> In the course of [voluntary] efforts there is at work a silent cycle of cause and effect which I call the 'genius of fulfillment,' meaning that the harder people work for the fulfillment of important social goals, the more fulfilled they are themselves.

And so our most basic understanding of the terms and phenomena of voluntarism has somewhat begrudgingly come to accept the notion of tangible or intangible incentives as a basis for individual participation in order to achieve collectively held ends. It is in the variation of those incentives and people's variable responses to them that difficulties are seen to arise which can have a profound impact upon nonprofit governance. As discussed in the beginning of this chapter, some theorists have emphasized the central importance of resources and their control as a basis for analyzing organizational goals and behavior. Both Zald and Perrow, for instance, take the position that organizational players—including board members—bring to their position resources comprised of knowledge and skills, contacts, money or access to it, manpower and the force of personality. As noted earlier, Perrow goes a step further than Zald, asserting that voluntary organization members themselves constitute resources or inputs. In his view also, they are frequently, though not always, the primary consumers of organizational outputs. To a greater or lesser extent organizational members make available to the organization their name, money, manpower and/or personality. As he sees it (1970a, p. 106), the nature of an individual's contribution is seen to decisively condition his role and power in the organization.

> Those groups which rely predominantly upon manpower for their resources tend to be either small or fairly autonomous parts of federated organizations. This resource cannot be easily stored and is specific rather than general—specific skills in a specific time and place are required. Furthermore, these resources are self–activating, sentient, and potentially recalcitrant as well as voluntary so they have greater say regarding the output of the organization, part of which they consume. Consumption varies as widely as the organizations themselves, from fulfilling the imagined obligations of a social position and using up leisure time, to satisfying burning resentments and desires for social change. . . .

> A significant element of most voluntary donations of manpower is also access to other's

> personalities through giving access to one's own. Furthermore, even those organizations which we would class as primarily personality or self–oriented must have an important element of manpower involved . . . The distinction is useful, since these are consummatory or internally directed groups . . . with almost all the production being consumed internally . . .
>
> As with manpower organizations, resources in personality–oriented groups are specific and cannot be stored—relationships deteriorate with lack of use. Even more than in manpower organizations, however, the resource is free to determine the output of the organization.

The situation is quite different when the primary contribution of an individual is their name, which was often seen to be the case in agency boards studied. The level of investment is not only lesser, but qualitatively different, allowing for far more discretion on the part of those in a position to provide ongoing, functional leadership. In this instance an organization is able to utilize the largely symbolic support of a credible member to bolster legitimacy. In return, the member receives both gratification and the option of using their association with the organization and its cause to serve their own needs for status or credibility. As Perrow suggests, "One of the pleasant things about voluntary organizations is that both the individual member and the organization can benefit from each other even with a minimal transformation or effort" (p. 103.)

The dilemma posed by differing motivations for voluntary association involvement has also been explored in depth by Fuller in an essay entitled "Two Principles of Human Association" (1969). In it he discusses the distinction between emphasizing means as opposed to ends as underlying motives for voluntary association or organization formation and cohesiveness—or the lack thereof. His logic can be applied equally to members, volunteers or trustees. In most instances shared commitment to mutual goals or activities often provides the initial, underlying impetus. Shared commitment is, in fact, Fuller's first principle of voluntary association. In cases where it is operative, shared goals or merely the sociability derived from participation in the organizational life of a club, association or service organization may be sufficient to capture and sustain the involvement of members and officers. This would be true, for example, in scholarly, professional or trade associations, where the promotion of member interests provides adequate motivation to actively participate and govern.

Unfortunately, it is not always true in service organizations, such as most of those reflected in the research described above. In many organizations, according to Fuller, an evolution is seen to occur, wherein the "formal rules of duty and entitlement" come to predominate. This Fuller refers to as the second or legal principle of association. In reality, he asserts, most human associations move inexorably toward domination by the legal principle as a basis for cohesiveness. In particular, he notes the variability of these two contrasting forces within varying organizational contexts (pp. 6–7):

> Even in the case of a society formed to achieve some stated purpose, it may turn out to be that the objective sought is unattainable, so that some other end, not merely smaller in compass, but actually different in nature must be substituted. Or, again an end originally selected, though attainable, turns out to require some unwelcome reordering of the internal relations of the group seeking to achieve it. This is frequently the case when an effective pursuit of the end originally sought is seen to require a formalization of the group's internal structure that is regarded as too high a price to pay for mere

efficiency. Finally, and most importantly, in an association formally dedicated to the achievement of some stated end, the strongest element of commitment may not lie in the end itself (which may be trite and wholly acceptable to any normal person) but in a belief in the efficacy of the means pursued.

It is important to add that in Fuller's view, no matter how much formally ascribed entitlements or authority may come to dominate, all associations depend upon the underlying existence of "internal groupings that are themselves sustained by the principle of shared commitment." (p. 13) To some extent, though, he sees the legal principle as existing in opposition to that of shared commitment.

> In most human associations the two principles stand in a relation of polarity—they fight and reinforce each other at the same time. As a shift occurs in the balance between them, this shift may both cause and reflect a corresponding shift in the quality of the human relationships encompassed by the two principles.

> When all goes well with an association, it is usually difficult to say how much its success depends on a sense of shared commitment and how much derives from a well–designed internal legal structure. When trouble develops and a schism occurs, however, the latent tension between the two principles may come plainly into view. (pp. 8–9)

In fact, it is this writer's belief that Fuller's point of view suggests subtleties which tend to be overlooked by some of our most prominent writers on nonprofit boards. Tracing its roots back to the writings of the grand theorist of organizations and bureaucracy, Max Weber (1946), formalization conceptually is the process whereby many if not all organizations tend toward ever greater designation of authority through written roles, rules and procedures. Its applicability to voluntary organizations was first systematically described by Chapin and Tsouderos (1955). Subsequently, Harrison (1960) noted its potential to engender conflict between the goals of individual self–expression and organizational maintenance through increased efficiency.

Weber viewed professionalization as one component or characteristic of formalization. Contemporary writers have noted the advent of professionalization within the field of voluntary organization management (Majone, 1980; Reisch, and Wenocur, 1981; and Milofsky, 1983). Milofsky (1980) has argued compellingly that the virtues of formalization and professionalization really depend upon whether their purposes lie primarily in "community building" or in the fulfillment of contractual obligations for service delivery. (N.B.: In a sense, the growth of a body of literature and training programs in nonprofit management reflect this, as well.) On the other side, writers such as Rothschild–Whitt (1976 and 1979) have contended that it is possible to sustain a non–professionalized or even collective leadership, but that certain kinds of conditions tend to render this arrangement of authority more or less difficult. It would appear as though one type of organization—the predominantly grant–funded, service oriented community based non–profit—does not fall under these conditions. Rather, it entails structures, decisionmaking and responses to environmental exigencies which may well bear greater resemblance to those found in many proprietary small businesses. At the least, as suggested by Zald, "An ideology of professionalism may lead to an effective abrogation of the role of the board. In such cases, the board serves to provide a mantle of legitimacy and community justification." (p. 176)

The Marginal Utility of Community Agency Boards

According to law the not–for–profit, charitable service organization is seen to belong to the community, rather than to any individuals. The so–called fiduciary role, or trusteeship, emanates from the perceived need for the public to have representative guardians of its interests such that the special status and privileges granted a non–for–profit are not abused and charitable purposes are upheld. But actual adherence to legal standards for the conduct of nonprofit directors would appear to trade heavily upon the investment of those directors in the purposes and activities of the organization which they oversee. Thus, one could hypothesize that, where organizational aims are "expressive" and achieved only through direct participation in what O'Connell has termed "the huzzah" of organizational life and activities, the existence, if not efficacy, of board involvement is more likely.

What of governance in organizations whose purposes are directed toward some type of charitable ends benefitting those other than the members or directors themselves? In these cases, the faith vested in directors presumes that their commitment to those ends is sufficient to allow the exercise of adequate fiduciary care, and this may well be a dubious proposition. That is, the same incentives borne of benefits tied to involvement may well be absent. To state it differently, much more weight must be placed on beneficence where organizational players are acting charitably on behalf of others.

Fuller in fact, comments on this directly, and he is not particularly optimistic. In his view, the more that formalization occurs, the less that essential ingredient of shared commitment is present to provide a basis for participation in organizational governance (p. 11):

> As a matter of sociological observation we may therefore assert that as an association becomes increasingly dominated by the legal principle, the element of shared commitment—though tacitly operative—tends to sink out of sight; any attempt to secure recognition for its role is likely to stir anxieties and meet with strong resistance. This reaction will extend, not simply to what may be called the element of shared substantive commitment, but to that minimum commitment essential to make the legal system itself function properly.

As has been observed in the field, within community service agencies where the benefits of organizational effort accrue at least partially if not mainly to staff or to persons who are outside of the organization, the level of "psychic equity" held by directors is less reliable. The basis for commitment sufficient to undergird active and attentive trusteeship is frequently absent largely due to *structural features* the organization has assumed i.e., the functional roles in which all organizational players are cast. Community service organizations with ideological or activist roots have by and large shifted to the delivery of hard services. Concomitantly, their internal arrangements and leadership have evolved to accommodate the demands of survival. As the data presented here suggests, the move toward organizational maturation through professionalism and also toward even greater complexity has left the board role in its ideal sense far less tenable than in the past. For trustees, technical knowledge, information and even familiarity with organizational life may well be at a premium, or at least increasingly dependent upon the agency executive. As Zald (p. 178) has asserted, *"the greater the complexity of the organization and the more technical its knowledge base, the lower the influence of board members"* [italics the author's].

CONCLUSION: THE NEED FOR DEVELOPMENT OF NEW FIDUCIARY MECHANISMS

There is every reason to believe that thousands of community service agencies throughout the United States are playing an important and even critical role in delivering services to both low and middle–income populations. Still, it is clear that many do so without the benefit of prescribed trustee behavior but are instead driven by professionals whose role is often heavily proprietary. In essence, many agencies seem to succeed quite well with "paper boards."

The advent of this development to the detriment of "traditional voluntarism" has caused one well known observer, Alan Pifer to toss up a red flag of caution (1967). Characterizing some grant funded nonprofits as either a "quasigovernmental" organization or "the nonvoluntary, voluntary association" also referred to as the private service organizations, Pifer warns against our abandonment of what he calls the "true voluntary organization." For Pifer, the nature of authority is the key to truly voluntary status. The quasigovernmental organization, created as a result of legislative appropriation (and exemplified by community action programs), is seen as financially dependent upon government with responsibility for its programmatic direction and lines of accountability running to government rather than voluntary auspices. (pp. 20-1) Other private service organizations are viewed as having become professionalized to the point where authority as a matter of practice is really vested in staff. Of these he writes: "Such voluntary organizations no longer exist to serve the individual, and he has little or no say in their management ... 'Voluntary' organizations such as these are, in a sense, severed heads no longer related to a body. They are answerable, not to a membership, but to themselves—that is, to paid professional staffs—and self–perpetuating boards of trustees. These organizations are legitimized in society by the social utility of their programs rather than by their status as the representative organs of defined bodies of the citizenry." (pp. 24-5) This he views as somewhat less onerous than the quasigovernmental organization in that the power to oversee it lies more clearly in the private hands of its trustees. For him, though, the bottom line is that "neither truly belongs within the great tradition of voluntarism in American life."

From a pragmatic standpoint, it is apparent that, for many community service agencies, needed policies and mechanisms for accountability are being increasingly wrought through funder regulation and the rigors of competition within the non–profit marketplace. That may not necessarily be so bad. For Pifer and others the primary concern continues to be with the issue of voluntarism as a key element within democratic society. The truth is that, under certain conditions, the values and strictures of voluntarism as we know them may not always be commensurate with the available means for or the reality of social provision. As governmental policies and involvement regarding human service delivery shifts away from public provision, the role of what Pifer calls "the private service agency" is increasing. In some instances where governmental services are especially scarce—including both inner city and rural areas—community based organizations may well be providing the only means to needed assistance in education, employment, health, seniors' and many other kinds of family services. Given this reality, perhaps we would do better to put aside some of the impassioned rhetoric of voluntarism and start defining clearer and more concrete standards of policy and oversight for agencies. To that end, nonprofit professionals themselves might well lead the way by attempting to codify key aspects of sound agency structure and management as a basis for policy, and by developing guidelines which can provide some basis for agency certification. In this way, they would not only demonstrate their own professional coming of age, but also provide their nominal employers—agency trustees—with a means of providing the oversight our society demands.

A METHODOLOGICAL FOOTNOTE

Sampling

The sampling procedure could best be characterized as an approach based upon opportunity. The research had its origins in a unique set of circumstances. As a state–funding provider of management assistance to several dozen community service organizations during more than four years, the researcher has been able to sample organizations, secure formal, written permission to study individual agencies, and gather substantial amounts of data in the service of the research design. In each instance, a letter of agreement was initialed by the presiding Board officer and top manager at each organization to be studied. Additionally, written release to utilize the data has been secured under the condition that anonymity be guaranteed.

Data Collection Procedures

Collection of data from agencies in the field was carried out according to a process synthesized in an initial pilot case. In this instance and most of the others, the researcher led a team of from one to four persons in the collection of data through extensive interviews, gathering and examination of documents, and direct observations on–site. The difficulties and rewards of gathering data in this fashion were much as have been described in the literature on "action research." (Foster; Seashore) Within the turbulent setting of ongoing organizational life, the varied frustrations of investigation are more than offset by the richness and utility of findings in vivo.

Collection typically required three to five days at an agency's location, as well as additional hours off–site for telephone interviews and documents review. In several cases, the researcher completed the data collection alone, and in one case, research assistants trained by the principal investigator completed the data collection without direct supervision.

In interviews questions were guided by, but not at all limited to a brief schedule constructed from a review of literature on nonprofit management. The guided interviewing was focussed upon items identified within categories such as by–laws; organizational structure; board responsibilities and practices; mission, goals and objectives; planning; communications; fiscal management; personnel management and supervision; and program evaluation. Interviewees were handled both singly and in groups of up to three, and interviews were often allowed to proceed in the style of the "extended conversation" (Schatzman & Strauss), lasting up to an hour or more. The team was instructed to utilize the guided interview to identify specific agency strengths and weaknesses, but also to take time to allow all interviewees to describe in detail their role and activities in the agency. Specific questions pertained both to areas individuals could be presumed to know about, for example, board–related items for trustees or issues of planning, supervision, etc., for managers, but also "non–sequitors" and open–ended items were used in an effort to elicit totally new material (i.e., to staff, "What do you see as the role of the Board?" or "If you could change three things here, what would they be?"). The examination of documents and records, as well as direct observations of operations were carried out in a similar guided but open–ended fashion such that the varied manifestations of agency life, structure and process could be "interrogated" to build obtain a detailed composite. Attempts were made to acquire independent verification of any particular finding through two or more sources (i.e., two interview statements from different persons and a document; a direct observation, verbal report, and documentation, etc.). While this was not possible in every instance, it was adhered to as a guideline for general practice.

Data Analysis

Data from each individual case was handled separately at first, and then later arrayed for comparative analysis. In the preliminary analysis, data from interviews, direct observation and documents review were handled using conventional inductive techniques to build categories pertaining to dimensions of goal definition, formalization of organizational structure and resource generation. In the secondary analysis, data from individual cases were arrayed on a simple grid for comparison across all cases. Additionally, individual case narrative information pertaining to such things as agency history, identified management problems at the time of the study, etc. was retained for later use.

REFERENCES

Blau, Peter M.
1964   *Exchange and Power In Social Life*. New York: John Wiley and Sons.
Blau, Peter M. and Scott, Richard
1962   *Formal Organizations: A Comparative Approach*. San Francisco: Chandler Publishing.
Blickendorfer, Richard and Janey, Jane
1986   "Policing the Commercial Nonprofit Corporation Director: A Dilemma of Fiduciary Law." *Proceedings of the Fourteenth Annual Meeting of the Association of Voluntary Action Scholars*, October 1–4, 1986, Harrisburg, PA, pp. 53–67.
Chapin, F. Stuart and Tsouderos, John E.
1955   "Formalization Observed in Ten Voluntary Organizations: Concepts, Morphology, Process" *Social Forces* (32), pp. 342–44.
Clark, Peter B. and Wilson, James Q.
1961   "Incentive Systems: A Theory of Organizations," *Administrative Science Quarterly* (6) pp. 129–66.
Connors, Tracy
1980   "The Board of Directors," in *The Nonprofit Organization Handbook*. New York: McGraw–Hill, 1980, pp. 2/35–63.
Conrad, William R. Jr. and Glenn, William E.
1983   *The Effective Voluntary Board of Directors*. Downers Grove, IL: Swallow Press.
Fuller, Lon
1969   "Two Principles of Human Association" in Pennock, J. Roland and Chapman, John W. (eds.) *Voluntary Associations*. New York: Atherton Press, pp. 3–23.

Gouldner, Alvin
    1960   "The Norm of Reciprocity," *American Sociological Review* (25), pp. 161–78.
Harrison, Paul M.
    1960   "Weber's Categories of Authority and Voluntary Associations," *American Sociological Review* (25), pp. 332–7.
Hartogs, Nelly and Weber, Joseph
    1974   *Boards of Directors, A Study of Current Practices in Board Management and Board Operations in Voluntary Hospital, Health and Welfare Organizations.* New York: Oceana Publications.
Homans, George
    1958   "Social Behavior As Exchange," *American Journal of Sociology* (63), pp. 597–606.
Houghland, James G. Jr. and Sheperd, Jon M.
    1984   "Voluntarism and the Manager: The Impacts of Structural Pressure and Personal Interest on Community Participation." Paper presented at the 1984 Annual Meeting of the Association of Voluntary Action Scholars, Blacksburg, Virginia, September 24–6, 1984.
Kramer, Ralph
    1969   *Participation of the Poor: Comparative Case Studies in the War on Poverty.* Englewood Cliffs, N.J.: Prentice–Hall.
Lerner, Max
    1983   "The Joiners" in O'Connell, Brian *America's Voluntary Spirit.* New York: The Foundation Center, pp. 81–9.
Lincoln, Yvonna and Guba, Egon S.
    1985   *Naturalistic Inquiry.* Beverly Hills, CA: Sage Publications.
Majone, Giandomenico
    1980   "Professionalism in Non–Profit Organizations," New Haven: Institution for Social and Policy Studies, PONPO Working Paper #24. New Haven: Yale University, ISPS.
Manser, Gordon & Cass, Rosemary Higgins
    1976   *Voluntarism at the Crossroads.* New York: Family Service Association of America, 1976, p. 42.
Mathiasen, Karl III
    1983   *The Board of Directors is a Problem: Exploring the Concept of Following and Leading Boards.* Washington, D.C.: Management Assistance Group.
Mauss, Marcel
    1954   *The Gift.* Glencoe, IL: The Free Press.
Milofsky, Carl
    1980   "Structure and Process in Self–Help Organizations," PONPO Working Paper #17. New Haven: Yale University, ISPS.
Milofsky, Carl
    1982   "Professionalism in Community Organizations," *Community Action.* Volume 1, Number 3, pp. 38–42.
O'Connell, Brian
    1981   *Effective Leadership in Voluntary Organizations.* New York: Walker and Company.
    1985   *The Board Member's Book.* New York: The Foundation Center.
Oleck, Howard L.
    1974   *Nonprofit Corporations, Organizations, and Associations,* 3rd Edition. Englewood Cliffs, N.J.: Prentice–Hall.
Perrow, Charles
    1970a   "Members As Resources In Voluntary Organizations," in Rosengren, William R. and Lefton, Mark *Organizations and Clients: Essays in the Sociology of Service.* Columbus, OH: Charles E. Merrill Publishing Company, pp. 107–8.
    1970b   *Organizational Analysis: A Sociological View.* Belmont, CA: Brooks/Cole Publishing.
Pifer, Alan
    1984   "The Quasi Nongovernmental Organization," in *Philanthropy in an Age of Transition.* New York, The Foundation Center, pp. 19–30.

Reisch, Michael and Wenocur, Stanley
    1981   "Professionalism and Voluntarism in Social Welfare," Washington, D.C.: Working Paper Series, Center for Responsive Governance.

Rosenbaum, Nelson and Smith, Bruce L.R.
    1982   "The Fiscal Capacity of the Voluntary Sector." Paper Presented at the National Conference on Nonprofit Management Assistance, Washington, D.C., June 9, 1982.

Rothschild–Whitt, Joyce
    1976   "Conditions Facilitating Participatory–Democratic Organizations," *Social Inquiry* 46(2), 75–86.
    1979   "The Collectivist Organization: An Alternative to Rational–Bureaucratic Models," *American Sociological Review* (44), pp. 509–27.

Sills, David
    1968   "Voluntary Associations: Sociological Aspects," in *International Encyclopedia of the Social Sciences.* Volume 16. New York: The Macmillan Company & The Free Press, 1968, pp. 362–3.

Smith, D.H.
    1981   "Altruism, Volunteers and Voluntarism," *Journal of Voluntary Action Research.* Volume 10 (1) pp. 21–36.

Van Til, Jon
    1985   "Mixed Motives: Residues of Altruism in An Age of Narcissism," in *Motivating Volunteers.* Larry F. Moore, (ed.) Vancouver: Vancouver Volunteer Center, pp. 243–61.

Weber, Max
    "Bureaucracy" in *From Max Weber*, H.G. Gerth and C. Wright Mills (eds.). New York: Oxford University Press, pp. 196–244.

Weitzman, Murray and Hodgkinson, Virginia A.
    1986   "Measuring the Size, Scope and Dimensions of the Independent Sector: A Progress Report." Paper presented at the Independent Sector Spring Research Forum, New York, March 14, 1986.

Widmer, Candace
    1985   "Why Board Members Participate," *Journal of Voluntary Action Research.* Volume 14, Number 4, pp. 8–23, and in this volume.

Young, Dennis
    1983   *If Not For Profit, For What?* Lexington, MA: D.C. Heath.

Zald, Mayer N.
    1974   "The Power and Functions of Boards of Directors: A Theoretical Synthesis," in Hasenfeld, Yeheskel and English, Richard A. (eds.) *Human Service Organizations.* Ann Arbor: University of Michigan Press, pp. 173–84.

Keys to Better Hospital Governance Through Better Information

Barry S. Bader

This piece is drawn from Keys to Better Hospital Governance Through Better Information, *published by the Hospital Trustee Association of Pennsylvania and is included here with permission by the Hospital Trustee Association of Pennsylvania.*

INTRODUCTION: THE CASE FOR IMPROVING BOARD INFORMATION

"An information bomb is exploding in our midsts, showering us with a shrapnel of images and drastically changing the way each of us perceives and acts upon our private world." So writes Alvin Toffler in his new book *The Third Wave* (1980:156), an exploration of the massive changes underway throughout society.

Hospitals, as a microcosm of society, reflect this exponential growth of information. "Ten years ago," recalls one hospital administrator, "when we wrote our hospital's annual budget, three of us got together in my office, worked all night, and the next day the budget was done. Now, it takes three months of meetings to sort through all the data."

The volume of hospital information has grown in response to a number of factors: the increasing complexity of medical care and therefore of the hospital setting; the demands of external regulators for information; the need for the hospital to cope with an uncertain economic environment; and increasing competition, which requires hospitals to use sophisticated market analyses in strategic long–range planning.

The volume of information showered on hospital boards has grown in proportion. Today's trustees are quite well–informed quantitatively—but qualitatively the information falls short of what is required for effective governance. Trustees receive so much information, in fact, that it becomes a major task to select those items that are essential to decision–making. And the format of presentation seldom offers much guidance through the maze.

The information explosion indiscriminately showers hospital management with both data and information. The two are not the same, as Professor Charles Austin points out:

> "... data refers to raw facts and figures which are collected as part of the normal functioning of the hospital. Information, on the other hand, is defined as data which have been processed and analyzed in a formal, intelligent way, so that the results are directly useful to those involved in the operation and management of the hospital." (1979:3)

Raw data is received by the hospital administration, which extracts from it the essential information it needs for planning, budgeting, and daily decision–making. Management information thus focuses on operational issues and is rich in detail; only in this form is it directly useful to management. However, this management information must be further refined so that it is useful for the board's unique responsibilities.

Survey of Information Needs

To pinpoint trustee needs for better information, a survey was conducted of board chairmen and CEOs in 161 hospitals. The results of the survey are printed in full in Appendix A, but the salient findings document the problems of providing board information.

- Trustees have limited time for information review. Nearly one–third of board chairmen spend up to ten hours a month reviewing hospital information, and nearly two–thirds spend more than eleven hours monthly. But two–thirds also believe that other trustees can devote less than five hours a month in this activity.
- Board chairmen and CEOs are dissatisfied with the format in which important information is presented to the board. We asked both board chairmen and CEOs to rank sixteen types of information as to how "important" the information is to governance, and how "satisfied" they are with the format of the information now provided. Below are shown the eight types of information with which CEOs and board chairmen, respectively, are most dissatisfied. They are listed in descending order of dissatisfaction.

CEO's are most dissatisfied with . . .	Board Chairmen are most dissatisfied with . . .
Annual operating budget	Quality assurance reports
Long–range plan	Recommendations for physician
Annual hospital goals	credentials and privileges
Annual capital budget	Annual capital budget
Recommendations for physician	Annual operating budget
credentials and privileges	Long–range plan
Quality assurance reports	Annual hospital goals
Monthly financial statement	Monthly financial statement
Committee minutes	Annual financial statement

- Trustees believe that more than one–third of what they receive is not essential. Board chairmen say that about 58 percent of what boards receive is essential information, 25 percent is important but not essential, and 18 percent is just "nice to know." This finding can be read two ways. On one hand, it says board members feel that nearly 60 percent of what they receive is essential. On the other hand, more than 40 percent is not.
While the survey did not indicate a need for improved board information, it also sent an encouraging signal about the chances for improvement. Two findings in particular seem to show that no real barriers exist:
- CEOs and board chairmen generally agree on what information is important and which types of information need to be better presented. With priorities already aligned, the board and the administration will not be working at cross purposes.
- CEOs, who are responsible for providing board information at more than 90 percent of responding hospitals, are more dissatisfied with its quality than are

board chairmen. The impetus for improvement, therefore, is already present among those who will be primarily involved in carrying it out.

The Hidden Information Problem

Sometimes, information problems are painfully obvious, as when a board is "surprised" by a sudden crisis: an emergency rate increase, a conditional accreditation, a six-figure legal settlement, an unexpected labor strike. Confronted with an unforseen and unpleasant contingency, board members may well confront the CEO or medical administrator and ask why they weren't kept informed.

More often, failures to communicate masquerade in other guises. They do not have definable "symptoms" of their own; they look like other problems, are experienced as other problems, and, indeed, often become confounded with other problems. For example:

Apathy: Is attendance at board meetings and committee meetings too low? Are discussions bland? Perhaps the information board members receive isn't sufficiently provocative and motivating.

Meddling: Do trustees question matters that are really management's concern, such as small expenditures and daily operating decisions? If so, the information given to the board may be too detailed.

Intimidation: Do board members fail to ask the tough questions they should about the hospital's financial condition or quality of care? Perhaps they feel intimidated by the technical or clinical jargon of the information they receive.

Distrust/Factionalism: Do board members feel that management is concealing "the true story" from them? This is an obvious information problem.

Myopia: Is the board focusing on narrow, operational issues rather than on broader, future-oriented issues and policy-making? One cause may be that the information received by the board lacks good analysis of trends, facts on environmental changes, and statements of long-range institutional goals.

Each of the above may be a symptom of an information problem. Information problems can remain hidden because board members have not been led to have high expectations for the information they receive about the hospital. They are not terribly unhappy with what they get because they have not seen examples of better ways of explaining and formatting information ... and because it is supplied in such large amounts that all the essential items are at least present, although not readily accessible.

Providing information in bulk is related to the tendency of many CEOs to think of a board as a "supermanager" which needs to be kept informed of the hospital's operations, and which occasionally must be consulted for major financial, policy, and planning decisions. The problem with this approach is that the board becomes over-supplied with management information, and is not receiving the appropriate board information.

The Governance Function

Because a hospital board exists to serve a very different function from management, it needs different information, or at least information presented differently from the manner in which it is seen and used by hospital management.

These information requirements derive from the unique attributes the board brings to the hospital (see Association of Governing Boards of Universities and Colleges, 1979).

Strong institutional leadership: Since the board typically has ultimate responsibility for the financial viability and quality of care of the hospital, it is in a position to assure management competence and require sound financial management and an effective program of quality assurance. In addition, the board acts as an advocate for the hospital's interests in dealing with the local power structure, other providers, and external regulators.

Different perspectives: Governing board members bring diverse backgrounds, often outside the health care field, to their trusteeship roles. This, coupled with the ability of trustees to be representative of the hospital's community, can allow a board to provide a valuable outside perspective on hospital decisions.

Resources for the future: Because the board is removed from daily operations, it can focus on the future of the institution. Through the strategic planning process, it can set an institutional direction that keeps the hospital financially sound and responsive to changing community needs. Through the political process, trustees can help the hospital secure the resource and affiliations it needs for the future.

If the board receives information tailored specifically to these roles, it can govern more effectively. If it receives management (operational) information, it will focus on operational issues to the detriment of its proper functions and responsibilities.

For example, asset preservation is a governance responsibility. Uncompensated care, including charity care and bad debts, gradually erodes the hospital's assets. It is the board's responsibility to preserve assets through the setting of policies, such as a policy on "percentage of charity care," or a policy on "desirable profit margin." To set policy, the board needs trend analysis information that shows the present and projected impact of uncompensated care on hospital assets. It needs information on relevant national regional trends and on viable options for the hospital.

Management, on the other hand, is responsible for keeping uncompensated care within board–approved guidelines; and as such, it needs detailed information on accounts receivable, collection schedules, and other areas of financial activity. Management's responsibilities and information needs are operational. The board's are policy–oriented. If the board receives operational informational on bad debts, it may begin to involve itself in the hospital's billing and collections procedures . . . or may instead lose interest in the entire matter because the information is too detailed and technical.

The Characteristics of Good Board Information

All information presented to the board should, to the maximum extent possible, be:

- Concise
- Meaningful
- Timely for the board's activities
- Relevant to the boards responsibilities
- Best available
- In context
- Graphically depicted, if appropriate

FIGURE 1

Characteristics	Examples	
	Poor	**Better**
Concise Is the information communicated as quickly or briefly as possible?	Departmental Variances for Month: ER—$2,994 Med/Surg—$5,443 OB/GYN—($44,533) Radiology—$55,110 Lab—$2,300 Pediatrics—$1,200 Orthopedics—($550) Fam. Prac.—$12,237	Departmental Variances Exceeding $10,000 Radiology—$55,000 OB/GYN—($44,500) Family Practice—$12,000
Meaningful Is the information shown in relationship to a significant factor, such as a goal set by the board, past performance, or comparative data?	Current Ratio: 2.96	Current Ratio: 2.96 Our Goal: no less than 2.9 Last Year: 2.6 Region: 2.67 Nation: 2.33
Timely Is the information relevant to the current agenda?	ER admissions dropped 34% last year.	ER Admissions down 14% in January. Cause: Friction with City Ambulance Service. Action: Meeting set with Mayor and Fire Chief.
Relevant to Responsibilities Does this information help the board or board committee discharge its responsibilities?	Board members receive all committee minutes and each chairman reports verbally at board meetings.	Board members receive summary of minutes, with action items highlighted. Routine reports by committee chairmen are discouraged.

Best Available
Is this information the best indicator available of the situation or condition being described? Can better information be collected/provided?

Proposed increase in Dietary budget to serve 30 new beds: $100,000

Proposed increase in Dietary budget to serve 30 new beds
Expenses:

Current	Proposed	% Increase
$500,000	$600,000	20%

Meals Served:

Current	Proposed	% Increase
54,000	86,400	59%

Meals/Full-Time Equivalent Employee:

Current	Proposed	% Increase
4.1	5.5	70%

Context
Is it clear why this information is important?

Current Ratio: 2.96

Current ratio monitors whether liabilities are becoming too great in relation to assets. Our current ratio of 2.96 means we have assets almost three times greater than our liabilities. The higher this ratio, the better.

Graphically Depicted, if appropriate
Can the information be better displayed graphically than in words? By using graphics, can we better communicate trends or show relationships between statistics?

Operating Surplus (Deficit)

1970	1.2%	$100,000
1971	1.4%	$115,000
1972	0.5%	$ 50,000
1973	1.1%	$110,000
1974	1.4%	$160,000
1975	0.9%	$140,000
1976	(1.2%)	($110,000)
1977	1.3%	$120,000
1978	2.1%	$210,000
1979	1.9%	$200,000
1980	1.5%	$180,000

Operating Surplus (Deficit) vs. Capital Replacement Costs

Estimated Cost of Capital Replacement

"The Gap"

Operating Surplus

1970	1975	1980

In contrast, the written packet of information which many boards receive prior to a meeting is anything but concise. Most of the information is heavily management–oriented—or just plain "heavy." The CEO often tries to add meaning and relevance to the data during a verbal presentation during the board meeting. However, verbal presentations do not help trustees prepare for a meeting or frame thoughtful, constructive questions in advance. One of two scenarios generally results: Either the board meeting produces little meaningful discussion of issues, or, at the other extreme, the meetings drags on endlessly with nit–picking and deliberation on minor issues, a situation directly attributable to the lack of pre–meeting preparation.

Board information that is meaningful, consise, relevant, and timely is an asset not only in full board meetings, but also at committee meetings. Most trustees and managers believe that the committee level is the appropriate place for in–depth exploration of issues and options. If committees receive good information and present good recommendations, the board as a whole does not have to waste time questioning the details of committee work. Full board meetings can focus instead on discussions of broad policy issues.

Figure 1 shows the seven characteristics of good board information and gives illustrations of both "good" and "poor" ways of presenting the same information to the board.

APPENDIX A

In the Spring 1981, the Hospital Trustee Association of Pennsylvania sent questionnaires to the chief executive officer and board chairman of its member hospitals. This appendix will describe the results of that survey. Specifically, the objectives of this appendix are to:

- Describe the types of information which CEOs and board chairmen, respectively, feel are important for effective governance.
- Describe how satisfied CEOs and board chairmen are with the information currently provided to their boards.
- Identify areas needing improvement.

Overview

To assess the state–of–the–art of information provided to trustees, HTA mailed a questionnaire in April 1981 to its 161 hospital members. Similar but not identical surveys were sent to CEOs and board chairmen.

Some 134 CEOs and 79 board chairmen, respectively, completed questionnaires. The salient findings of the surveys were:

- In more than 90 percent of the hospitals, the CEO is the individual responsible for providing information to the board.
- CEOs and board chairmen generally agree on the types of information which are most important for the board to have. Leading this list are the Annual Operating Budget, Annual Capital Budget, Monthly Financial Statement, Annual Financial Statement, Recommendations for Physician Credentials and Privileges, and Committee Minutes.
- A "dissatisfaction" score, computed by comparing importance and satisfaction

scores, indicated a need for improving information in a number of areas, including the Annual Capital and Operating Budgets, Recommendations for Credentials and Privileges, Quality Assurance Reports, Productivity Reports, Annual Hospital Goals, and the Long–Range Plan.

- Hospital size and type appeared to have little effect on the importance and satisfaction scores, indicating that some generic models for board information would be appropriate.
- Nearly one–third of board chairmen spend up to ten hours a month reviewing hospital information, and nearly two–thirds spend more than eleven hours monthly. However, board chairmen believe that two–thirds of other trustees spend less than five hours a month on this activity.
- Board chairmen believe about 58 percent of what boards receive is essential information: the rest is either "important but not essential" or simply "nice to know."
- Most board chairmen would like to have information two weeks before a board meeting, although one week is acceptable to many.

Generally, CEOs and board chairmen agreed on the importance of various types of information. The chairmen did feel Quality Assurance Reports were more important than CEOs, and that committee minutes were less important, compared to CEOs rankings, but even these differences in opinion were not marked.

In addition, the "spreads" or dissatisfaction scores again identified the need for improvement with regard to the Annual Capital Budget, Annual Operating Budget, and Long–Range Plan. Also, board chairmen were more dissatisfied than were CEOs with Quality Assurance Reports and Recommendations for Credentials and Privileges.

Implications

What implications can be drawn from the survey data? The editorial committee Pennsylvania hospital board members which guided this project drew the following conclusions:

- Board members are less than fully satisfied with much of the information they receive, or with the way in which the information is presented.
- Their dissatisfaction is best described as "moderate," and certainly not severe. One explanation for this is that board members have not been led to have high expectations in terms of the information they receive about the hospital. They are not terribly unhappy with the information, because they have not seen examples of better ways of explaining and formatting information.
- There seemed to be a lack of familiarity with certain types of information, such as Financial Variance Reports, Energy Management, and Productivity Reports. It may be that many hospital boards simply do not receive information on these items.
- The opportunities are great for improving the information that goes to the board, because CEOs and board chairmen generally agree on what information is important and on which types of information need to be better presented. When the response of CEOs and board chairmen from the same hospital were compared, only five out of eighty showed sharp differences of opinion.

A critical issue, however, is whether management wants to have a better informed board. Some cynics believe that the typical CEO wants to keep the board unin-formed. Since few contemporary boards will tolerate a dearth of information, some administrators overload the board with voluminous data. This gives the impression of keeping the board informed, but it actually may conceal information about the true condition of the institution and its future.

Information is power, and some CEOs may be reluctant to enhance the power of their boards. Some feel their boards flex their muscles too much already. The major-ity of CEOs, however, recognize the value of an informed, involved board. They know that trustees bring a perspective and other attributes found nowhere else in the institution, neither within administration nor the medical staff. They also under-stand that for the board to do its job, it needs to be well–informed.

Summary

This article has developed the argument that:

- Hospital board information is quantitatively strong but qualitatively weak.
- A major cause of qualitative weakness is the presentation of what is essentially management information, which is oriented toward operations.
- Quality can be improved by tailoring information to the board's unique respon-sibilities as the hospital's governing body.

Responses from CEOs

1. Is one individual primarily responsible for selecting, organizing and disseminating information to governing board members?
   Yes, the CEO—91.8%
   No—6%
   Other/No response—2.2%
2. Do you, as chief executive officer, deliver a report to the board at its regular meetings?
   Yes—96.3%
   No—2.2%
   No Answer—1.5%
   If yes, which topics does your report address most of the time?
   Updates on important hospital projects—100%
   Financial Outlook—89.1%
   Environmental Trends—49.6%
   Personnel Changes—43.4%
   Status of Litigation involving Hospital—40.3%
   Quality Assurance/Medical Staff Matters—12.4%
3. How much of your time is consumed by matters concerning the board, its ac-tivities and members?
   0–9%—10.4%
   10–19%—32.1%
   20–30%—24.6%
   31% or more—29.1%
4. Different chief executives have different styles for guiding board decision–making; how would you describe your style?

CEOs were given five statements describing different management styles for decision-making. They were asked to indicate, on a scale of 1–5, how well the statement described their style.

The statements ranged from a very structured management style to a highly participative one in terms of board involvement. The answers clustered in the mid–range, with a majority of CEOs indicating strong preference for relying on effective committee work.

The table below shows the pecentage of CEOs who marked a "5" ("most like me") for each statement:

Style	Statement	Percent Saying "Most Like Me"
Structured	Board prepared gradually for impending decision	20.4%
	Strong committee work	59.8%
Mid–Range	Close relationship with board Chairman	37.1%
	Strong reliance on staff work/board review	37.0%
Participative	Board reviews range of options	15.9%

Reinforcing these findings, the most participative style of guiding board decision-making—allowing the board to review a range of options, any of which the CEO could live with—drew the largest percent of "least like me" scores. Some 26.5% of CEOs said the "range of options" operating style was "least like me."

Style	Statement	Percent Saying "Least Like Me"
Structured	Board prepared gradually for impending decision	6.8%
	Strong committee work	1.7%
Mid–Range	Close relationship with board chairman	9.0%
	Strong reliance on staff work/board review	8.9%
Participative	Board reviews range of options	26.5%

5. With regard to various types of information commonly provided to boards, rate each one as to its importance to the board and your satisfaction with the information as now provided.

These findings have a number of implications. Clearly, CEOs feel financial information is most important, followed by information on quality of care. The satisfaction levels generally dropped along with how important a CEO felt each piece of information on quality care. The satisfaction levels generally dropped along with how important a CEO felt each piece of information was. For example, although only 15.6% of CEOs were "fully satisfied" with the Productivity Reports provided to the board, only about 14% felt this information was "most important."

For this project, the most meaningful finding concerned the spread between impor-

CEOs Rank of Importance	Type of Information	Percent Saying "Most Important"	Percent Saying "Fully Satisfied"
1	Annual Operating Budget	92.5%	65.6%
2	Annual Capital Budget	77.6%	55.2%
3	Monthly Financial Statement	74.6%	61.9%
4	Annual Financial Statement	72.3%	69.4%
5	Committee Minutes	64.1%	57.4%
6	Recommendations for Physician Credentials and Privileges	62.6%	44.7%
7	Long–Range Plan	50.0%	23.8%
8	Annual Hospital Goals	46.2%	21.6%
9	Financial Variance Reports	41.7%	36.5%
10	Quality Assurance Reports	39.5%	26.1%
11	Fund Raising/Development Reports	24.6%	21.6%
12	Contracts for Physician Services	23.8%	44.7%
13	Labor Contracts	19.4%	29.8%
14	Productivity Reports	14.1%	15.6%
15	Marketing/Competition	13.4%	14.1%
16	Energy Management	11.1%	29.1%

tance and satisfaction scores, which might be termed a "dissatisfaction" score. "Dissatisfaction" scores were noted for the following types of information:

Type of Information	Importance/Satisfaction "Spread"
Annual Operating Budget	26.9%
Long–Range Plan	26.2%
Annual Hospital Goals	24.6%
Annual Capital Budget	22.4%
Recommendations for Physician Credentials and Privileges	17.9%
Quality Assurance Reports	13.4%
Monthly Financial Statement	12.7%
Committee Minutes	6.7%
Financial Variance Reports	5.2%
Fund Raising/Development Reports	3.9%
Annual Financial Statement	2.9%

Responses of Board Chairmen

1. About how much time do you, as chairperson of the board, devote each month to reviewing information from the hospital? About how much time do you think other trustees spend?

	Time Board Chairman Spends	Time Other Trustees Spend
1– 5 hours	8.8%	64.5%
6–10 hours	31.6%	26.5%
11–15 hours	18.9%	3.7%
16–25 hours	22.7%	1.2%
more than 25 hours	17.7%	(—)
don't know	—	3.7%

It is not surprising that board chairmen spend more time than other trustees reviewing information from the hospital. However the estimate that two–thirds of trustees spend the least amount of time may be disheartening to some.

The findings imply that ten hours a month is the outside limit for trustee reading; information provided to the board must comply with that constraint.

2. How much of the information which board members receive is "essential," versus "important but not essential" and "nice to know"?

Response	Mean Scores
Essential	58%
Important but not Essential	25%
Nice to Know	18%

This finding can be read several ways. On one hand, it says board members feel that nearly 60% of what they receive is "essential." On the other hand, more than 40% is not essential.

3. How far in advance of a board meeting would you like to receive information?

Response	All Hospitals	Community Hospitals	Religious Hospitals
At least two weeks ahead	36.7%	48.3%	6.6%
At least one week ahead	55.6%	48.3%	80.0%
Several days ahead	7.5%	3.4%	13.3%
	100.0%	100.0%	100.0%

Most board chairmen wanted information a week before the meeeting. On this question, there was a significant difference between community and religious hospitals, with the chairmen of religious institutions being more comfortable with one week's notice.

4. Regarding various types of information commonly provided to boards, how would you rank its importance and your satisfaction?

Trustees Rank of Importance	CEOs Rank of Importance	Type of Information	Percent Saying:		
			"Most Important"	"Fully Satisfied"	Dissatisfaction Spread
1	1	Annual Operating Budget	84.8%	68.3%	16.5%
2	3	Annual Financial Stmt	77.2%	72.1%	5.1%
3	2	Annual Capital Budget	74.6%	53.1%	21.5%
4	4	Monthly Financial Stmt	73.4%	65.8%	7.6%
5	6	Recomm for Physician Credentials & Privileges	63.2%	43.0%	20.2%
6	10	Quality Assurance Reports	56.9%	27.8%	29.1%
7	7	Long–Range	56.9%	40.5%	16.4%
8	5	Committee Minutes	54.4%	65.8%	—
9	9	Financial Variance Report	48.1%	46.8%	1.3%
10	8	Annual Hospital Goals	45.5%	35.4%	10.1%
11	12	Contracts for Physician Services	30.3%	32.9%	—
12	14	Productivity Report	29.1%	21.5%	7.6%
13	11	Fund Raising/Development Reports	26.5%	21.9%	4.6%
14	13	Labor Contracts	25.3%	27.8%	—
15	16	Energy Management	18.9%	27.8%	—
16	15	Marketing/Competition Reports	7.5%	11.4%	—

Board–Staff Planning and Implementation Processes in Innovative Performance–Benefit Plan

Gary Baker

Crittenton Center is a mental health facility, located in Kansas City, Missouri, serving children and adolescents with serious psychiatric disorders. Over the years senior management and key members of the board have worked diligently to create effective board selection, recruitment, training and work processes. Crittenton now has a thirty–member working board of directors. The purpose of this section is to describe the board–staff processes that have led to the creation and effective implementation of an innovative performance–benefit plan.

Approximately ten years ago the board determined that two critical board committees—Policy and Long Range Planning and Personnel—needed more substantial staff representation. Until that time the chief executive officer was the only staff member on the committee. The members of the board believed that policy would be improved by the infusion of more information and a staff perspective. The board decided that both committees should have equal representation from staff and board members. The board members on each committee are appointed by the Chairman (Chief Volunteer Officer) and the staff members are appointed by the President (Chief Staff Officer).

All committee members have a vote. Discussions are often lively and open exchange of ideas is encouraged. Recommendations reached by the Personnel Committee are presented to the Board of Directors by the Chairman of the Personnel Committee who is a board member. The President, Vice Presidents and Medical Director routinely attend the Board meetings. Other key staff periodically make presentations, provide information for Board education, and serve on Board task forces as requested by the Board or the President.

The remainder of this section will focus on the work of the Personnel Committee, and later the work of the Trust Committee.

THE WORK OF THE PERSONNEL COMMITTEE IN DEVELOPING THE PERFORMANCE-BENEFIT PLAN

Historically the Personnel Committee focused its work on formation of personnel policies, employee evaluation forms and formats, salary range, studies, grievance procedure, and other related personnel matters. Approximately six years ago, by studying various Crittenton issues (the organization had recently gone through a major growth from approximately 100 employees to over 200 employees) there was a general consensus that three problem areas existed. (1) We had a relatively young and short-tenured staff and there was a need to create systems that would reinforce tenure and continued length of employment at the center. (2) We wanted to find ways that would create a greater sense of ownership or commitment to the organization and lessen the impact of the "burn–out" that occurs working in a mental health facility with severely disturbed children. (3) We needed to find a way to reward or reinforce those employees who were going the extra mile and finding creative solutions to problems through individual and group initiative. Through a series of personnel committee meetings we began discussing and assimilating the structure of what would ultimately become known as the Performance Benefit Plan (P–BP).

The Ideas Are Formed

The P–BP really had its beginnings when the committee discussed, in 1981, a benefit that was given to steel workers in a local steel mill. After employees worked at the mill for ten years, they would then become eligible for an extended vacation every five years. This allowed the employee to earn an additional ten weeks of vacation and gave the employees thirteen weeks off once every five years. It was noted that this had a profound rejuvenating benefit and was of significant interest to the men in the mill. Crittenton's employees needed similar rejuvenating time to counter the effects of burn–out. No sabbatical or extended leave policy existed. It was determined that it would be very desirable to deal with the problem of burn–out if some similar kind of benefit structure could be determined and provided in the Crittenton Center setting. After a number of discussions with employees, it was determined that time off in an earned and planned for fashion would be extremely important and of substantial benefit to the employees.

As we began exploring the incentive portion of this idea, it was noted that not–for–profit organizations lacked ownership of stock or payment of dividends which is fairly common in business profit sharing plans. Not–for–profit organizations really have nothing that would be equivalent to this benefit. We began exploring the notion of how we could create a similar effect of ownership in a not–for–profit organization. A board member put forth the simple notion of issuing shares of the organization, have them resemble a stock certificate in their official appearance, and assign the share some predetermined face or par value. The shares would then create a sense of ownership if a method of earning these shares could be determined which would be fair and respected among fellow employees.

The next breakthrough came as the committee explored how we could set up a system of issuing these shares which would address the problems previously stated while reinforcing the positive behavior of savings and esprit de corps as well as the sense of ownership that we were after. A staff member suggested setting up a nomination process. Fellow employees could put forth a simple, straightforward, factual presentation of a nomination that would outline exemplary or extraordinary work performance that was meritorious and deserving of both recognition and monetary reward. The committee also decided that an employee could nominate himself or herself. (In practice, 95 percent of nominations are made by others.) A bonus would be paid of some determined amount in the form of these shares which would have a predetermined face value. At first it was an idea that seemed too simple to work, but the general reaction of the personnel committee was, "Why not?" These are the people who know the work best; these are also the people who can best determine excellence and extraordinary performance, especially if this concept could be bottom–up and oriented towards line staff or direct care staff.

The Plan Takes Shape

The committee determined, after much deliberation, that the way to administer or monitor these nominations would be through a Trust Committee made up of two Board members appointed by the chairman, two staff members of supervisory rank and tenure qualifications elected by staff, and the President of the organization, who would be exempt from any consideration in the Performance Benefit Plan. Staff members of at least supervisory rank with at least three years of tenure are eligible to be on the election ballot. The supervisors who agree to serve form the actual ballot. All full and part time permanent employees vote. The staff member with the most votes serves three years, second most votes two years, third and fourth alternates. A reelection occurs as warranted.

Election to the Trust Committee is seen as an honor and a respected responsibility. It is hoped that the staff comprising the committee come from different parts of the organization. Staff elected to date have been well thought of by fellow employees and, internally, most trusted. After much thought, the Plan started to take form. Each share would have a $10 par value. Basically we determined four ways to earn these shares.

Earning Shares

The first way shares are earned is for years of service. Each time an employee achieves another year of employment, he or she would receive a fixed amount of shares. In the first through the fifth year of employment ten shares are awarded annually; during sixth through the tenth year, fifteen shares are awarded annually; the eleventh year and up, twenty shares are awarded annually. We felt this was important because we wanted every employee at the center to earn shares and participate in the Performance Benefit Plan to at least this extent. It also reinforced tenure and seniority with a relatively young and growing organization, an important component to be reinforced.

The second earning category is called Fiscal Year End Performance. The committee recognized that each and every employee played a role in the financial health of the organization. While this may not be a value traditionally emphasized by most not–for–profit organizations, clearly this corporation was like any other corporation in that it could not do anyone any good if it was bankrupt and each and every employee could certainly contribute to the savings of expenditures if not the enhancement of income for the organization. Thus, the second category of earnings was created. At the end of each fiscal year, if the organization operates with a net surplus, 4 percent of that net surplus is divided equally among all share holders on the date of record of the issuance of the Fiscal Year End Performance statement. The issuance is made in additional shares. For example, in 1986, each employee received nine shares, referred to as the "Robin Hood Benefit," that is, one for all and all for one. We felt it was important to establish the principle that we are all in this together. It would come as close as anything that we could think of to emulating a profit sharing plan, give a real sense of ownership and enhance the importance of financial performance.

The third way of earning shares would be for *individual merit* for exemplary or extraordinary performance; and the fourth way would be for *group or team merit* for exemplary or extraordinary performance. The committee decided that the nominations for these awards would be submitted to the President at anytime during the course of the year as they occurred. The President would record them and present them at quarterly meetings of the Trust Committee. The nominations would be determined and reviewed against a predetermined criteria established in three categories: effort, performance, and achievement. The smallest award that would ever be given to an individual nomination would be five shares or $50. The largest award would be fifty shares or $500, but no other restrictions on issuance of merit shares would be made. An individual employee could be nominated as many times in a quarter as deserving and could receive as many shares as determined by the Trust Committee.

The Committee first reviews each nomination to determine if it fits with in the category of exemplary or extraordinary performance in either individual or group merit. Generally the Committee is looking to the basic question: Is this nomination within the normal expectations of job description or routine performance, or is it a nomination for simply being a good employee over a length of time? If either situation is determined to be applicable, the nomination is rejected. Nominations are also rejected if they are considered fallacious or not significant enough to warrant consideration. As a general routine a consensus of opinion and attitude is formed as the Trust Committee works, yet one does see each of the three different perspectives coming into play in the decision making process. Staff generally have more specific and detailed knowledge of events that occur on a day–to–day basis within the organization. Board members generally have a more objective or non–prejudicial view of events and tend to look at nominations from a perspective of community importance, perception of overall board objectives. The President's focus would be routinely more along the lines of nominations that are consistent with organization mission or guiding philosophies that have been determined as significant in the ongoing management of the organization.

Specific nominations that are considered meritorious are grouped into the following three categories:

The first category is Extraordinary Effort and has a range of five to ten shares. This category is for the performance of tasks which fall into one's job description, and are situational as opposed to requiring extra effort over an extended period of time. Nominations falling into this category are ordinarily recognized by a "pat on the back" and "thanks for helping out," but merits recognition for the Extraordinary Effort.

The second category is Extraordinary Performance and has a range of ten to thirty shares. This category is for performance of a task which may or may not be clearly within one's job description, but requires a significant amount of effort, time, and creativity to complete that task. Performance in this category would reflect a significant amount of commitment and action which goes beyond the day–to–day job routine.

The third category is Extraordinary Achievement and has a range of thirty to fifty shares. This category is reserved for tasks performed which are clearly outside or in addition to one's job description. This kind of performance requires a high degree of initiative, dedication and commitment of time.

A range for awarding shares is determined for each category. Each Trust member determines the number of shares he or she feels is appropriate within the category, then the five numbers are averaged and that total becomes the final number of shares actually awarded to the employee. No one member of the Trust Committee dominates the process. There has been an amazingly cohesive give and take. Occasionally board members argue in favor of a nomination that other members do not at first concur with. Occasionally Trust Committee members will declare themselves in a conflict of interest position and excuse themselves from considering any nominations of staff members who serve on the committee. The staff members of the Committee have a tendency to have the most input because they routinely have the greatest amount of knowledge of events and occurrences that generally would relate to the specific nomination under consideration.

The Chairman of the committee notifies employees of the Trust Committee awards and the share certificates are prepared and distributed. There is a detailed recordkeeping system maintained, and the shares are treated much like a stock certificate of a corporation, numbered, dated and recorded. A computer program is used to perform recordkeeping functions, as well as the basic reason for the share award. This is very useful information for the Trust Committee in their deliberations. There have also been a number of practices developed that publicize and celebrate these awards. A newsletter is prepared in which it is reported who received the shares, for what purpose, and who nominated them. However, we never report the number of shares awarded. This is a confidential matter much like the amount of one's paycheck. The Committee also determined that the rest of the top management and the physicians of Crittenton Center would be ineligible for the Plan. We wanted this incentive system to be a bottom–up process that focused on the direct care staff.

Spending of Shares

The question next faced by the committee was the best use of these shares. The personnel committee decided that a formal survey would be conducted of the employees to determine what they would like to be able to have in the way of additional benefits. What came back was not especially surprising. They wanted to have opportunities for additional time off, additional income (cash), help with educational expenses, help with day care, and the ability to participate in various activities that the Center might assist individual employees with, as well as other uses such as deductibles for health insurance, or car insurance, air travel to meetings, professional dues, journals, periodicals, and so on.

Based on the long shopping list of additional benefits, it was determined that the highest value to employees and to the personnel committee would be the employee's ability to save the shares earned and use them for time off, especially extended or sabbatical use. To reinforce this value, we set a discounted use for a vacation day at five shares. Most employees average income would be more than $50 per day, but it would only require five shares to be cashed in to take one day off, with no restriction on the number of days that could be saved and used. An employee, if he or she wanted to save long enough, could save enough shares to take the entire summer off or a month off to work on writing a book or whatever they might be interested in.

On using the shares for cash, the personnel committee felt just the opposite. The committee members felt it was important to permit employees this use, but they wanted especially to reinforce savings and tenure. Thus, the committee established a rule that during the first ten years of employment, if an employee chose to use the shares for cash, each share would be worth 50¢ on a dollar. But, after ten years of employment, it would be worth a full dollar value. It was in effect a plan that would encourage savings and would create a "nest egg" for future use, perhaps to send a child to college, help buy a home or, if saved long enough, a cash fund to assist at retirement.

The third category approved was educational assistance. If employees wanted to use their shares they could do so for any educational matter, from Ph.D. work to taking a class in auto mechanics.

The fourth approved category was day care assistance. Each month employees could turn in their shares to be reimbursed for their own day care cost. This is an important issue in a children's treatment center and, since we do not provide day care services on site, a way to help individual employees who needed assistance in this area.

The fifth approved use was in Crittenton sponsored activities. This was general and loosely defined. An example of some of the activities that have been approved and used are staff sponsored ski trips, where the fee and the cost could be paid for through shares, staff sponsored warm weather vacations, sporting teams, and so on.

We continue to look at additional benefits which could be added to the use side and every other year poll employees as to what changes they would like to see made to the usage of the shares or what additional benefits they would like to see permitted. For instance, this coming year we are going to permit employees to transfer their shares permanently into their tax deferred annuity plan to act as a formal way of retirement planning if this is important to them. We are also seriously considering allowing shares to be used to pay for medical deductibles.

The shares are recorded in the gross number an employee earns. Twenty percent of the gross number (rounded up to a whole share) is withheld at the time of issue to satisfy tax withholding requirements. The net number of shares earned is the amount issued on the share certificate. This permits the employees maximum flexibility in the future use of their shares.

Observation About The Plan

We did determine that after the first year most of the objectives we had hoped we would achieve were indeed occurring. People were saving their shares and using them for special events, rather than immediately or frivolously. For those employees saving their shares, a dividend check is issued in the spring of each year, based on the interest earned from the shares saved. This comes as a somewhat unexpected windfall and provides a tangible reminder of future benefits. Employees in the first three years of the Plan have received anywhere from $6.50 to $160 in annual dividend earnings and it comes at a time that it has a very positive effect on the organization.

What else have we seen occur? We are now completing three years of use of the Plan. We've seen it work almost to the letter of our expectations. The Trust Committee process has worked amazingly well. It is a relatively simple system to administer from a personnel standpoint and it may require, based on the size of an organization, a computer program. The program runs very effectively on a minicomputer system. Our organization currently has 250 employees; in a much smaller organization a manual system would work fine. I could also go through a long list of creative ideas, incentive ideas, work–smart ideas, cost–saving ideas, income–producing ideas— ideas that a few years ago I would have almost had to force employees to implement and now I see them opting to do them because of a great change in commitment based on the Performance Benefit Plan. I know there have been a number of times that employees have taken on projects knowing that they would be nominated for shares. There have been many occasions when I've seen employees go an "extra mile" or do work above and beyond the call of duty. Part of what has been positive and somewhat unexpected is the way employees feel about the nominations themselves. Even if they are not rewarded with shares or the number of shares they thought appropriate, the feeling of having a co–worker take the time to write out a nomina- tion and in effect provide a tangible "pat on the back" is greatly satisfying. It's as though the employees hand each other "little Oscars" for a good idea and hard work.

From a management standpoint, it's almost a dream. The positive "can do," "let's solve the problem," "what if," kind of attitude that exists in this organization is just nothing short of amazing. It's had an absolutely electric effect. The Center is a "popcorn popper" of ideas day in and day out. The Plan literally reinforces the best in work performance. It is "catch them being good" in the very best of that idea. This whole concept is positively focused and has had virtually no negative effects what- soever.

On the use or earning side, what the employees appreciate most is being treated as adults with freedom of choice. The shares often take on a psychological value greater than their monetary worth. I see employees taking their shares and putting them in their safety deposit boxes and being very respectful of their earning worth. We've come up with a number of practices that, in effect, reinforce the earnings. We have an annual employee excellence dinner where board and staff get together to rejoice in the last year's accomplishments and highlight the people who have had key annivers- aries, five, ten, fifteen years, and so on, as well as any other real significant events that have occurred during the year. We recreated a "Golden Oak Tree" and each em- ployee, after earning the first merit share of each year, signs a brass leaf and places it on this beautiful tree as a way to recognize our corporate motto, "Together We Grow." This, by the way, was an idea of one of the employees who was nominated for shares *for* this idea, as you might expect.

Summary

The beauty of this plan is that it is employee driven, it was employee generated, and employee administered. This is a wonderful partnership between Board and staff. In particular the Board members that sit on the Trust Committee absolutely love these committee meetings because it gives them and the President an opportunity to see the very best ideas at least four times a year, the most creative solutions, and the most positive outcomes of this organization. Overall, the Plan costs approximately 1 per- cent of the Center's annual operating budget, an amazing return for the amount expended.

We have learned that this Plan is very flexible. It was recognized nationally in March of 1986 by the *Independent Sector*. Since that time we've had sixty–four organizations request detailed information about *The Performance Benefit Plan* and there are approximately a dozen organizations in various stages of implementing the idea in their own corporate personnel policy structure. Our first for–profit organization has implemented the program here recently. What we have learned is that it is a very effective idea, in both motivating and rewarding excellence. It is a positive program and very flexible in that all or parts of the Plan can be used—maybe only the merit portions or only the fiscal year end or years of service category or really any combination thereof.

The concept of the nomination, while incredibly simple, is very effective. The freedom of choice on the use of these shares is appreciated and valued, and the Share itself takes on a value that is greater than its financial worth. It creates a sense of ownership. It will have the long term effect of reinforcing and building tenure in this organization and it will also have, I think, the long term effect of permitting people to work for many years in a very challenging mental health field and, because of the sabbatical possibilities, take the time to recharge their energies in a positive and proactive way. I think I am most proud of this idea because it does reward excellence, extraordinary and exemplary performance by those employees who choose to go the extra mile. It is a unique incentive system, clearly well thought out, for the not–for–profit world. I think this idea is an outstanding demonstration of what can occur when board and staff members of an organization decide to set down and creatively problem solve together. Literally, Together We Grow.

Minority Participation on Boards of Directors of Human Service Agencies: Some Evidence and Suggestions*

Candace Widmer

A preliminary draft of this paper was presented at the 1986 Annual Conference of the Association of Voluntary Action Scholars in Hershey, Pennsylvania and appears in the Conference Proceedings.

INTRODUCTION

For the seven years that I have been studying boards of directors of nonprofit organizations and working with board presidents and executive directors on board development, the issue of diversity of board membership has been raised frequently by both board members and agency staff members. Many organizations believe that the image of the agency, ideals of fairness, and/or the need for appropriate representation require diversity among board members. Some organizations recognize the need for diversity, particularly racial diversity, in order to make effective decisions, to design and deliver appropriate services to minority clients, to compete, and to survive. But participants on boards of directors, like other citizen participants, come disproportionately from upper status groups. (Johnson and Ross, 1979; Milbrath, 1965, Milbrath and Goel, 1977; Rosenbaum, 1979; Shingles, 1981; Verba and Nie, 1972; Widmer, 1984; 1985). Board members of human service agencies are primarily white, middle class or upper middle class, well-educated, professionals (Widmer, 1984). How can organizations achieve diversity on their boards? In order to begin to address this question, I have, in turn, begun to ask many other questions: Who are the minority participants on boards? How are minority board members recruited? Do minority board members participate in the same ways and for the same reasons as white board members? Do minority board members represent the minority community? Can minority participants represent the minority community? Do minority board members experience stresses that get in the way of effective participation? This paper will present preliminary evidence addressing these questions and will suggest some steps toward achieving diversity.

METHODS

The subjects for the research presented here are members of the boards of directors of ten human service agencies located in upstate New York. Agencies were selected to differ in type of service, client population, size of staff, board, and budget, and sources of funding. The boards ranged in size from thirteen to forty-one members. Ten members of each board were randomly selected to receive a mailed questionnaire. The rate of return on the questionnaires was 69 percent. A first round of interviews was conducted in 1983 with three members of each board, including the board president and two other board members who were known to be community leaders, agency clients and/or to represent minorities on their boards. Five of the boards were also observed at regular board meetings.

A second round of interviews with members of the same ten boards was conducted in 1986, approximately three years later. All current board presidents—in all cases a different individual and again in all cases white individuals—were interviewed as were a sample of minority board members. The second round of interviews focused on issues of recruitment and retention of board members and on the experiences of members who were racial minorities on their boards. Additional interviews were conducted with selected past and present minority board members of affiliate agencies of a national human service organization. Data from all the interviews and questionnaires and analysis address the questions outlined above.

All comparisons of black and white board members are based on data from the questionnaires returned and interviews conducted in 1983. The study focuses on black and white board members because there were no Asian, Hispanic, or other members of racial minorities in the 1983 sample, and only one Filipino and two Indian board members in the 1986 sample. The population of the county in which the study was conducted is, according to the 1980 census, 92.5 percent white, 3.0 percent black, 2.2 percent Asian, 1.5 percent Hispanic, and .8 percent other. The population of the city in which the majority of the agencies were located is 86.7 percent white, 6.4 percent black, 3.6 percent Asian, 2.2 percent Hispanic, and 1.1 percent other.

It is important to note that this research, including all interviewing, was done by a white, female, middle class, college professor. While it is difficult to predict exactly how this may have affected the data and its interpretation, it undoubtedly has had an effect.

RESULTS AND DISCUSSION

Minority Participants

Ninety-five of ninety-nine board members in the initial sample identified their race, nationality, or descent. Seven or 7.4 percent of the board members were black and eighty-eight or 92.6 percent were white. Six of the black board members were women, one was a man. Of the ninety-nine respondents in the initial sample, forty-seven were men and fifty-two were women. Three years later, in 1986, the presidents of the boards identified nine black members (4 percent) among the 217 members of the ten boards. Seven of the nine black board members were women; two were men. Thus, there is some evidence to suggest that black board members, but not white board members, of human service agency boards of directors are more likely to be women.

In addition, the black board members, who ranged in age from 28 to 45 years, mean age 34.1, were younger than the total population of board members who ranged in age from 20 to 77 years, mean age 41.9. The black board members were also all well–educated professionals. All were college graduates; all but one had a master's degree or higher. They were somewhat better educated than their white counterparts, only 53.5 percent of whom had that much education.

The median family income of black board members was the same as white board members, but while only one black board member reported a family income in excess of $40,000, 45 percent of the white board members had incomes greater than that amount. And although none of the black board members came from the business sector, 17 percent of the white board members did. In addition, while 84.8 percent of the white board members owned their own homes, only one of the six black board members who responded to this item owned his home.

The black board members were also more likely to be newcomers to the community. Two of the black board members were students who had came to the area to attend school. Two others had lived in the area for less than a year. The black board members, excluding the students, had lived in the area for an average of 4.8 years. The average length of residence for all board members was 15.1 years.

Both black and white board members came from upper status groups; neither were representative of the community from which they came. Social class is clearly an issue in board participation, though one that is, for the most part, beyond the scope of this paper. In addition, although the number of black board members is very small, the above data suggest that black board members are more likely to be younger, to be better educated, to rent their homes, and to be newer to the community than white board members. Furthermore, black women seem more likely than black men to be members of boards of directors of human service agencies. It is impossible to know from this study if black individuals of this description are more acceptable to boards or more likely to accept invitations to join boards. It is likely, however, given the manner in which board members are recruited, that these are the individuals most likely to be known by white board members. Recruitment of board members is discussed in the following section.

Recruitment of Minority Members

The data indicate that black board members were recruited the same way other board members were recruited, predominantly through friendship networks. (See Widmer, 1985, for a more complete discussion of this finding.) Some boards put out feelers for new board members by announcing openings in a newsletter or asking staff members. Some board members contact friends and friends of friends for suggestions. But most names of potential board members are, according to board presidents, suggested by existing members. Almost half of the board members (43 percent) in this study reported that they talked first about board membership with a friend on the board. Only 6 percent were first approached by someone they had never met. Only two of the black board members in the first sample talked first with a person who was not a friend. All of the black board members in the second sample were first approached by a friend. Boards tend, the presidents reported, to send the "person who knows them" to speak to potential members.

This "friendship–network" method of recruitment has obvious limitations. Boards which recruit in this manner are unlikely to recruit new members who are significantly different than current members. Indeed, it is often possible to construct "family trees" of board membership, and trace the lineage of friend and colleague relationships. There are, of course, also advantages to this method of recruitment. Current members tend to have more information about potential members whom they know. New members are therefore more likely to be compatible, both because they are like and because they are liked by old members. Members are also more likely to share values and such boards may function more smoothly with fewer disruptions and disputes than more diverse boards. Friends may also be easier to recruit. Members are more likely to be explicit with a friend about the benefits of board membership and to be more knowledgeable about the incentives that will motivate a friend to participate.

Although all of the boards used the friendship–network method, some boards selected new board members in a more purposeful fashion than others. While some seemed to welcome almost anyone with a willingness to serve, others sought board members with specific expertise, for specific roles, or to represent specific constituencies. Some paid more attention to diversity than others. When interviewed, board presidents were asked not only "How does your board recruit new members?" but also, "Has your board been successful in finding the board members it needs?" and finally, "Has your board had any difficulty recruiting the kinds of board members it needs?" Four of the ten board presidents responded with comments about the desirability and/or difficulty of achieving racial diversity on their boards. The other six board presidents either reported no difficulties or identified other categories of board members they wished to attract. It is important to note that seven of the nine black board members in the second sample are members of the four boards whose presidents expressed concern regarding minority recruitment. The other six boards had recruited few minority board members and did not, apparently, consider that a problem.

Board presidents were also asked specifically if their board had any difficulty recruiting or retaining minority board members. Two presidents said that no efforts had been made or that they didn't know what efforts had been made to recruit minority members. The other board presidents and the black board members interviewed made a variety of observations and suggestions regarding the recruitment, retention, and participation of minority board members. Those comments which focus on minority recruitment are discussed below; minority participation and retention are discussed in the sections which follow.

Some board presidents reported that members of their boards were simply not interested in minority recruitment. Other board presidents, white board members, and executive directors reported that although they had tried to recruit black board members, they had been unsuccessful. One board president explained:

> Our executive director and board president have gone to [the black community centers] and to black individuals we've encountered. They're not interested, or we're not asking them right.

This board president raises two quite different possibilities. Are black persons less interested, for one reason or another, in board participation? Or does the problem lie with the manner in which black members are recruited? Some board presidents supported the view that black people were less interested in serving on the boards of human service organizations. One explained:

> Blacks in this community and historically do not get involved in social issues on a small scale. There are not too many active black people in this community.

Yet black people in the community studied have been very active, for example, in efforts to improve educational opportunities for black students. Another board president suggested that black people are unlikely to participate on boards because board participation is irrelevant to their lives.

> I'm sure we are a little irrelevant to their lives. The agency needs an approach to services that would appeal to black clients. We don't have the ability to serve that population. If we did then maybe black board members would make a serious effort.

Certainly the degree of participation in school–related activities suggests that black people do participate in areas which effect them or their children directly. One black board member suggested that there is pressure within the black community to belong to "our own organizations and make them as strong as possible." But there are people, including black people, who participate on the boards of organizations that have little relevance to their lives or the lives of those who are like them. In the community studied, middle class people serve on the board of an anti–poverty agency which serves predominantly poor clients, gay people serve on the board of a family planning agency which serves predominantly heterosexual clients, and black people serve on the board of a mental health agency which serves predominantly white clients. These individuals serve for a variety of reasons, one of which is not, apparently, to represent their group. Indeed research into incentives for participation indicates that very few board members, black or white, serve in order to represent their interests as clients or the interests of their class, ethnic, or racial group.[1] Some people may decline board membership because the work of the board is "irrelevant," but others serve. They clearly have other incentives.

If at least some black persons are interested in serving, perhaps the board president quoted above is right: Some boards may be asking the wrong way, or the wrong people. More than one board president suggested that, "It's the same little bunch of minorities who are approached to join boards." Another said, "The black people we know have enormous demands on them." Some black board members agreed, that the market had been saturated, that all the black professionals, those who were traditional board material, were already serving on boards. One black board member recommended that I test this hypothesis by contacting all of the black professionals in the community and asking if they served on a board. She belived that I would find that they did. Although this is certainly a valid approach to the question, it is important to note that the black board member who made this suggestion was in her forties, had a doctorate, had lived in the community for more than ten years, and had served on a board for only one year. She had never served on another board and had never declined to serve on a board. Despite her "perfect" board profile and her ability to contribute, which I noted in observations of her board, she was not, to say the least, inundated with requests to serve. Nor were other black board members in this sample. Of those who were asked, only 17 percent currently served on another board, and only 42 percent reported that they had declined an invitation to serve on a board. The black board members were, in fact, in less demand than their white counterparts. In the sample of both white and black board members, half of the board members currently served on another board, almost a third served on two other boards. Of 115 board members who were asked if they had ever been asked to join a board and had declined, 62 percent said that they had. Thus, although there may be a number of highly visible black community leaders who are asked repeatedly to serve on boards, there also seem to be a number of black professionals with board experience who are not in such demand.

Several board members, both black and white, believed that boards could, if they tried, recruit more black board members.

> Saying there's a difficulty recruiting minority board members is a crock! But it is a problem if white people do not interact with blacks on a personal level. There are enough black professionals. Those boards that make an effort can recruit blacks. Those who say they can't find them are lying.

> Difficulties [with recruitment] are the fault of the white majority who don't make an effort to get to know minorities. We need to go talk to people, that's what we have to do.

Preliminary evidence supports these observations. The data suggest that there are potential black board members who are both capable and available. And some boards have successfully recruited black members. These black board members were recruited the same way other board members were recruited, primarily by friends and colleagues, black and white, who served on the boards, and occasionally by board members who had talked with people who knew other people who might make good board members. These black board members were recruited primarily by boards with concerns about racial diversity. As noted above, the four boards whose presidents identified recruiting minority board members as a problem recruited 78 percent of the black board members. Those boards whose presidents indicated that no eforts had been made or that they didn't know what efforts had been made recruited none.

Participation of Minority Members

Although the recruitment of black and white board members is similar, their experiences serving on the board were not identical. In this section, the incentives for and the benefits of participation, the roles of minority participants, and the stresses of minority participation are addressed.

Incentives and benefits of participation—One board president suggested that black board members may not be able to achieve some of the same incentives as white board members.

> Black board members know that board participation won't really make a difference in their career or social standing.

This statement implies that black board members have very different careers and social experiences than white members. The demographic data on black and white board members suggest that this is not the case. This is not to imply that black and white board members lives look or feel the same, but because black and white board members share similar educational and professional backgrounds, they also share many of the same incentives for participation. Like white board members, black board members reported a variety of material, social, developmental, and ideological incentives for participation.[2] Several of the black board members specifically mentioned community service and employment–related incentives. The opportunity to develop and use skills was cited by most. The opportunity to meet people and learn about the community was particularly important to those board members who were new to the community. Black board members reported such benefits of participation as: "met people;" "gained contacts;" "learned about the community;" "let me use my skills;" "enriched my ability to understand what I can do, to differentiate my skills;" "learned how a good board operates;" and "provided me an outlet for living my personal convictions and my politics." Neither the incentives of black board members nor the benefits which they reported were discernably different than those of white board members.

Roles of minority participants—Black board members also played roles similar to the roles played by white participants.[3] Several contributed specific expertise; some spoke as human service professionals; others contributed time and energy rather than specific skills or perspectives. The major difference in the participation of white and black board members was that in many cases black board members represented or felt that they were expected to represent the minority community. Some felt this was an opportunity to represent their group and viewed this as a positive role. Others resented the assumption that they knew what other black people felt or wanted or that they would or could represent the minority community.

> They [the board] hoped I'd represent more of the minority population than I do. It's an impossible job for a minority person.

> The minority community probably wouldn't see me as a representative, and I don't speak for them.

Several black board members pointed to class differences in explaining why it was impossible for them to represent all of those whom they were expected to represent. Others explained that they spoke as a black person, not for black persons. The pressure to speak for others of their group is directed only at those individual members who are perceived in some way as different from the majority of board members. It is one of several stresses reported by black participants.

Stresses of minority participation—Although some of the board presidents suggested that black board members may be less comfortable on boards than white board members, they were unclear about what might make black board members uncomfortable. Black board members, however, reported a number of stresses in addition to the pressure to represent the minority community. Some black board members reported feeling patronized. One said that she felt that white board members assumed she didn't understand complex issues. Another reported that if a black board member didn't understand what was going on, other members appeared to assume that was because she was black; while if a white member didn't understand, that was because she was new. Some board members occasionally felt alienated or alone. Some noted that they experienced hostility when minority issues were discussed. One reported an assumption on the part of white board members that she couldn't be objective, like them, on "black issues." Several felt invisible.

> Other board members seem to forget that I'm black. This feels both good and bad. When I speak out on a minority issue, they look shocked. That bothers me.

> People are color blind. They haven't had to deal with ethnic or cultural differences. Because I'm a middle class professional they can think I'm like them. [Yet] if issues come up, I'm expected to speak the truth for all minorities.

Another black board member felt like she was in charge of absolving white board members of their guilt or discomfort. Black board members reported feeling both used and forgotten, highly visible and invisible. Some commented on the energy required to deal with white people who were inexperienced or insensitive in working with people of color. A few talked specifically of racism. (See Font, 1982, for a discussion of the experiences of people of color in the work place.) A number of black board members, however, reported no stresses associated with being a black person on the board. More than one commented that they experienced being a minority everyday and that board participation was no different than their experiences in most of the rest of the world.[4]

Despite the fact that some black board members and some white board presidents report discomfort on the part of minority participants, only one board president suggested ways to make black members more comfortable. "I think it might be a good idea to have more than one. One of anything might feel out of place." Being a numerical minority is in itself stressful (Kanter, 1977), although not necessarily because of "feeling out of place," and attempts to avoid putting individuals in this position are helpful. But both racism and minority status contribute to discomfort and alienation. If boards wish to achieve a "comfortable" environment for minority board members, both must be addressed.

In addition to the stresses described above, some black board members, like some white board members, expressed disappointment that their abilities and skills had not been utilized by their boards or that their recommendations had not been heeded. Black board members, however, also rated their influence on the agency somewhat lower than white board members. Asked to rate their influence on a scale of 1 to 4, black board members responded with a mean rating of 2.0; all board members, a rating of 2.7. The difference may be due in part to the relatively short tenure of the black board members. The average length of time served by black board members at the time of the study was 8.5 months, by white board members 2.9 years. The issues of retention and length of board service are discussed below.

Retention of Minority Members

Some board presidents reported that black board members were less active participants and served for a shorter time on the board. Some black board members themselves indicated that they were not active participants. Others were very active, they served on board committees, held board offices, and participated actively in board meetings. Some black board members (and some white board members) left after only a few months; others served for years. It is important to keep in mind in drawing conclusions about black participation that, as one board president pointed out:

> There are so few black board members that when normal things happen—they move or change jobs and leave the board—it's a problem, we lose our black membership, [and] we notice.

One measure of retention of black and white board members in this study was available. The initial sample from 1983 could be compared with the board lists from 1986. Of the seven black board members in the 1983 sample, three appeared on the 1986 list. Two, or 29 percent, of the black board members still served on the same boards; one served on a different board. Four of the black board members, including the two students, had left the community. Of the sample as a whole, 31 of 137, or 22 percent, of the board members still served on the same boards. It is important to note that most of the boards have a limit on the number of consecutive years a board member may serve—in most cases two three-year terms—and a number of board members may have completed their terms. Some boards, however, reported that many board members left the board before they were required to by the by-laws. One agency had only one board member, a black board member, still serving on the board three years later.

IMPLICATIONS FOR PRACTICE AND RESEARCH

Some of the questions addressed by this study, as outlined in the introduction and reiterated below, have been answered, at least in part. In this concluding section, this evidence will be summarized and suggestions for practice will be addressed. But, as is appropriate for a preliminary investigation, the study has raised more questions than it has answered. These research questions, which are a principal contribution of this work, will also be a part of these conclusions.

Who are the minority participants on boards? The minority board members in this study were predominantly black. These black board members, and the white board members, came disproportionately from upper status groups. Like the white board members, the black board members were not representative of the communities from which they came and did not serve as client or consumer representatives. The black and white board members were not, however, identical. The black board members tended to be younger and better educated and more of the black board members were women than men. Why? Are younger, more educated, black women more likely to be asked to join the boards of human service agencies? Are they more likely to serve? To serve longer? Are they more likely to achieve their incentives? We need to look at those minority individuals who accept and those who refuse invitations to join boards, and at those who are never asked. And we need to continue to pursue the questions of why citizen participants come disproportionately from upper status groups.[5]

How are minority members recruited? How can boards improve minority recruitment? The black board members in this study were recruited in the same way other board members were recruited, primarily through friendship networks. Black board members were recruited most frequently by those boards most concerned with racial diversity. These boards appear to identify more carefully the kinds of board members—including minority members—they want and to go to greater lengths to recruit them.[6]

Boards which want to achieve racial diversity must make such "affirmative efforts." Many organizations have affirmative action plans for staff recruitment; boards should develop affirmative action plans for board recruitment and retention. Boards should identify the kinds of board members they wish to recruit and take steps to locate them. Board and staff members should continue to ask their friends and colleagues, but they should also ask their friends about their friends and their friend's friends. In other words, they must "network." In order to locate new board members, boards may have to look harder and in new places. Boards might try the staffs of other agencies, schools, colleges, hospitals, churches, government, unions, and minority associations. They should avoid asking only "the most visible" leaders in the minority community, but they should ask "visible" community leaders for suggestions of others they might contact. Contrary to conventional wisdom, there is evidence to suggest that minority professionals are not deluged with invitations to join boards, and are, in fact, in less demand than many white board members.

Boards should also keep records of potential members and get back to those who say "not this year." The nominating committee of the board should be charged with identifying minority candidates and should itself include minority representation. Board leadership, the president or a member of the executive committee, should be responsible for monitoring and evaluating the board's affirmative action plan.

The above are suggestions of ways to recruit the kind of minority board members described in this study. If boards wish to achieve class diversity, the task is likely to be considerably more difficult and to involve substantial changes in recruitment and participation.

Do minority members participate in the same ways and for the same reasons as white board members? The black board members in this study sought the same incentives and realized the same kinds of benefits as white board members. Black board members performed the same roles, with the exception of the role of minority representative, as white board members. This is not surprising considering the similarities between white and black board members. If board members were more diverse, in educational backgrounds and occupations for example, more differences in incentives and roles would undoubtedly be apparent.

Do minority board members represent the minority community? Can minority board members represent the minority community? The concept of representation is extremely complex. (See Pitkin, 1967 and 1969, for one of the more lucid discussions.) The minority board members in this study are representative in the sense that they are modal representatives, "individuals who are representatives in the statistical sense—that is individuals whose characteristics or behavior parallel or reflect the central tendencies of a group or class." (Alexander, 1976:6) These black board members "represented" a race, but did not, in most cases, represent the experiences of most members of the black community. Some boards accept black board members as modal representatives; others hope or expect that they will be more than that—that they will speak for the minority community. Some black board members accept or even seek the role of spokesperson; others are unable or unwilling to fill this role and may resent expectations that they will perform it. All black board members, however, speak for themselves as people of color, which in itself provides a different perspective than that of white board members. Board members, both black and white, may also speak as advocates for, rather than representatives of, community interests.

Representation on boards of directors and in other forms of citizen participation deserves more critical attention. It may be that current forms of participation are unsuitable for representative participation. It may be that advocacy, rather than representation, is all we can hope for from boards of directors.

Do minority members experience stresses that get in the way of effective participation? How can these stresses be reduced? A number of the black board members in this study reported stresses associated with being minority members of boards. What effect these stresses have on their participation and on their ability to achieve incentives is not clear. We do know that being a numerical minority alone results in pressures which make performance more difficult. If boards expect to successfully recruit and retain active board members, they must work to reduce stress and increase the comfort of minority board members. This will require the efforts of all board members. Board presidents, and executive directors, should encourage recruitment of more than one or two of any minority group, and should discourage "tokenism." They should be aware of the stresses of minority participation and treat sensitively the role of minority representative, neither expecting nor rejecting representation from minority members. And, they should facilitate open discussions of minority issues.[7]

White board members should be aware of their own behavior, including the assumptions they make about minority members' roles and abilities. White board members must learn to confront other white board members about their assumptions and behaviors. Minority members can be clear about their ability or willingness to speak for the minority community. They can develop the ability to confront productively white board members who are contributing to their stress. They can also talk with other minority members about the stress they experience.

Can boards achieve diversity? The suggestions presented above are intended to help organizations work toward diversity. But experience has shown that there is one critical element which must be stressed. If agencies and their boards are to work successfully toward achieving diversity, they must believe that diversity is important. Almost all board members speak of diversity as a good thing—a beneficial, fair, helpful, noble thing to achieve. But when board members are asked why diversity is good, many aren't sure or can't say. If board members are to act to achieve diversity, they must have incentives to act. They must expect something valuable to come of their efforts. Before boards of directors and individual board members can or will work toward diversity, they must find their own answers to some very difficult questions: Is diversity important? Why? What kind of diversity? What are the benefits of diversity for the organization, the board, the board member? Should achieving diversity be a priority? Why? Perhaps social scientists can help answer some of these questions and can contribute some practical suggestions, but if diversity is to be achieved, those who must act, must believe that there is reason to act.

NOTES

1. See Widmer (1985) as well as Ostrander (1980) who suggests that the "community service" of upper class participants may be related to group and self interest in maintaining order and stability in society.
2. Widmer (1984) proposes a conceptual model of citizen involvement, which suggests that individuals participate in response to material, social, developmental, and ideological incentives. The incentives of members of the boards of directors of human service agencies are described in "Why Board Members Participate," *Journal of Voluntary Action Research,* October–December 1985, 14(4): 8-23.
3. See Widmer (1984) for a discussion of participatory roles.
4. I learned inadvertently—for it had not occurred to me to ask—that some of the black board members whom I interviewed had white spouses. This finding has interesting implications for recruitment. Such minority individuals may be more "visible" to whites. And, of course,

they bring their own experiences as members of interracial families to their board participation.

5. There are several explanations for the low rate of participation of lower status individuals. The "needs" approach suggests that lower status individuals have unmet lower level needs, while upper status individuals have met these needs and are free to seek to fulfill upper level self–esteem and self-fullfillment needs through participation. (See, for example, Milbrath and Goel, 1977.) The "civic culture" approach suggests that higher status individuals are part of a culture which instills in them a sense of the importance of participation and their duty to participate. Lower status individuals do not believe in the importance of participation and do not see it as their duty to participate. (See, for example, Verba and Nie, 1977.) The incentive approach (Widmer, 1984) does not reject needs or culture as a link between high status and participation, but suggests some additional possibilities. The incentive approach proposes that individuals participate in response to incentives, the expectation of valued outcomes. Individuals who do not participate differ in that they have no incentives to participate, they expect no valued outcomes. It is reasonably easy, of course, to demonstrate that individuals participate in response to incentives. It is considerably more difficult to demonstrate why people do not participate.

6. In looking at boards which recruit or do not recruit minorities we must consider the organization in addition to the individuals and the processes. Davis (1982) suggests that diversity can be achieved only through organizational change. I agree. Real change in board membership will require significant changes in organizational structures and procedures, and real changes in the world in which we live.

7. The videotape "A Tale of O" (Goodmeasure, Inc., 1980) is a valuable tool to use with agency boards and staff to raise consciousness of the stresses experienced by minority members of organizations.

LITERATURE CITED

Alexander, Chauncy
    1976   "What Does a Representative Represent?" *Social Work*, 21 (January): 5–9.
Davis, King E.
    1982   "An Alternative Theoretical Perspective on Race and Voluntary Participation." *Journal of Voluntary Action Research*, 11, April–September, (2–3): 126–142.
Domhoff, G. William
    1980   *Power Structure Research*. Beverly Hills: Sage.
Font, Ora D.
    1982   "Racial Diversity in Organizations and Its Implications for Management." *Personnel*, September –October: 60–68.
Johnson, Carl F. and Joann Ross
    1979   "Underrepresentation of Minorities in Citizen Participation." in Langton (1979) pp. 156–159.
Kanter, Rosabeth Moss.
    1977   "Some Effects of Proportions on Group Life: Skewed Sex Ratios and Responses to Token Women." *American Journal of Sociology*, 82 (March, 1977): 965–990.
Langton, Stuart (ed.)
    1979   *Citizen Participation Perspectives*. Medford, MA: Lincoln Filene Center for Citizenship and Public Affairs.
Milbrath, Lester W.
    1965   *Political Participation*. Chicago: Rand McNally.
Milbrath, Lester W. and M.L. Goel
    1977   *Political Participation* (2nd. edition). Chicago: Rand McNally.
Ostrander, Susan A.
    1980   "Upper–Class Women: Class Consciousness as Conduct and Meaning." In Domhoff (1980) pp. 73–96.
Pitkin, Hannah
    1967   *The Concept of Representation*. Berkeley: University of California Press.

Pitkin, Hannah (ed.)
   1969   *Representation*: New York: Atherton Press.
Rosenbaum, Walter A.
   1979   "Elitism and Citizen Participation." In Langton (1979) pp. 174-179.
Verba, Sidney and Norman H. Nie
   1972   *Participation in America*. New York: Harper and Row.
Widmer, Candace
   1984   "An Incentive Model of Citizen Participation Applied to a Study of Human Service Agency Boards of Directors." Cornell University, unpublished doctoral dissertation.
   1985   "Why Board Members Participate." *Journal of Voluntary Action Research*, 14, October–December (4): 8–23.
   1986   "A Preliminary Study of Minority Participation on the Boards of Directors of Human Service Agencies." *Proceedings of the Fourteenth Annual Meeting of the Association of Voluntary Action Scholars*, October 1–4, 1986, The Pennsylvania State University.

The Importance of Board Effectiveness in Not-For-Profit Organizations

John P. Mascotte

Revision of an address delivered March 11, 1985 in Kansas City, Missouri, sponsored by the Kansas City Association of Trusts and Foundations.

The business community in every city has an important stake in the effectiveness of not–for–profit organizations. Not–for–profit arts organizations are increasingly important in attracting new businesses to a city and not–for–profit social service organizations are crucial to efforts to improve a city's quality of life. Of course, businesses frequently provide important resources for the not–for–profit sector: direct contributions, executives as board members, sites for federated fundraising efforts, and programs that encourage employee volunteering. Thus, the business community should be committed to improving effectiveness in the not–for–profit sector. And, given the time and effort business executives are asked to give to board service in the not–for–profit sector, the effectiveness of not–for–profit boards is an especially significant issue. I'd like to address this topic by discussing two questions. The first of these: Do boards of directors really play a significant part in the overall operation of not–for–profits? In other words, do boards really matter? And if they do, the second question concerns what steps can be taken to ensure their increased effectiveness.

The first question is really not rhetorical. I think it's one that perhaps the not–for–profit organizations might well benefit from focusing on before we talk about how the boards might be improved. I'd like to present some ideas on that most fundamental question of whether boards matter in the first place.

It seems to me that any not–for–profit organization possesses three resources as it attempts to address the functions for which it was organized. The first, of course, would be the whole range of financial assets that a not–for–profit possesses—be it cash or its opportunity to obtain cash from committed supporters, its facility, or other capital assets. The second category of resources are those human skills represented on its staff and on its board. What I think is largely overlooked in analyzing performance of not–for–profits is that third resource category—the "ownership" of a social problem or the responsibility for meeting a community need.

I would suggest that in answering the question whether the boards of not–for–profits really matter, you can look at the three resources of any not–for–profit and reach some rather significant conclusions. First, the board clearly is charged with the responsibility of overseeing the financial resources of a not–for–profit. Secondly, through its executive director, a board is clearly charged with overseeing the effective utilization of its staff resources. In both of these instances the board is largely delegating the responsibility to those who are directly associated with the organization on a full time basis. However, the third resource, "ownership" of a problem is a resource that only the board can effectively control. I would suggest to you that the creation and nurturing of that third resource cannot, in fact, be delegated to the staff.

I'd like to speak rather specifically today about what I mean by the "ownership" of a problem, that third resource of a not–for–profit. I'd like to tell you what I believe that really means and why it is so critical for boards to understand their key role in managing it.

I think there are three observations with respect to the so called "ownership" of the problem issue. The first, of course, is the definition of what many of us call "turf." What is the proper way of defining the role of a given not–for–profit in any community? For example, does the board correctly perceive its mission consistent with what is needed in the community? Does it take into account the positioning of other not–for–profits which might be in similar or, at least, related areas of concern?

It's been over five years now since I've had the great privilege of being heavily involved in activities in Kansas City, but I will suggest to you that there are many areas such as hospital care, drug abuse programs, and certain inner city and neighborhood revitalization efforts which clearly indicated to me a significant amount of overlap exists. I'm sure the same phenomena occurs in other cities. Only a board of a not–for–profit can adequately examine the issue of definition, if you will, of purpose. Only the board can really stake out and articulate what is the proper "turf" of a not–for–profit, and I think that's a critical issue.

Just as critical, and the second of the three "ownership" of the problem pieces, relates to the issue of legitimization. It is increasingly evident to me that by visibly and vocally committing oneself to a not–for–profit, a board member is placing his or her personal stature at the disposal of that not–for–profit and, in effect, is legitimizing its role. How often have you received a letter requesting that you financially support an organization and your eyes rather quickly glance down to see who's associated with this organization? Who are the board members that feel this particular not–for–profit is important enough to make it worthy to be associated with their names? A board member is really making sort of a public statement about what is important to him or her in the very process of becoming affiliated with an institution. We expect things from not–for–profit board members in terms of their affirmation of the validity of a not–for–profit's goals, so that the legitimizing role, I would suggest, is an extremely important one. It is important not only because it gives the agency its starting legitimacy, but also because it is necessary to sustain this whole notion of "ownership" of the problem.

The third point on this business of effective "ownership" of a problem has to do with the community's respect for the organization's contributions to solving a perceived need and with the critical issue of self–evaluation. However well defined a not–for–profit's objectives might have been when it was set up, has the board taken the time to go back and look squarely at whether or not the agency or institution is really meeting its objectives? In my choice of words, is there really a job to be done today of the kind that was envisioned when the not–for–profit was set up? I have probably seen or participated in the creation of at least ten not–for–profit organizations in my seven-year span in Kansas City. I cannot recall a single elimination of a not–for–profit. Unfortunately, these institutions tend to take on a life of their own because, in my judgement, boards are all too frequently willing to skip over their responsibility for sitting down and asking the tough questions—is there a job to be done and does this not–for–profit have the resources, both human and financial, to do it well? Both this question and that of the quality of service are ones you can't ask the staff to do. You'd be asking someone to pass judgement on his or her own activities, and it would be grossly unfair of not–for–profit boards to allow staff of the organization to justify their own continued existence. Yet, how many times have you participated in a not–for–profit in which there's sort of a general sense of smiling and back–patting once a year, typically at the time the budget is approved, and an assertion that somehow those lofty goals that we all want were in fact achieved.

I guess what I'm focusing on here is something that Peter Drucker summed up pretty well in a distinction he made a few years ago in a text that he was writing for managers. He asked his readers to distinguish between two very critical things: DOING THINGS RIGHT AND DOING THE RIGHT THINGS. It seems to me that it is clearly the function of the staff of a not-for-profit organization to DO THINGS RIGHT, to understand the charge as it has been sketched out and flushed out by the board and to take those steps in the utilization of the human and financial resources available to execute the strategy of the board effectively. At the same time it is absolutely imperative that the board assign to itself the question of what is the RIGHT THING TO DO? So, in summary, it is the board's job to make sure that the organization is DOING THE RIGHT THINGS and that it is the staff's responsibility to make sure that those THINGS ARE DONE RIGHT. In my judgement board members in that regard are often not hard enough on themselves. There is typically an assumption that the purpose and values of the institution are somehow predetermined or are givens. If one is not coming in at its beginning, one tends to accept a position on a board almost by saying, "I'll simply live and work inside whatever boundaries this organization is already operating in." Further, members may fear it would be perceived as sort of ungentlemanly or unladylike to analyze at the end of the year what the organization is trying to accomplish and whether it is really doing the best job of accomplishing it?

Why is it important to ask the hard questions? The answer is simple—public confidence determines public support. Many of the problems in funding the old Kansas City Philharmonic grew out of a sense that somehow that institution was simply not doing the job of meeting community needs as sufficiently as I think the community believed they needed to be achieved. I think there are a number of organizations that chronically complain of the difficulty of achieving their objectives, of the difficulty of finding new people to support it, of meeting budgets, and of getting effective community response to their programs. They'd do well if they sat down and said, "How accurately do we measure our performance as opposed to how the community perceives the delivery of that performance?" As you could imagine, if the staff and, particularly the board, is giving itself A + in delivery when the community is in fact rating it D − , there is going to be a huge problem of perception that will begin to manifest itself in dozens of ways—difficulty in getting new board members; a tendency on the part of the staff to become more entrenched; certainly a tendency not to strike out and establish new agendas for the organization, but to stay inside the hardened little shell of the initial activity. Finally, and worse than anything else, there develops a "Bunker" mentally that becomes very defensive and says we must guard against all intrusion even if it appears that someone else is beginning to offer an alternative to what we do that is in fact more efficient, more effective, and better for the community.

Let me conclude my answer to this first question, are board members important? I think they are absolutely critical because they provide an orderly and necessary review and control of financial resources and because they select and monitor the executive director. Like an old washer woman, they exist to constantly nag, probe, and challenge the initial thrust and charter of a not–for–profit. They exist to examine critically what the size and scope of the "ownership" of its particular problem is and how the delivery of service is working.

Given the need for the board, how do we go about making boards better? I think there are a series of things that can and should be done. First, there ought to be *criteria for selecting board members* and those ought to grow out of the nature of the problem being addressed by the organization. There are lots of different people in every community with different skills. Some have access to certain fund raising capabilities, others have excellent communication capabilities, still others have important contacts with various segments of the community such as the public sector and various minority groups. For example, I would suggest that you might well look for different criteria if you were recruiting for board membership at Children's Mercy Hospital or the Folly Theatre than you would if you were seeking to obtain a strong neighborhood presence for a neighborhood improvement association. Uniform criteria for board membership completely misses the point about that all-important role of the board to define and keep analyzing and testing the organization's reason for existence.

As you begin to develop that list of candidates who might be true believers and who might be board members that could really commit themselves in a meaningful and effective way to the success of your particular not–for–profit, you might want to take a leaf out of one of Kansas City's most effective and certainly one of its wisest superstars in the not–for–profit arena. That is Dr. Charles Kimball. Dr. Kimball came to Kansas City with a vision of the Midwest Research Institute and I think has taught all of us a great lesson with respect to how to effectively utilize board members.

What Charlie Kimball did was to develop a large advisory board of one hundred which provided Midwest Research with varied insights, great contacts, and a broad base for legitimizing the agency's role. The advisory group also became a training ground and cadre for appointment to the Executive Committee, a group of twelve to fifteen people who actually became involved in the day–to–day running of the Institute. This was an excellent way to screen the true believers and still have the advantage of the broader group's limited involvement.

Secondly, I think it is perfectly fair, appropriate, and indeed necessary when recruiting or evaluating board members to have *performance objectives*. What are the specific duties you want each board member to participate in (fund raising, helping to manage the staff, and so forth)? How much time is going to be asked of a board member—all day, once a month, two luncheons a month? Do you intend to expect more from the chairman of committees in your not–for–profit than you do from other board members? I believe there are only a small number of people who are likely to be deeply commited to any cause. A not–for–profit would be really successful if it can aggregate a small number of people who are so dedicated and so committed to the goals and objectives of the not–for–profit that they can take their bundle of particular talents and consistently energize the organization. Thus, it seems to me, that it is perfectly legitimate to test someone's commitment by saying, "We'd like you to become interested in this and we think that a good measure of your interest would be your willingness to commit X hours a month to do this particular kind of work." The great risk, of course, is that when you begin to establish standards and suggest performance objectives, a great many folks that you might ask to become board members are going to turn you down. They're going to say, "If it's going to mean that much commitment, I'd rather not." So be it! If there is a single point I'd like to make here, it is that not–for–profits traditionally waste too much time getting lukewarm consent in board memberships and then pay a heavy price for not having the kind of drive in those institutions that they really need in order to be successful. If the job isn't worth doing well, it isn't worth doing at all and you're much better off using the screening process that allows you to determine that up front. If you are going to have standards of performance and if you are going to ask for performance objectives, I think you have to be willing to appraise board members each year. In a very careful and in a very, I hope, sensitive way, you have to deliver messages to non-performing board members that if they have found that their interests have shifted elsewhere, they really ought to consider leaving the board. This is an enormous problem with deadwood in institutions. I would also suggest to you that, in many cases, there are not–for–profits in every community that exist for the simple reason that the board members involved are too embarrassed because of social peer rela-tionships to shut them down, or fold them into another not–for–profit, or coordinate their activities more effectively with other not–for–profits.

The third issue with respect to what steps you can take to increase board effec-tiveness has to do with the *selection and management of the chief executive.* In no case is the risk of success or failure perhaps more clearly pinpointed in one specific board act than in the selection and the annual review of the performance of the executive director. I'm afraid that in the selection process of executive directors, there is a tendency to be misguided as soft as opposed to hard and disciplined. Any job, even one that sometimes has as broad a charter as many not–for–profits do, needs a set of selection criteria. Without criteria, it will be impossible for the board to effec-tively evaluate the incumbent in that position. More importantly, it will be impossi-ble for the incumbent to understand whether he or she is adequately doing his or her job. It is simply not enough to say that you wish the position to provide neighborhood housing support for the city, that you wish the position to contribute to the arts activities of the city, that you wish it to tackle the issue of child abuse. Of course, it all goes back to that issue of what is the problem and what is the need that this organiza-tion is trying to seize "ownership" of? The more specific the charter of the organiza-tion; the more specific will be the criteria for the selection of its chief staff officer.

Before we move away from how to select and how to manage the chief executive, I want to share a few thoughts on age, enthusiasm and insight. I think age is misun-derstood in not–for–profits. I will say that my own bias suggests that age and enthusi-asm are frequently linked. I have known a number of chief executives of not–for–profits in their late 50s and 60s, and some even in their 70s, who bring such an intense level of commitment to their work, that they are able to generate the kind of enthusiasm that is necessary to fuel a not–for–profit. But, on the other hand, I must tell you that they are exceptions and that the most effective staff people that I have found in not–for–profit organizations tend to be those who are young enough and enthusiastic enough to sustain the emotional drive of a not–for–profit. Each case will differ but this issue needs to be carefully examined. The real effectiveness of the not–for–profit has to come from a very strongly motivated full–time staff person.

I think most not–for–profit work is frankly a good deal more difficult than most of us in the business community realize. It is hard to be motivated and to run an organization effectively when it exists in an environment that is frequently highly uncertain. The most striking successes have typically come when motivated board members with the right kinds of objectives have been able to associate themselves with staff people who have an enormous amount of energy to focus on a specific problem. I believe boards should give enthusiasm a very high priority in selection and evaluation of the chief executive.

With respect to insight, let's look at the third of those criteria for the selection of a chief executive. I think it is awfully important to be comfortable with what Denver psychologist, Dr. Robert Merrill, calls the Platinum Rule. All of you know the Golden Rule. Dr. Merrill, who has been dealing with interpersonal relationship issues in the management area for years and years, has evolved one called the Platinum Rule which briefly stated says, "Do unto others as they would do unto themselves." I think it is very important for the chief executive of any not–for–profit to have a sufficient amount of insight into his or her own character to really be able to put themselves in the board members' shoes. There is no other area in which fundamental disagreement on policy can be so cleverly hidden than in a not–for–profit. If people disagree, those disagreements simply do not surface well because there is a great desire not to be offensive. There's frequently a feeling that, "Gee, I don't really own this problem on a full time basis as a board member, whereas the staff person has to live here everyday. I feel very strongly about this, but I just don't think it's worth my time to run the risk of engaging in confrontation to really open up and air this issue." If a staff person can be exceptionally insightful to those kinds of signals from a board member, I would suggest that is a quality and a resource that is literally without measure.

In terms of managing the chief executive, I would return to exactly the same three criteria that I used in suggesting the selection of board members. That is, you have to have performance objectives, they have to be laid out, preferably in writing for the chief staff person. There has to be an appraisal against those objectives each year, and finally, you have to decide (and this is somewhat different than with a board member, although certainly related) what your chief staff person's primary function is—such as being a fund raiser or being a service provider. This is a decision to which there is no right answer, but a board would do well to understand what it is really looking for from a chief staff person. Many chief staff people are good because they are very effective at raising funds. There is nothing wrong with that. Indeed, if that is one of the primary needs of the not–for–profit organization, it may be critical; but there are many other not–for–profits which legitimately can say that the board members can, in some aggregated fashion, work to achieve the funding goals of the organization. What we need is someone to be able to provide a superb level of service. If that's what your not–for–profit needs, a superb provision of service, then you might do well to focus in advance on the fact that your chief staff person may well have more skill at service provision than at fund raising, and you ought not to beat that person over the head if, in fact, they deliver one of those skills as opposed to the other. Understand what you need and make sure you recruit and manage with that in mind.

One last point before I conclude and that is one that I would file under the general category of fighting bureaucracy. Just a couple of observations about how to make boards more effective beyond the initial selection of board members and then the selection and management of the chief executive of the organization. There are several golden rules: (1) set administrative cost goals, and (2) decide in advance what percentage of your gross receipts is really an appropriate amount for you to spend to simply sustain the institution. I'm not going to suggest any arbitrary figure (that will obviously vary by necessity based on the goal of your not-for-profit), but if you find yourself at the end of three, four, or five years, paying a larger and larger percentage of your gross receipts into the mere administrative activities of the not-for-profit, I think you are getting a flashing red light that says the board ought to go off in a corner somewhere and begin to ask some tough questions. Good jobs tend to get done very efficiently. You have to decide what the proper level of efficiency is for your institution, commit yourselves to trying to deliver that level of service inside that guideline, and begin asking the hard questions when you fail to reach your goal. Number two, and this might seem somewhat contradictory to my last point, do not manage to a business oriented bottom line. The whole notion of not-for-profit, it seems to me, is embraced in that rather casual but descriptive title. If you are engaged in supporting a not-for-profit organization, remember that title—do not use a business type of mentality which somehow seeks to maximize bottom line efficiency. I think there is no such thing in not-for-profits. Not-for-profits ought to be measured on a proper definition of the goal or objective they are seeking to achieve and the efficiency with which they can achieve it and not on whether they have managed to somehow use a business technique in the management of the activity. I would further suggest to you that perhaps the greatest reason for steering clear of too much profit-oriented or bottom line mentality is that, frankly, you will begin to erode the very principal of the not-for-profit. The ownership of a problem that is truly a social (or cultural or educational) problem by definition lies outside the ability to maximize the bottom line. When you begin to discuss a genuine social need in terms of profit orientation, you begin to undercut the very moral strength which leads the organization to operate in the first place. Third, and last, do not allow the administrative structure to trivialize the goals of the organization. If you have a staff that spends a great deal of time worrying about how it's organized, if you have a staff that spends a great deal of time worrying about how many meetings it's going to have to attend with other groups in order to ally efforts and link arms to achieve broad scale goals, if you find yourself spending too much time concerned with administering the costs of the not-for-profit instead of analyzing and being able to see clear-cut achievement of its goals, then you are allowing the process to become more important than the output.

I guess all of this could be summarized by simply saying that it is very critical to make sure that you constantly go back to the source—what are we trying to accomplish, what are the resources we need to accomplish it, both human and financial? Where are those few true believers, those people in this community that have such a passionate commitment to this problem that they will be willing to energize this institution and legitimize this institution by their own hard work?

In my view, quite candidly, there are too many not-for-profit organizations in the United States, too many in most cities. Many of them were started by well-meaning, but misguided people who after the initial energy and enthusiasm of getting started, failed to continue to sharply define what they were trying to achieve, and have wound up defending a small piece of sometimes irrational "turf". In many instances, not-for-profits should reexamine their very reason for existence, reexamine whether or not they really can find enough committed true believers to sustain that not-for-profit at the board level. If they can, that reenergizing should occur, and if they cannot, then that not–for–profit, it seems to me, should seek another institution with which it can align itself or it should go out of business.

I realize that I have set some very tough conceptual standards. People who are not committed, who accept board jobs for social or ego reasons, are not doing the organization or the community a favor. I don't mean to denegrate or minimize the good efforts and the contributions of anyone associated with any not–for–profit. Having said that I want to come back to the original point. Any not–for–profit that is really worth its salt, that really seeks to achieve something, is going to succeed only if and to the extent that it can obtain a seasoned, tough disciplined board that will commit itself to articulating and then rearticulating the goals for which it was brought into existence. There are not lots of people who will make that commitment. I suggest that as you examine your own not–for–profit, you ask yourself that question, however terrifying it may be, and then analyze your future in light of the honest answers you give yourself.

The Characteristics and Influence of Intraboard Networks: A Case Study of a Nonprofit Board of Directors

Melissa Middleton

The author would like to gratefully acknowledge comments on a previous draft of this chapter from Clay Alderfer, Paul DiMaggio, Robert Herman, Marion McCollom, and David Thomas.

INTRODUCTION

This research project focuses on some of the less examined aspects of board functioning within nonprofit organizations. The chapter makes the argument that these aspects, which primarily include the social and instrumental needs of trustees as expressed through their relationships with each other and with the organization, bear significantly on how a board performs its governance and trustee responsibilities.

In contrast to the argument presented here, much of the existing literature on nonprofit boards stresses their explicit activities. Practitioner–focused material provides prescriptive descriptions of their internal administrative responsibilities such as supervising executive–level staff and setting policy for the organization. The scholarly literature, drawn primarily from organization–environment theory, examines the external functions nonprofit boards fulfill in linking organizations to crucial informational and financial sources in their communities (Pfeffer & Salancik, 1978; Aldrich, 1979). An important assumption of this theory is that organizations use their boards *strategically*, that is, organizations use their resource needs as strategic criteria by which to recruit board members and to direct the board's primary activities, e.g., fundraising. Several studies conclude, therefore, that nonprofit boards perform important external functions which reduce organizational resource dependence. (Price, 1962; Pfeffer, 1973; and Provan, 1980).

There is some indication that board members strategically select nonprofits as well. Philanthropic work has increasingly become a career expectation for managers seeking to advance within corporations (Fenn, 1971). One can assume, therefore, that the more visible the work (for instance, a board officer position) and the more prestigious the nonprofit, the more advantageous board membership will be to a manager's corporate career (Zald, 1967).

I have suggested elsewhere that the strategic needs of nonprofits for access to crucial resources combined with needs of trustees for prestige and career enhancement lead some boards to be dominated by trustees from upper and upper middle socioeconomic classes (Middleton, 1983). The paper raises two principle questions about the potential consequences of this domination: First, to what extent does it suggest a conservative role played by nonprofits in maintaining a community's current system of resource allocation; and, second, how might this phenomenon influence a board's ability to perform necessary functions for its own organization? For example, regarding this latter question, if trustees represent homogeneous groups in racial, gender, age, occupation, and social organization affiliations (and there are data to support this; see Nason, 1977; Kohn & Mortimer, 1983; Salzmann & Domhoff, 1983; Ratcliff et al., 1979), then one may hypothesize that these similarities, while serving certain trustee needs, will detract from a board's ability to gather a diversity of information from a changing environment.

Some arts organizations may be especially prone to maintaining a homogeneous board. Historical data on early nonprofit organizations (Hall, 1975; DiMaggio, 1982) suggest that these organizations, particularly those involved with high culture and the arts, were convenient mechanisms used to separate upper and upper middle socioeconomic classes from lower ones.

Furthermore, even today, when high culture organizations face the need to diversify their financial base, boards frequently resist management's suggestions to recruit business professionals and broaden their audience mix. Boards view diversification as a threat to their control over an important elite screening and socialization mechanism (DiMaggio & Useem, 1982). This may indicate that the social relationships among board members, instead of serving the strategic needs of organizations as proposed by the organization and environment theorists, may in fact impair an organization's capability to attract new resources.

To better understand the content and influence of trustee relationships, this research examines the board of a performing arts organization. The research draws on two primary theories. The first of these is a network theory which relates tie strength between network members (that is, the intensity and depth of relationship between members) to their ability to access diverse information (Granovetter, 1973, 1974). This theory provides a general framework for examining in detail the *content* of trustee relationships. Its focus on the issues of information access and networks also allows one to hypothesize about adaptive and nonadaptive consequences of these relationships for an organization. The second theory used is intergroup theory which explains dynamics between groups in terms of the memberships individuals have in various identity (i.e. biologically determined groups such as race, gender, age, and ethnicity) and organizational (i.e. hierarchical or functional position) groups (Alderfer & Smith, 1982). Intergroup theory provides additional information on the nature and substance of ties as they relate to these types of group memberships and allows one to conceptualize certain tie patterns at the group level.

In Granovetter's work on the job search process (1974), he determined that job seekers with weak ties or connections to a range of employment information sources were more successful in the search process than those seekers who relied only on strong ties to gather information. To describe these networks, he makes a distinction between strong and weak ties among members where "the strength of a tie is a (probably linear) combination of the amount of time spent, the emotional intensity, the intimacy (mutual confiding), and the reciprocal services which characterize the tie" (1973:1361). One can further refine the notion of reciprocal services by viewing them in economic (or instrumental) and social exchange terms. Economic exchanges involve exchanges of equivalent resources, such as money, information, and tangible products. Social exchanges entail the extending of oneself to another as part of the exchange, such as giving and receiving love or friendship, status and respect, and services (Foa, 1971). They have an on–going quality where what is given is not necessarily repaid with an equivalent resource. The line between social and economic exchange relationships is not clear as many on–going economic relationships become overlaid with social content (Granovetter, 1984). This definition of ties then includes a historical dimension, a socioemotional component, and a description of the kind of exchange patterns which characterize the relationship.

Granovetter (1973) hypothesizes that the stronger the ties between members, the more likely they will be tied to the same individuals and the more likely they will be similar to each other. In other words, they will maintain fewer group memberships as defined by intergroup theory. In terms of the job search process, seekers who relied on strong tie networks (e.g., family members or close friends) had less access to information about potential job openings because of the tendency for strong tie members to share the same information. Weak ties permitted access to more remote parts of the information network and therefore increased the diversity and range of information channels available.

Drawing on Granovetter's work, among others, R. Coser (1984) makes a broader argument in describing the "greedy nature of *gemeineschaft.*" Gemeineschaft groups are characterized by strong ties among members who are cognitively and emotionally oriented toward each other. The group energy is a centripetal one, thereby heightening a sense of belonging and membership and decreasing the group's interest in and awareness of external factors. It becomes a closed system and loses its ability to sense and adapt to external changes.

A similar argument applied primarily at the organization or subunit level is made by intergroup theory in describing overbounded and underbounded systems (Alderfer, 1980a). An overbounded system, characterized by rigid boundary conditions between itself and external elements, impedes the flow in both directions of resources across its boundaries and thus may become less adaptive to external change. One could conceptualize the organization or a subunit as a network of relationships where transactions across boundaries represent extensions of the network beyond the organization or subunit. Strong internal network ties reduce the likelihood of these transactions (because of the similarity of members and the centripetal forces created) and help create situations of overboundedness.

The similarities of these theories, while appealing, should be qualified with regard to this research project. Granovetter's theory of networks does not stop at the level of the single organization boundary; for example, he would make explicit the connections between trustees and external groups. On the other hand, intergroup theory would not necessarily say that networks are systems or groups or that they would be amenable to overbounded/underbounded system analysis. Networks could qualify as groups, however, if they met the definition of groups posed by these theorists. They define a human group as one where members have significant interdependent relations with each other; where members and nonmembers can identify who is part of the group and who is not; where roles in the group are differentiated; and where group members have interdependent relations with other external groups (Alderfer, 1977). This research is not meant to test either theory. Rather it uses elements from each to illuminate important aspects of board behavior. Specifically, research questions focus on determining the content of ties between trustees, the relation of these ties to board structure and the influence ties have on board functioning.

There are two content–related questions. By extending Granovetter's definition of the strength of ties to include more explicit attention to social and economic exchange components, I hypothesize that:

> 1. Weak ties between trustees will emphasize an instrumental or economic exchange component and, by definition, strong ties will emphasize social exchanges.

Further, Granovetter cites empirical evidence that "the stronger the ties connecting two individuals, the more similar they are, in various ways" (1973:1362). Applying intergroup theory to this concept, I hypothesize that,

> 2. The more homogeneous trustees are, particularly with regard to identity groups, such as race, gender, and ethnicity, the more likely they are to develop strong ties between each other.

Three hypotheses relate to board structure and functions. First, with regard to trustee recruitment,

> 3. The greater the homogeneity and the stronger the ties between trustees, the more likely are trustees to be recruited on the basis of shared salient characteristics rather than more objective criteria that reflect changing organizational needs. The recruitment strategy is likely to emphasize interpersonal networking, or the recruitment of people already known to current trustees. The effect of this criterion and strategy will be to recruit trustees who are similar to existing trustees on many dimensions.

I would also argue that the formal board power structure (board officers and committee chairpersons) will relate to the strength of ties because this structure provides opportunities for such ties to develop by increasing the amount of time spent together, for example, at meetings and special functions. In this regard,

> 4. Trustees who hold positions in the formal board structure will be more strongly tied to each other than those who do not hold these positions.

Because of declining public sector support and changes in patron giving, crucial functions for arts boards include fundraising and marketing. Following from the previous discussion of the adaptive and nonadaptive qualities of various tie strengths, I would hypothesize that,

> 5. The stronger the ties among trustees, the more resistant they will be to expanding the diversity of the organization's financial and audience base, and, importantly, the less able they will be to do so because of their narrow range of connections. Conversely, the weaker the ties among trustees, the greater the number and types of resources available from which to launch fundraising and marketing strategies.

Finally, while boards depend on and interact regularly with management and other organization members, boundaries separating the board from each of these units are necessary for the clarity of the organization's authority structure and for the adequate coordination of responsibilities. Therefore,

6. The stronger the ties between trustees and members of these subunits, the less clear the boundaries and hence authority relationships will be between them and the board.

The chapter discusses first the methodology and the results from the study of the board of East Coast Orchestra (ECO). The chapter ends with a reassessment of the theory as applied to board behavior.

METHODOLOGY

My overall methodological approach derives from Glaser and Strauss' (1967) notion of "grounded theory" which emphasizes the importance of allowing concepts, hypotheses, and eventually theory to emerge from various interpretations of the data, rather than imposing a tightly conceived framework on those data. Through immersion into the data, I discovered the relevance of networking and social exchange theories to explaining board behavior. Working between these theories and the concepts that emerged from the board data, I hope on a modest scale to expand upon those theories used.

Organizational Diagnosis Methodology

The specific methodology I chose is that of organizational diagnosis described by Alderfer (1980b and elsewhere). Diagnosis gives an organization a snapshot of itself from the perspective of key organizational groups. It is a clinical approach in that it recognizes the importance of the relationship between the researcher and the client system, uses multiple levels of analysis, (i.e. individual, interpersonal, group and intergroup), views the organization as a holistic entity with interdependent parts, is concerned with depth and subtlety, and is interested in change (Alderfer, et al., in press). I chose this clinical methodology for several reasons. First, gaining entry and establishing a relationship of trust with a board of directors can be problematic if they see the board as an "inner sanctum" which protects its own work and that of the organization from outside interference. Because I wanted specifically to study board functioning and member relationships, both potentially threatening topics, I needed a methodology which explicitly addressed relationship–building between the researcher and the client system. Second, a key underpinning of this diagnosis methodology is intergroup theory. As discussed in the Introduction, this theory added important dimensions to the general framework used. Third, because I wanted the research work to be beneficial to the organization, I needed a methodology which included a change component. A diagnosis prepares the organization for change if it decides that change is desireable.

There are three primary stages in a diagnosis that follow sequentially from each other, although some overlap and interrelationship exists among all three. These stages are entry, data collection and analysis, and feedback to the organization.

To gain initial acceptance and understanding of the project, I held the entry meetings (listed in sequence) with the following organization members: Trustee/Director of Development, General Manager, General Manager and Board President, Founder/Conductor, Executive Committee, and full board. After board approval, I also met with the staff, the orchestra and the board of the volunteer group to explain the project. Each group was enthusiastic and excited about the potential benefits of the project.

The second phase of a diagnosis is data collection where the researcher uses a variety of unstructured and structured methods. I used unstructured observation, participant observation, semi–structured interviews and archival research.

I began by observing a full board meeting and a meeting of the board of the organization's auxilliary group, the Volunteers for ECO. Shortly thereafter, I attended an orchestra rehearsal, and two fundraising events in which I participated as a volunteer worker. I subsequently observed four regular board meetings.

Interview questions were jointly determined by my research needs and critical organizational issues. Staff and board members helped me compile the final list of fifteen questions. I had planned to interview all board members and to sample from the rest of the organization. In the end, I interviewed the following:

> Board—15 current members (26 total)
> 2 former members
> Staff— 4 staff (4 total)
> Volunteers— 6 members of their board (20 total)
> Orchestra— 4 musicians (15 total)

I reduced the number of board members interviewed because several were virtually impossible to reach, a few (implicitly) refused to be interviewed, and the fifteen represented key subgroupings in terms of board tenure, centrality, and gender ratios. Interviews lasted from one to two–and–a–half hours and were conducted in homes (eleven), offices (sixteen), and restaurants (three). I relied on extensive notetaking, staying as close to verbatim statements as possible.

After completing all interviews, I then reviewed closely the board minutes from the inception of the organization to the present. It was wise to save this task until the end since I knew enough about the board and its history to interpret the often cryptic summary of those meetings.

Data analysis took place in two stages, representing the differences in the consulting and research parts of the study. (For the purpose of this chapter, I will describe only the research analysis and will do so at the end of the feedback description below.)

Using the intergroup theory framework, feedback design usually involves a series of meetings with groups in the organization whose composition is determined by the results of data analysis. Feedback is also a time when members react to and check the "validity" of the researcher's interpretation of data; thus, it is an interactive process among organization members and between the client systems and the researcher.

Feedback to ECO took place in four stages covering a six week period. I formed a liaison group at this stage in the process, comprised of three board members and one representative each from staff, orchestra and Volunteers. The purpose of this committee was to check the soundness of my interpretations of the data from each of their perspectives. They, therefore, were the first group to receive the feedback. In following the organization's pattern of how issues are presented to the board, the Executive Committee was the next group to receive the feedback. That group also helped me plan how to present the most important material to the full board. The feedback to the full board spanned two meetings. At the first, I presented the material for board reaction, and at the second, I facilitated a discussion of their recommendations for changes. In the interim between the two meetings, I mailed to each board member a written report detailing the findings.

During feedback, trustees described the material I presented as "devastatingly accurate" and as "moving the board ahead three years in its development." The board had lively and at times heated discussions at both meetings and was already making several changes that interviewees had recommended. This burst of energy is gratifying to the consultant part of me. I also anticipate that it will wane over time but hope that it will become part of a longer–lasting process of change.

Measuring the Extent of Interpersonal Ties Among Board Trustees

The research analysis, while including much of the material from the consulting work, examined in more detail the nature of ties between board members and the influence of those ties on board functioning. To analyze board ties, I translated the components of Granovetter's (1973) definition of the strength of a tie to the board context and developed a quantification system that allowed me to differentiate between strong and weak ties among members. The components of Granovetter's definition include:

amoung of time spent
emotional intensity
intimacy (mutual confiding)
reciprocal service.

The time component is particularly important to board member ties as board and committee meetings provide the temporal structure and boundaries within which relationships can be developed and sustained. I quantified, therefore, overlap in attendance at board meetings, joint committee assignments, and length of tenure with the board. Members dyadic relationships with each other received two points if their attendance at board meetings overlapped two–thirds of the time during the past twelve months and one point if they overlapped less frequently; one point for each committee assignment they currently shared; and one point for each year they overlapped on the board.

Determining and quantifying "emotional intensity" and "intimacy" were more difficult, although very important for the strong tie–weak tie distinction. I decided on a proxy measure which was interviewees' answer to the question, "Are there members in the organization with whom you share a particularly strong relationship, one that exists outside of organizational activities?" As described by interviewees, these were social relationships where at least the possibility of a deeper emotional component existed. Members received five points for these relationships if both members of the dyad named each other as strong relationship partners. The scoring, therefore, assumes reciprocity in the relationship. (Data on nonreciprocal, strong relationships are also used in this study but not to determine the strength of ties. I also address the reciprocal services component in a separate section that examines how trustees describe their "exchange" relationships with the organization, that is, what they feel they gain and receive from their work with ECO.)

The score given to each dyadic tie is a linear summation of four components. In other words, the dependent variable is a score which represents the strength of the tie.

The independent variables are overlapping meeting attendance, committee assignments, years on board, and reciprocal social relationships. Strong ties were those that received nine or more points and thus included a reciprocal, strong relationship. This is in keeping with Granovetter's emphasis on the social and emotional components of a strong tie between two people. Weak ties involved less than five points and thus could not include these reciprocal relationships. Some trustees received no "tie points"—these were trustees who had not attended a board meeting in two years or more and thus it was reasonable to assume that no ties existed between them and other board members. Dyads with points between five and eight I termed "moderate ties," a distinction not made by Granovetter. This category seemed important to include because the amount of points indicated a substantial time commitment to board work but perhaps without the social relationship factor.

To test the robustness of the weighting system, I dropped and added one point to each dyadic score. The distinction between strong ties and other kinds of ties remained largely unchanged. The most affected area was that differentiating moderate from weak ties. Five cases were particularly volatile in this regard where the addition or subtraction of one point significantly changed the proportion of types of ties they had with other trustees. The pattern across three of these cases related to their length of time on the board which is two years. The other two cases appear to involve sporadic meeting attendance. These data suggest that the distinction between moderate and weak ties may be problematic. Other data from the interviews, however, appear to lend more credibility to this distinction as the results sections will describe.

In this article, the relationships among the independent variables are examined qualitatively in order to provide a rich descriptive case study of the board. Because of this qualitative focus, I have extensively used quotations from the interviews to allow the reader to make his or her own interpretations. I have also used several charts that categorize and quantify member responses to allow the reader to see the basis for my analysis and conclusions.

THE ECO BOARD OF DIRECTORS

This section describes the board of a medium–sized performing arts organization. East Coast Orchestra (ECO) is a relatively new entity with its history very much alive in the cognitive and emotional systems of the organization. According to member reports, the orchestra was begun by musicians and a novice conductor who had a vision of how to develop an orchestra that placed musicians at the center of the organization and not at the periphery serving a status–conscious board and audience. Several members of the original musician group and of the first formal board are still full participants in the organization.

The orchestra has been extremely successful in terms of artistic reputation and recognition, and its growth has been remarkable. In its American Symphony Orchestra League category it ranked high nationally in the amount of dollars and work it generated for orchestra members. Partly because of this growth, members from all parts of the organization feel it is going through a transition period in terms of what is needed to make the leap from start–up to maturity as an established entity.

With the increasing recognition and growth of the orchestra, some board members began to express concern over whether the board could meet expanding organizational needs for resources and managerial sophistication. In the opinion of the current board President,

> The orchestra is growing at an exhilerating or alarming rate depending on what day of the week you talk to me. As the orchestra goes through stages of development, and it is crossing them quickly, its needs change. What's expected of the board changes as well . . . Currently the board is unable to live up to its obligations as trustees in the literal sense.

The conductor/founder who is also a trustee added that "the board is growing behind the orchestra and not in front of it. The board we have now would have been great two years ago."

What follows is a description of the results of the study of the ECO board which spanned an eight–month period.

Ties and Networks

Using the quantification system presented at the end of the methodology section, the following table depicts ties among this organization's board members and summarizes board membership and demographic information about each member.

The names listed vertically are board members at the time of data collection. (All names are fictionalized, as is the name and some information about the orchestra in order to protect their identities.) The first three columns list the numbers of strong, moderate, and weak dyadic ties each trustee has with all others. The history column is the length of time each trustee has been on the board, rounded off to the nearest year. The next column lists who recruited each member, as described by that member or from other records. The description "former trustee" is one individual who was a founding board member and past Chairperson, no longer on the board. The average attendance record, drawn from the minutes, is the averge for each member's board tenure. The category "official positions held" include current and past positions, as recorded in the minutes. The age column is my approximation of members' ages although in some cases, members volunteered the information. Profession is drawn from verbal reports by members. I made a distinction between corporate business and other (i.e. small) business careers because that information becomes important in the analysis.

Information on the table allows one to distinguish four distinct groups relative to tie patterns. The first four trustees have the most strong ties and these are predominantly with each other—of the eighteen strong ties listed, twelve are with each other (which means that each member of this foursome is strongly tied to each other member). The remaining strong ties are with members of the next group who have a preponderance of moderate ties—most of these moderate ties are with each other and with members of the strong tie group. The third group is characterized by a pattern of weak ties to everyone. The moderate ties that exist within this group link these two trustees to the strong tie or moderate tie group. The one strong tie that exists is between a husband and a wife. The fourth group has no ties with the rest of the board relative to the weighting scheme because of their total absence at all board meetings in the last two years.

I have labelled these tie patterns "groups," which seemed warranted by the strength of the patterns; as described in the Introduction, an important component of the

TABLE 1
Trustee Ties and Characteristics

Name	Ties to Others			Tenure	Recruited by	Average Attendance	Official Position[1]	Age	Job
	Strong	Moderate	Weak						
Paul	4	7	10	Founder	NA	96%	EC, 1st Pres.	30s	Conductor
Mary	5	8	8	5 yrs.	Former T.	91	EC, past Pres.	40s	Housewife
Joan	5	8	8	Founder	Paul	96	past Dir. Dev.	40s	Housewife
Walter	4	7	10	Founder	Paul	80	EC, NC, MC, past Pres.	40s	Lawyer
Dan	2	11	8	4 yrs.	Paul	85%	EC, Sec.	30s	Lawyer
Ed	1	9	11	2 yrs.	Mary	89	EC, Pres.	40s	Academic
Tony	1	10	10	Founder	Former T.	76	EC, VP, MC*	30s	Lawyer
Chris	1	13	7	3 yrs.	?	81	EC, VP, DC*, NC	40s	Architect
Ira	1	13	8	4 yrs.	Tony	65	EC, Treas.	30s	Accountant
Irene	2	7	12	2 yrs.	Joan	68	EC, VP, NC, DC	40s	Bus-corp.
Nancy		12	9	4 yrs.	Paul	93		30s	Housewife
Arlene		8	13	3 yrs.	Former T.	48		50s	Housewife
George		8	13	4 yrs.	?	57		40s	Dentist
Leona		3	18	3 yrs.	?	59%		70s	Housewife
Tom			21	2 yrs.	Paul	32		40s	Lawyer
Angie	1	2	20	2 yrs.	Joan	84	Past Pres. Vol.	30s	Housewife
Kitty			19	1 yr.	Joan	64	DC	40s	Bus-corp.
Bob			21	1 yr.	Tom	18		30s	Business
Margery			21	1½ yrs.	Joan	29		30s	Bus-corp.
Gordon			21	1 yr.	Paul/Joan	33		30s	Bus-corp.
Ken			21	1 yr.	Joan	61	MC	50s	Bus-corp.
Bob			21	1 yr.	Vol. Bd.	33	MC	30s	Bus-corp.
Pat	no ties			3½ yrs.	Michael	0%		50s	Doctor
Michael	"			4 yrs.	Joan	0		50s	Bus-corp.
James	"			4 yrs.	Paul	0		50s	Celebrity
Roy	"			5 yrs.	Joan	0		50s	Bus-corp.

1. EC = Executive Committee; DC = Development Committee; MC = Marketing Committee; NC = Nominating Committee.
* Chairpersons of those committees.

behavioral definition of what constitutes a group (Alderfer, 1977) includes that members and nonmembers can identify who is part of the group and who is not. To a large extent this is true for these tie groupings based on trustees' own descriptions of the "inner circle, the middle range, and the outer fringe" that they used to distinguish degrees of board involvement. Interviewees labelled certain trustees and themselves as belonging to specific groups and these labels correspond well with the patterns depicted here. Systematic data were not collected on trustee perceptions of internal groupings; the responses just referenced were spontaneously given. Therefore, I cannot claim complete overlap between perceptions of groups and chart data. The indications are strong enough, however, to allow me to use these tie pattern groupings for further analysis, and I will do so throughout the body of this article.

Table 1 also provides important descriptive information concerning the nature of ties among trustees. First, table data plus interviewee data illuminate the *hierarchical nature of internal board networks*. That is, networks or tie groupings coincide with power differences among trustees along several dimensions. First, in all strong tie dyads but one, at least one dyad partner is a member of the strongly tied grouping. (This exception is Chris and Angie who are one of two married couples on the board.) Second, not shown on the table are asymmetrical social relationships where only one member of the dyad describes having a strong relation to another. Most of these asymmetrical ties exist between moderately and strongly tied members where moderates feel closer to members of the strongly tied group than those members feel toward the moderates. In instances where the relationship is reciprocal, the moderately tied trustee holds a position in the formal board structure. Those trustees with no strong ties hold no officer positions and few committee seats.

These are two possible explanations for this pattern. One is consistent with Hypothesis Four that strong ties result from relations developed among trustees holding positions in the formal structure. In the past, this appears to be the case where the initial board officers formed significant relationships with each other because of their work together on the board. An alternative explanation, however, seems more consistent with current trends. Moderately tied trustees hold positions in the formal structure because of previously existing strong ties with one or more members of the strongly tied grouping. Data from the interviews suggest that in all cases, the current officers and committee chairs were well known to members of the strongly tied group prior to or at the time of their election to office. Furthermore, the Nominating Committee chairperson, who is a member of the strongly tied grouping, proposes the slate of officers and committee chairpersons. While he could use primarily objective criteria in selecting trustees for these positions, it appears that personal relationships in addition to these explicit criteria strongly influence his decisions. Data described below on the strongly tied group and in the section on recruitment discuss this pattern further.

Strongly tied trustees. The group of four trustees who are strongly tied to each other is an older group relative to the board as a whole. Three are WASPS (white, Anglo–Saxon Protestants), one is from an old Italian family in the city and two have prior connections to the local college. Two of its members, Walter and Joan are married to each other and were both founding trustees. I interviewed each of these four trustees.

A history of commitment to ECO is striking across the whole group as the group's average tenure of six years and its average attendance record throughout that tenure is 91 percent. Three members are former Presidents of the board and one is the former Director of Development, a position she held while still retaining her board seat. Only one currently holds an official position as a committee chairperson. Their Executive Committee memberships derive from a tradition of having past Presidents invited to those meetings.

Their current influence is concentrated primarily in the area of recruitment of new members. Thirteen out of eighteen people outside of the strongly tied group (data are missing on four other members) were recruited by these trustees. For many trustees, therefore, the initial contact or at least central contact with the board came from within this one group. The chairperson of the Nominating Committee is a member of this group, a position either he or his wife has held for several years. This position is a critical gatekeeping one as the chair not only nominates new trustees and suggests who should be dropped from the board, but also proposes the annual slate of officers. It may not be surprising that current officers have strong ties to this group. While strongly tied trustees are not, therefore, overly represented within the board's current formal structure, they determine it. A fuller discussion of this gatekeeping role is given in the section on recruitment.

The importance of intra–board social relationships for these strongly tied trustees is represented by a "family" theme which ran throughout the interviews. Paul described frequently having Sunday dinner with Walter and Joan. Walter said of his and Joan's relationship with Mary and her family.

> It has become a family affair, with Jay, their kids and even their friends. It still befuddles me, given their global backgrounds and financial success, why they selected us.

Paul is single and has no family nearby. Walter and Joan have no children and Mary and her family were new to the community when she began her involvement with ECO. The organization therefore have provided a focus and a sense of familial connection for these members.

Other interview data suggest that the role of these trustees was changing. They sometimes described the family theme in past tense terms, referring frequently to activities they did with each other two or three years ago. The orchestra's first general manager, who left the organization around that time and to whom all felt strongly tied, is an important absent member of this group. His leaving coincided with a change in board leadership (away from this group), greater growth in the orchestra, and hence more formalization of roles. In response to these changes, strongly tied trustees expressed a feeling of loss and also annoyance that decisions were being made by staff or the Executive Committee without them. As a group they were very critical of the present leadership with whom they did not have strong ties. They claim that the general manager does not have the same interpersonal skills as the former manager, and that some members of the Executive Committee are overly protective of the committee's influence and decision–making process.

Moderately tied trustees. Trustees moderately tied to each other and the board in general hold most of the formal leadership roles in terms of board officer positions and committee chairs and may be characterized as the "doers." They are diverse with respect to ethnicity with a mix of WASP (3), Jewish (2), eastern European (1), and Italian (3) surnames. A sizeable number of this group are in their early 30s, and are probably just beginning to fill positions of some influence within their firms. Their youthfulness in addition to their ambition may enhance the general "doer" quality of this group. Their activism is further underscored by the fact that while they represent ties to few corporations, they described using the connections they do have to help the organization raise money and establish internal administrative systems.

I interviewed six out of the nine moderately tied trustees. A theme from these interviews was a concern that the board and staff need to be better organized to handle the workload. Their descriptions of problems were more task–focused and, in contrast to the strongly tied trustees, they were not as critical of individual trustees or staff. In particular, they saw the Executive Committee, of which many are members, as the appropriate decision–making and leadership group within the board because of the lack of steady involvement from others.

Unlike the friendships and sense of familial relations that the strongly tied trustees emphasized, these trustees spoke of their involvement as an alternative to their daily occupational routines. Work with the organization gave them a different set of people with whom to interact. Thus, while intra–board social relationships were important, they were in addition to ones which existed externally.

Weakly tied trustees. Trustees weakly tied to each other and the board are relative newcomers. One exception is an older woman who has been on the board for four years. Ethnically they are predominantly WASP (5) with two Italian, one Jewish, and one eastern European member. I interviewed six of these nine trustees.

They also represent a number of substantial local, regional, and national business corporations. Their board membership signals an effort on the part of the board to recruit management expertise and corporate connections. However, their lack of committee memberships, their low average attendance record (44 percent as compared with 73 percent for the moderate tie and 91 percent for the strong tie groups), and their lack of strong ties suggest that their current influence is minimal.

Weakly tied trustees were very critical of the board overall and specific in their criticism of its lack of focus, planning, and follow–through, of a committee system which often does not work, and of immaturity on the part of the staff. Several felt that they had important fundraising connections that were not being used by the board because of its general disorganization.

A feeling of being outsiders on the board underlay many of these criticisms. One trustee said he felt unable to make suggestions because he "doesn't have the social legitimacy" on the board. Another who has made suggestions at board meetings said she "felt like they haven't heard me." A third hasn't tried to recruit any trustees because she is "too new." And a fourth, who led an effort at a recent board meeting to change the name of the orchestra for marketing purposes said he hoped "the balance of the board doesn't look on that gregariousness as being a smart ass," refering to his perceptions of his style at that meeting.

Related to seeing themselves as outsiders was their notion of an "inner circle." Three of these interviewees explicitly discussed this. One looked to the inner circle to solve the organization's financial problems—"there's an inner circle. In my heart I believe there is someone there who'd come up with the money if the organization needed it." Another was more critical of what he saw as the dynamics caused by there being an inner ring of influence,

> Joan and Walter created this organization and encouraged Paul. They have a great deal of clout and I think the people on the board are afraid to break the image. If Joan wants

to do something, she'll be able to. I'm afraid there's an unconscious stifling of ideas. On the other hand, others with ideas won't get off the dime and do anything.

It is difficult to ignore that these "outsiders" are predominantly business people. Characteristics of trustees not tied to the board provide further evidence of the seeming connection between corporate trustees and an outsider status.

Trustees with no board ties. They are an older group of well–established and wealthy businessmen and professionals. They have a lengthy board tenure and represent one of the first attempts by the board to recruit "heavy–hitters" and big names. In the earlier years, three of these four members sporadically attended board meetings; however, in the past two years, they have attended none, as recorded in the minutes. From verbal reports, the board or staff has involved them once or twice in fundraising efforts.

I attempted to set up interviews with two of these people; however, I was unsuccessful with each because of their busy schedules and unreturned phone calls.

This descriptive information on tie groupings begins to test some of the hypotheses related to the content of ties and the relationship of tie strength to board structure. As Hypothesis One proposes, the stronger the ties between trustees, the more emphasis they place on social relationships. Trustees more weakly tied to the board were concerned with task–focused or instrumental issues. An important similarity across these weakly tied trustees was their careers in business which may explain their more instrumental focus. However, their outsider status limits the extent to which this kind of perspective is brought to bear on board matters.

Tie strength related most clearly with similar identity groups (Hypothesis Two) among the group of trustees strongly tied to each other where these trustees were predominantly WASP and from a similar age group. Greater diversity was seen among moderately and weakly tied trustees.

The data on ties further suggests that there is a hierarchy of tie groupings that relates strong, social ties to internal power (Hypothesis Four). This relationship is less direct, however, than that implied by the hypothesis. The most strongly tied trustees do not hold the formal positions of power except for the position of Nominating Committee chair; rather, those trustees who do hold these positions have significant connections with the strongly tied trustee group. Furthermore, the direction of this relationship appears to be opposite from that suggested by the original hypothesis— that is, the data described above indicate that strong ties influence board position rather than office–holding creating strong ties.

The next section examines the social and economic exchange components of tie strength in more detail and therefore adds more substantive data to the hypotheses concerning the content of network ties.

Exchange Patterns—Trustee Relationships with ECO

To relate the reciprocity notion included in Granovetter's definition of ties to an organizational context, I examined the kinds of exchange patterns members have with ECO. I determined generic categories from interviewees' responses to the question, "What do you gain from and what do you give to your work with ECO?" Once I determined these common categories, I then coded each member's responses accordingly. These are described in Table 2. In some cases members gave more than one

TABLE 2
Categories of Exchange Responses by Trustee Grouping

		Strongly Tied Group	Moderately Tied Group	Weakly Tied Group	Total
Gained:	Being involved (s)	4	4	5	13
	Friendships (s)	3	3	3	9
	Learning (i)	6	1	0	7
	Assoc. with music (s)	2	0	1	3
	Career enhancement (i)	1	2	3	6
	Having influence in the organization (s)	3	0	0	3
Gave:	Personal qualities (s)	2	6	1	9
	Prof. skills (i)	0	3	3	6
	Moral support to orchestra (s)	3	4	0	7
	Personal sacrifices (s)	3	1	0	4
	Time (s)	2	3	1	6
	Connections (i)	1	2	4	7
	Money (i)	2	1	4	7

response which fit into the same category; for example, if a member said he or she gave "enthusiasm" and "common sense," I coded each of those as personal qualities. The cell numbers, therefore, represent the coding of total responses.

To look at general trends, one could apply these categories to Foa's (1971) components of social and economic or instrumental exchanges. For example, his three social components include the giving and receiving of love or friendship; status or respect; and services. These can be compared with respondents' categories of personal qualities, personal sacrifices and friendships; being involved and having influences; and support to the orchestra, time, and association with music. His three instrumental components are money, information, and products or goods. These correspond to money; connections and career enchancement; professional skills and learning new skills described by trustees. The (s) or (i) notation next to each category on Table 2 is my translation of respondents' categories into social or instrumental exchange components.

Table 3 breaks down the percentage responses between social and instrumental components for the board as a whole and for each tie grouping. These figures suggests that, on the whole, trustees describe having more of a social exchange relationship with ECO than an instrumental one. Important economic or instrumental components exist, however, such as career enhancement and learning new career–oriented skills.

In comparing responses across groups, patterns emerge that support the group descriptions given in the previous section. For example, the percentage of social to

TABLE 3
Percentage Comparisons of Exchange Responses by Trustee Grouping

	Total Board	Strongly Tied Group	Moderately Tied Group	Weakly Tied Group
Social Components	62%	69%	70%	44%
Instrumental Components	38%	31%	30%	56%

instrumental exchange components for strongly and moderately tied trustees is more than two to one, higher than for the board as a whole. Percentage comparisons for the weakly tied group, on the other hand, show a domination of instrumental components. This provides further support for Hypothesis One regarding the relationship of tie strength to social vs. instrumental qualities and is consistent with Granovetter's finding (1974).

Instrumental components were not absent for strongly tied trustees, however. "Learning," a particularly important category for these trustees, was often described implicitly as "career enhancement." For the women, the responses had to do with learning skills for a *new* career or new position in the community. For example,

> When I was President, it gave me a role in the city at a time when I had only just come. Now I am perceived to be a part of the community and am continually asked to be on boards.

And another female trustee from this group said,

> I am a different person. I had no real skills and now I can earn a living. I've established credibility.

The men described the learning more in terms of their *emerging* careers, as "enhancing leadership skills." These trustees, unlike others, also described as a gain, "having some influence within the organization" which could be interpreted as a way they began to apply their new learning in an organizational context.

In exchange, strongly tied trustees mentioned having made what I called personal sacrifices for the organization. Responses in this category included, "I have given them a lot of my spirit" and "I have given my life to the organization." They mentioned less frequently "giving" instrumental exchange components such as connections or their professional skills. These things, it appears, they were gaining from rather than giving to the organization.

In contrast, trustees weakly tied to the board often spoke about their involvement as a challenge, a place where they could put their *already existing* skills to work in a different setting. One member said,

> It's a personal challenge away from work. Can I bring in new money, sell an orchestra? I know I can do that in the oil business. Can I be part of a group that brings this orchestra to new heights and acceptance?

Another said,

> I see myself as a professional manager—I get a helluva kick in seeing organizations grow. I like people to respect me because I'm carrying my share of the weight to make things happen. The ECO thing is fun because I believe I can make a difference.

What these trustees feel they give to the organization are their professional skills, money and connections, all instrumental components. For example, they described giving "24 years of marketing sales know–how," "good comments regarding the financials and long–range planning," and "putting my reputation behind them." They infrequently discussed giving social exchange components such as personal qualities or moral support. What they gained also had strong instrumental overtones. "Being involved" represented for some enhanced visibility for their organizations; and they, more than any other group, mentioned board membership as enhancing their careers.

The patterns of trustees moderately tied to the board resembled those of the strongly tied trustees in terms of gaining a sense of involvement in the community and friendships. However, where strongly tied trustees felt they were gaining more than they were giving to the organization, moderately tied trustees felt they were giving twice as much as they were gaining from their involvement. They described themselves as giving a great deal of personal qualities and professional knowledge, and particularly spoke of giving support to the orchestra or to the conductor. On the whole, they were most aware of the time they gave. These trustees are predominantly "givers" and do so in social exchange terms.

Examining exchange relationships more fully describes the nature of ties between board members and ECO. For example, one can see the centrality of the organization along several dimensions for trustees who are strongly tied to each other. The organization has given them a place in the community, a circle of close friends, and skills for new or emerging careers. For weakly tied trustees, the organization is not as central to either their social or professional lives but rather represents another context in which to put their already existing skills to work. Moderately tied trustees may feel they are receiving neither the benefits from having the organization central to their lives nor the ability to use existing skills to push the organization ahead. Instead, in their positions of responsibility they experience most of the trustees' and staffs' frustration with the board's inability to mature to the next stage of development.

The recruitment and selection of trustees has an important influence on how these exchange patterns are established and perpetuated. The next section describes this process, how it is changing and how inertial forces within the board are resisting the change. It specifically examines Hypothesis Three which states that the stronger the ties are among trustees, the more likely the recruitment process will follow an interpersonal networking pattern.

Recruitment, Selection, and Composition

It is reasonable to describe the recruitment of board members as a process which combines the use of strategic criteria for selection and interpersonal networking. Strategic criteria represent organizational needs for access to certain types of resources such as information and money. Categories of board members that follow from these criteria include, for example, lawyers, accountants, wealthy patrons or corporate executives. Other criteria, such as how potential members will "fit in" with the existing board are also important. Interpersonal networking, or bringing in members already known to others, provides an important screening function for these criteria and is likely to enhance the social relations among board members.

On the ECO board, most interviewees described the recruitment process in interpersonal networking terms:

> anyone who knows someone, as long as they are recommended
>
> always a friend of somebody's

> Joan cultivates us as friends before we become board members

The current Nominating Committee chairperson describes the underlying basis of this process,

> We discourage snobbery at all levels, that's the theory of the receptions where the audience interacts with the musicians. It's part of the soul of the organization. I don't know if it came from anywhere, we just knew we didn't want to be like the symphony.
>
> Am I conscious of it in recruitment? No. The original group had it. People who came on the board are associates of those already there. Matching spirits. So the original spirit has just come marching along.
>
> The converse is a consideration. Someone who is unfriendly or cynical isn't likely to be considered, even if he's loaded to the gunnels.

According to this quotation, therefore, the interpersonal networking process provides an important screening function that protects certain organizational values. The protective function appears to be more important under some circumstances than gaining access to needed resources.

As described by interviewees, the recruiting process is an informal one. Board members contact the Nominating Committee chair with suggestions and he calls the other two committee members to discuss the possible candidate. Without any formal recruitment process or structure, the influence of the interpersonal networking among a small number of trustees may become particularly strong.

Data in Table 1 regarding who recruited current trustees implies that most have been recruited by trustees strongly tied to each other. Two former board members discussed this pattern and raised the question of whether it displays an exclusionary quality. One of them linked the exclusionary quality to the current Nominating Committee chair, among others—"The true founders portrayed a protectiveness and sense of ownership almost as if it was their own orchestra." A current trustee said that the chair of the Nominating Committee decides "who's worthy," implying an unspoken standard applied to potential candidates. In contrast, the Nominating Committee chair and other trustees strongly tied to him described the board as "non–snob types," "populist," and "not stuck in set roles or status differences." These data suggest that recruitment is an informal networking process controlled by a small group of board members. Whether one perceives this process as protecting organizational values or as protecting an organizational elite depends on whether one strongly tied to this small group of trustees.

Interviewees' perceptions of the board's current composition lend interesting support to the notion of there being an internal elite. In widespread convergence across interviews, trustees described board members as city college–affiliated, professional, or "low–level business types." This latter phrase was used to connote lower or middle range managers as opposed to top level executives. Data on the actual composition contradicts their description:

> College-affiliated—three members, all in the strong tie or high moderate tie group.
>
> Professionals—eight members, all but two in the strong tie or moderate group.
>
> Business—nine members, all but one in the weak tie or no–tie group and representing six major corporations, two banks and the head of the city's Chamber of Commerce.

"Low–level business types"—five upper or top level executives, all in the weak or no tie groups.

The perceptions of board composition relate to trustees who are strongly or moderately tied to each other but *not* to the board as a whole. The college–affiliated and professional career members are virtually all strongly or moderately tied trustees. "Low–level" business types include executives from major corporations and banks who are weakly tied to the board or not tied at all. Given this perceived composition, it is not surprising that trustees spoke of the need for more "heavy–hitters" on the board, meaning members with corporate connections or ties to wealth. Note, however, that such members currently sit on the board but are visible to the board as a whole.

In discussing the need for a more influential board, two strongly tied trustees spoke of fears they have about that transition. One said,

> One selection criterion should be a fundamental interest and awareness of the art form because their motivations have got to be in improving that. Otherwise, their motivations will be to enhance their own prestige—that's not bad if they aren't using the board just for that purpose.

And another described how,

> We don't have those types of fundraisers on the board. We are not comfortable with them. We are more like a cottage industry. I like to feel we are all friends because it is life–enhancing and we're all civilized human beings, not that it's a business. I like this lovable feeling, but we need a tougher component, a United Jewish Appeal type of approach. (She then mentioned a weak tie and a no–tie member who are "like that").

> If I had to make a choice, I'd go with the way we are now. If the board changed, I wouldn't go to meetings.

These quotations demonstrate an ambivalence that some strongly tied trustees expressed regarding the recruitment of trustees with the ability to do necessary fundraising. Again the dual themes of production and exclusion emerged.

Hypothesis Three regarding the recruitment of trustees who are similar to existing board members is not upheld. While the board uses an interpersonal networking strategy, new trustees are not as similar or as socially connected to the board as in previous times. A significant pattern, however, that illustrates the complexity of this transition is that while new trustees are being recruited more for the strategic needs of ECO, they maintain a peripheral status on the board. Their board attendance records are poor and they hold few positions in the formal structure. Bringing these trustees onto the board but not including them in the formal structure or the inner circle may be a way that strongly tied trustees are trying to satisfy both the organization's needs and their own social relationship needs.

The next section on trustee functions focuses on Hypothesis Five which links strong ties among trustees to resistance to diversifying financial and audience bases of support. In this section we will be able to examine the ramifications of the ECO's recruitment strategy which seems to leave corporate or business–oriented trustees weakly tied to the board as a whole.

Trustee Functions

Table 4 summarizes trustee responses to the question, "What are the board's current functions?"

Functions 1, 2, and 3 are externally focused, that is, they require that the board use connections and ties outside of the organization. Functions 4 and 5 are internal ones that relate to the governance of the organization. The dominant response pattern from all three groups related to externally focused functions, although moderately tied trustees emphasized both external and internal types of functions. They also had the highest volume of response which again indicate their heightened awareness of board responsibilities.

Members were very critical of the board's abilities to perform these functions and thus their answers took on the flavor of what the board *should* be doing, rather than what the board currently is doing very well if at all. Many of these criticisms related to the lack of planning and fundraising direction.

Fundraising. The ECO board has had a problematic history with fundraising, and there have been several unsuccessful attempts to organize the board more effectively to fulfill this function. As described by trustees, other parts of the organization have been more reliable in this area—for example, the fundraising events of the Volunteers, unanticipated profits from the orchestra's tours and gigs, and grants from a large, local corporation that has underwritten unprofitable concerts.

The strong and moderate tie groups focused on the Development Committee's lack of leadership in this area. The strong tie group in particular emphasized problems with the chairperson. They expressed resentment at his asking for the job and that it be made a Vice Presidential position and then not following through with tangible results.

General board resistance to fundraising was also an important factor. All strongly tied trustees described how the board as a whole did not like to fundraise and often did not know how. One person from this group and two moderately tied trustees admitted that they personally disliked it—"I just detest fundraising," "It's not my thing," "I don't have the connections."

Trustees weakly tied to the board emphasized less the centrality of the Development Committee chairperson and more the lack of planning by the whole board as well as the Committee. Several felt that their connections were not being used effectively because of a lack of overall fundraising direction and follow–through.

The historical as well as current problem with fundraising may significantly relate both to the exchange relationship members have with the organization and with the

TABLE 4
Categories of Board Functions by Trustee Grouping

Functions:	Strongly Tied Group	Moderately Tied Group	Weakly Tied Group	Total
1. Fundraising	4	5	3	12
2. Promoting ticket sales	1	2	3	6
3. Increasing visibility	0	1	2	3
4. Est. policies and planning	0	3	1	4
5. Fin. and admin. oversight	0	3	1	4

strength of their ties to each other. As one member said, "I'd like to think of ECO's success as artistic and not financial." If the relationship with the organization for some trustees has emphasized the social components of an exchange, then fundraising adds instrumental qualities such as increased professionalism and managerial competence that may fundamentally contradict the basis of that relationship. Foa (1971) points out that it is difficult to add economic exchange components to a relationship that is essentially a social one.

Second, as Granovetter's theory describes (1973), to the extent that members are strongly tied to each other, they may not have the variety of external connections needed to raise money from a variety of sources. In addition, if existing relationships among some trustees have an exclusionary quality, then they may resist opening organizational boundaries to include nonmembers in fundraising efforts. These ethnocentric dynamics reduce the board's adaptive capacities by reducing the number and breadth of connections to needed resources. As the data on recruitment suggests, the ECO board may have implicitly made the trade–off between creating a loyal and compatible inner group and expanding its fundraising capacity. The marketing function of the board provides additional information on the ramifications of this trade–off.

Marketing an Orchestra. The marketing issue for the ECO board includes developing an audience and establishing a musical emphasis. Stated one way, the issue is "filling the seats" of a two thousand–seat theater for the local subscription series. The series averaged only four to five hundred subscriptions per year over the last four seasons. Looked at another way, the issue is to whom does the organization want to appeal, which has important socioeconomic class overtones.

Audience development and musical emphasis are interrelated. Which one takes on greater significance depends on how one frames the marketing question. If one asks first, "what's our audience?" then one is more apt to tailor the music to the tastes of that target group. If one instead asks, "what do we want to play?" then one finds an audience who will listen. ECO, founded by musicians, has historically asked more of the latter question. Subscription series tickets sales have not grown, however, and thus the former question has gained more emphasis. As it has, some tension has begun to surface on the board relating to the balance between fine–art music and "pops" in the repertoire. Two quotations from the interviews summarize the extreme points of view on this issue. The board President said,

> I hope the orchestra can survive playing the music it set out to rather than just finding work for musicians. Greater attendance by university people would balance out the quasi–philistine interests who want to see more pops music.

A new, weakly tied corporate trustee emphasized,

> ECO could grow from four hundred season ticketholders to one thousand. Target the 25–40 year old market. Play the Beatles. If ECO played the Beatles, there'd be an immediate appeal.

Most members did not express such clear opinions and felt that the orchestra should continue its diverse and flexible programs. Patterns which point to important group differences did emerge, however, when members discussed the future of ECO.

Strongly and moderately tied trustees saw ECO in five years with a national reputation, touring in Europe, and using highly respected guest conductors. Some members compared ECO to the prestigious Academy of St. Martin–in–the–Fields and the St. Paul Chamber Orchestra. While the weakly tied trustees hoped for national recognition as well, they stressed more the issue of audience diversity, for example,

> It is safe to say a truck driver doesn't like classical music? You need everyday people to tap into a broader audience. If you aren't going to go after that audience, then you may not be able to fill the auditorium.

Marketing issues, strongly related to fundraising ones, illuminate critical tensions for arts boards. As described in the Introduction, the separation of high culture from popular culture has historically been important to the differentiation of the upper classes from lower ones. The recent reduction in public subsidies for the arts has meant, however, that some in the arts community perceive a strong need to diversify their audiences, boards, and even artistic performances in order to expand their economic base. Corporate members of these boards can more readily see the issues in economic terms and have the expertise to make concrete suggestions for change. These changes clash with the social desires of other members who may want to maintain greater homogeneity throughout the organization and its audience base. It is precisely this conflict that is beginning to surface on the ECO board and was feared by strongly tied trustees when describing the needed changes in composition.

It is too simplistic, however, to say that ECO's present needs are entirely economic and therefore it is faltering because of nonadaptive qualities expressed by the strong ties among its formal and informal leadership. The social content of these trustee relationships is important as it provides the glue which binds people together and enhances commitment to the values and mission of the organization. Furthermore, it is not altogether clear that trustees weakly tied to the board are proposing a diversification strategy that fits best with the core values and mission of the organization. More accurate perhaps is to say that economic considerations *in addition to* social concerns are now crucial if the organization is to become an established entity.

The final section on trustee relationships with the rest of the organization draws on material about ties and subnetworks which exists in other parts of the organization and which influence internal ECO dynamics.

Relationships With the Rest of the Organization

This section describes the perceptions of trustees, staff, orchestra, and Volunteer of ECO regarding the role of the trustees and current relationships between each unit and the board. It examines Hypothesis Six that connects tie strength between trustees and members of these other organizational units to clarity of the boundaries separating them. The staff group consists of four people—the music director/conductor, the general manager, the assistant general manager, and the administrative assistant, all of whom were interviewed. The orchestra includes a core group of fifteen musicians plus additional players as needed. Three core musicians and one additional player were interviewed. The Volunteers group is a membership organization which holds social, fundraising events for ECO and has a board of twenty. It is not separately incorporated and reports to the trustees. I interviewed six of their board members.

Board–Management Relations. Relations between board and management of a nonprofit are often difficult because the board, while in a hierarchically superior position, consists of part–time volunteers who must rely on staff's expertise about the daily operation of the organization. This paradoxical relationship can lead to unclear lines of authority where the top executive is held accountable by a board who knows little about his or her management responsibilities. Social ties between some members of management and the board can further obscure the hierarchical relationship. In many arts organizations the situation is further complicated by a triadic authority structure consisting of the general manager, the artistic director, and the board president. Splitting staff leadership functions between business and artistic responsibilities may also parallel organizational tension between these two functions.

ECO board members and staff were each asked to describe the relationship from their perspectives. While most members from each unit described the relationship as good and mutually respectful, some also discussed problem areas including the personality, behavioral style, and management expertise of the general manager, Don.

In examining these interviews, an interesting trend emerged. The four trustees who most strongly criticized the general manager as a person were all women and strongly tied to Joan. She has just resigned as the Director of Development, a staff position which worked closely with Don. As she described, she left that position because of a continuing personality conflict with him. Knowledge of this tension plus some of these trustees' own frustrations in working with Don translated into harsh, personally focused criticisms. For example, from three of these trustees,

> He just dismisses people. He won't talk to me.

> Don is not a good manager in that he doesn't keep the spirit up. Bill (the former general manager) was an extraordinary man. He knew what Joan's strengths and weaknesses were.

> Joan made us feel really cared for. Don doesn't know how to work with volunteers.

As one quotation illustrates, Don was often compared with Bill, the first general manager and absent member of the strong tie group. These trustees described Bill as not only able to work with Joan but also as someone who made the office–board relationship a familial one. They did not evaluate or discuss his management skills.

In contrast to the criticism of Don, these trustees praised Paul, the conductor, to whom several felt strongly tied. Some expressed the fear that if Paul left the organization, "the ballgame is over."

These data portray a split in the office that staff described as consisting of Paul and Joan on the one hand, and Don, Pete (the assistant general manager), and Liz (the administrative assistant) on the other. Data on strong ties supports this. Paul and Joan have strong ties to each other and to other trustees but are not tied to the rest of the staff. Pete, Don, and Liz are tied strongly to each other but to no one else in the organization. Staff described the rift in terms of Paul and Joan's emphasis on the social and family atmosphere in the office while the other three have a more businesslike attitude toward their work. The following quotations from each of the four staff are illustrative:

> *Don*: For Paul, it's a love not a job. It's abhorrent for him to think it's a 9–5 job or that there's a life after work. This causes tension between Paul and me and Pete . . . Paul lives

in the office. His clothes are there, all his music is there. He spends from 10am to 11pm there and only sleeps at home.

Pete: What do you do with one–and–a–half years of frustration and anger? There are problems with Paul that are similar to Joan. He's comfortable with old ways and equates the business side with the social side. Some of us like going home at 5 pm. There is no separation for Paul and he may see us moving away from him.

Liz: Joan's been with the orchestra since it was born and that makes a strong tie between her and Paul.

Paul: The office used to operate as a group, a 24–hour–a–day relationship when Joan was there and Bill. I don't like to see different people. That's changed a lot now.

In all these quotations, one can see clearly the tension between familial and social values and a more professional and businesslike orientation. The tension parallels similar tensions at the board level that surfaced regarding recruiting, fundraising, and marketing functions. Through ties between the board and staff, it is reasonable to suggest that office tensions are carried up to the board and that board tensions make their way into the office.

Unclear boundaries between board and staff regarding certain functions, responsibilities, and authority may also increase the level of conflict within the office. The relationships among the leadership triad, (the general manager, the music director, and the board President) are particularly confusing. As Don, the general manager, said "I have no sense of authority. I don't work for Paul but it's Paul's orchestra. Also, he's on the board, so in fact, I do work for Paul." Don feels relatively close with Ed, the board President, but feels that Ed is more interested in the artistic end than in business matters. The President substantiated this description of himself—his greatest satisfaction from his work with ECO is "the exposure to Paul and the musicians." Most of his time, however, is spent working with Don and because of Don's lack of experience, Ed described himself as "more like a chief operating officer than the chairman of the board." Paul, the conductor, sees his role as "shephardship and control, influence and access toward shepharding the organization. To say something at the right time." He prefers to work behind the scenes so as not to appear too controlling; however, from several examples he gave, he maintains a great deal of influence in all phases of the organization's activities.

Staff described this confusion with a great deal of frustration, particularly with regard to fundraising and development. Because of lack of board follow through, they felt that much of the work landed on their shoulders and was *in addition to* the work they had in managing the growth of the orchestra. The fundraising must get done, however, as it is the source of their own salaries. Staff reported feeling tired and overstretched, and they asked for more direction and leadership from the board. The general manager explained,

The problem is I never had the chance to work for someone and now I must provide leadership and I don't know how. It can't afford to be a learning experience for someone anymore . . . The board should be actively and constructively overseeing what I do. I'd pay a lot of money for that, to provide me with some direction.

Some trustees recognized their lack of leadership relative to the office. The board President stated,

> The real growth of the orchestra has been met by management and not the trustees. Without them, the efforts of the trustees would have been shown to be inadequate.

Much work fell through the cracks, however, with the board being unclear about its direction and responsibilities, the founder/conductor maintaining influence in areas outside of the artistic realm, and the general manager being young and relatively isolated from key board members. As with the fundraising issue, some trustees preferred to see the problem as located within one individual. It is doubtful, however, because of system level dynamics based in historical relationships and ties, that anyone in the general manager's position would have an easy time. As a result both the board and the office often felt they were flourishing.

Board–Orchestra. The relationship and degree of interaction between the trustees and members of the orchestra have been unique and important components of the organization's life. As described by several trustees, their respect for and attention to the orchestra is a crucial part of the anti–elitist attitude they foster on the board. The board holds receptions after the concerts for audience, musicians, and board members. Trustees invite players to their homes for dinner and have arranged for special services to be donated to orchestra members. The orchestra members interviewed appreciated these activities and felt that their relationship with the board made a difference in how they perform,

> It's a wonderful feeling to get out on stage and project the fact that you are having a good time. There are a lot of reasons for that—one is the board. If it stops happening, ECO will be in a lot of trouble, when it stops being a give and take between the people who fund it and the people who play.

Trustees in the strong tie group and a few of the musicians from the original core group maintain social connections. Newer trustees mentioned no such connections but described interacting with the orchestra primarily after concerts and at one or two ECO parties a year.

More than the social relationships, however, orchestra members recommended that there be a "business" connection to the board where their views regarding the direction of the orchestra could be heard on a regular basis. Aside from occasional social interaction, the only conduit between the board and orchestra at ECO occurs through Paul, the conductor.

Underlying this recommendation for more of a business relationship may be the issue of what kind of role the conductor should play relative to the board–orchestra interaction. One staff and one musician implicitly stated this and several trustees raised the issue of whether the board should have a role in musical programming and in making more direct contact with the musicians. In my interviews with the conductor, he stated that he was adamantly opposed to any board role whatsoever in programming. Instead he preferred discussions that took place "over brandy after dinner" between himself and one or two trustees whose musical judgment he respected.

The control issue surfaced directly through the question of, "Whose orchestra is this?" Several trustees discussed this issue in general terms. One approached it explicitly—he is a founding trustee, socially tied to several musicians, and has a substantial background in classical music. He stated,

I have taken on the role of 'spiritual godfather' and invite myself to Executive Committee meetings to raise the question of whether this is Paul's orchestra . . .

Two years ago we would have had a divided board, many would say 'fold the orchestra if Paul dies.' But now there is unanimity that it's not Paul's orchestra. He probably acknowledges that.

There are better conductors around and I wouldn't be adverse to considering that . . . It's not Paul's outlet. It is an acceptable and accepted facet of the arts community on the East Coast.

This issue, when raised at a feedback session, was a volatile one. The trustee just quoted, when he heard that some board members still feel "it is Paul's orchestra," said that these trustees should be "re-educated" and if that did not change attitudes, they should be "purged from the board." The use of such terms as "godfather," "re-educated," and "purged," however, underscore the issues of power and control.

It is doubtful that this trustee alone has questions concerning the appropriate role of the founder/conductor. If the board begins to acquire a sense of its hierarchical position and responsibilities, and if the musicians begin to deal more directly with the board, Paul's central mediating role is likely to be challenged and changed.

The original coalition of founding trustees core musicians, and the conductor, all of whom *were* strongly tied to each other is changing. While a few trustees and musicians remain strongly tied, the conductor does not describe having close relationships to any of the current musicians. Growth has necessitated a separation of roles. However, the separation is not clear and coordination mechanisms are not fully in place. In this ambiguous situation, questions of ownership may represent deeper issues of control to which all three groups can claim a historical right.

Board–Volunteers. Data on the trustee–Volunteers relationship provide another view of the business–artistic tension and of the exclusivity dynamic.

The Volunteers of ECO were founded by Joan, one of the original trustees, and actually existed prior to the formal board. The purpose of the Volunteers is to raise money for ECO through various social events such as subscription series, cocktail parties and a winter ball. The structural link between the Board of Trustees and the Volunteers' Board is made by having the President of the Volunteers sit as a trustee during his or her tenure. The Volunteers have asked that a trustee regularly attend their meetings and that has happened sporadically. Other connections exist through Volunteers' membership on the Development and Marketing Committees and by Volunteers' making presentations at trustee meetings. Additionally, four current trustees were previously on the Volunteers board before becoming trustees. Informal friendships also exist between some trustees and members of the Volunteers board. Most of these ties are with Joan who is still very involved with their activities.

Despite these formal and informal links, confusion over responsibilities and a perceived status differential create tensions between the two units. Both groups agree that some Volunteers feel that the trustees have a higher status in the organization and in the community even though the internal perception is that the Volunteers raise more money than the trustees.

Most of the Volunteers I interviewed acknowledged this perception but felt it was ill–founded since the Volunteers are "where the action is." The trustee board was seen as distant, inactive, and "a different group to fire up." They also saw themselves as better organized than the trustees. (The Volunteers' board meeting I attended corroborated that opinion as the President presented the board with goals and objectives, and committee and board officer job descriptions.) In turn, Volunteers criticized the trustees for their lack of direction, particularly in fundraising and marketing which are the two areas where the groups overlap the most. Several Volunteers said they felt that their work was appreciated by the trustees in a broad sense, but that they had difficulty getting trustees to support their specific fundraising activities:

> The Volunteers' board gets a lot of accolades about all their hard work, so it's not that we are unappreciated. Some Volunteers think 'that and a dollar bill will get me a ride on the subway—why didn't you help us sell tickets?' The Board of Trustees is not viewed very positively.

One Volunteers members said that she thought the trustees were "committed to the music and the Volunteers were committed to the organization." This may be further data to support the general split within the organization concerning artistic and business or professional values.

Another part of the status differential is an undercurrent of male–female dynamics. The Volunteers' board and membership is predominantly, although not exclusively, female. Some current trustees described the Volunteers as "a women's auxilliary," "women who don't work," and as the organization's "cheerleaders." Two men who sat on that board later became trustees and some Volunteers remarked that that was seen as a "step up" for them, although neither is a part of the formal or informal trustee power structure. In addition, the strong ties that are maintained between the Volunteers and the trustees exist primarily among women. The female trustees, while not peripheral members, are also not part of the formal power structure which is dominated by men. Male–female dynamics may inhibit the forming of ties between the Volunteers and the formal power structure. It is reasonable to assume that this directly and indirectly contributes to the confusion surrounding the Volunteers' role in the organization and the continuing perception of its being a lower status group relative to the trustees.

CONCLUSIONS

In this final section, the research results will be drawn together in two primary ways—first, differences in the content of strong, moderate, and weak ties will be discussed as these differences relate to the trustee–board and organization relationship; and second, the adaptive and nonadaptive qualities of these differences for the organization will be examined. Table 5 summarizes these results.

Differences in the Content of Ties

With regard to strong ties, the importance of the social component had several ramifications. The emphasis on social relationships appears to have influenced the perceptions of strongly tied trustees regarding significant organizational problems such as fundraising and board–staff tensions. Their perceptions are person–centered, that is, trustees who are strongly tied explain organizational problems in terms of the personal characteristics of certain individuals, for example, the prestige motivations

TABLE 5
Organizationally Related Characteristics of Ties

Differences:	Strong	Moderate	Weak
Perception of organizational issues	Person-centered	Task-focused	Task-focused
Role of ECO in their lives	Central	In addition to other interests	Not focal
Degree of exclusivity	High to moderate	Moderate	Low, stresses diversity
Role on board	Informal power Hierarchical position Gatekeepers	Formal power structure	Peripheral Outsiders

Adaptive Qualities:	Strong	Weak
Positive for organization and board	Enhanced commitment Binding together	Access to diverse range of resources
Negative for organization and board	Exclusivity leads to reduced access to resources	Less attention to values and personal relationships
	May promote ambiguous internal boundaries	

of the Development Committee chairman or the lack of social skills and immaturity of the general manager. They less readily seek system–wide explanations for the difficulties.

The emphasis on social relationships also relates to the importance of informal structures for the accomplishment of activities. Strongly tied members spoke more frequently than others did about preferring to "work behind the scenes" and emphasized the advantages of the interpersonal networking approach to recruitment of new trustees. For these trustees, strong ties may substitute for a formal structure. That is, an informal structure is more congruent with the type of dense and frequent interaction that represents these trustees' experiences with each other and with the organization. They may see a more formal and rationalized structure as unnecessary *and* as threatening to the current interpersonal relationships.

Another characteristic of strong ties is the kind of central role played by the organization. For strongly tied trustees, ECO provided them with a surrogate family, a sense of belonging in a new community, and with skills that have enhanced or created career opportunities. The psychological boundary that separates the person from the organization may be attenuated by strong ties—for strongly tied members, ECO *is* these relationships and personal opportunities. Organizational problems which arise, therefore, cannot be separated from the individuals involved because of the person–organization overlap. In addition, a formalized structure would more clearly separate the person from the organization as specific roles, responsibilities, processes, and procedures would exist external to the people involved.

A third important characteristic of strong ties is the tendency of those relationships toward exclusivity. This surfaced most strongly during discussions of recruitment strategies and board composition and seem to relate to issues of club or family membership. Identity group characteristics, in this case, ethnicity, appear to be a particularly salient although subtle, component of exclusivity.

Connected to the exclusivity property is the hierarchical position of strongly tied trustees within this organization. As described in the section on Ties and Networks, data on asymmetric strong ties and on the relation of symmetric strong ties with board leadership positions indicate that the strongly tied group maintains a hierarchical position relative to the board as a whole. This may be due to their long history and founding status within the organization. I would hypothesize, however, that the hierarchy exists because other trustees, particularly those moderately tied, perceive the person–organization overlap that equates ECO with these strongly tied trustees. For those wanting to have influence within the organization, therefore, they seek out relationships with the strongly tied group.

While strong ties emphasize informal operations, there is formal structural reinforcement for their characteristics described above. They are the gatekeepers and the boundary enforces through the role they play in recruitment of board members and selection of the annual slate of officers. On the positive side, this role involves protecting the organization's values or "spirit." On the other hand, it also allows them to perpetuate an exclusivity quality which may hinder long–term board effectiveness.

Much of the content of weak ties contrasts with that of strong ties. There is a significant instrumental component to these ties. For example, weakly tied trustees describe giving to their board work money, professional skills, and connections and gaining career enhancement. They therefore have a very different range of qualities to offer the organization than strong tie members.

The importance of the instrumental component also relates to how weakly tied trustees view organizational problems which is in task–oriented, not in person–centered terms. As described earlier, these members applied a corporate management perspective to solving board problems.

The role of the organization in the lives of weakly tied trustees also contrasts with that for strongly tied members as ECO is not a focal point for them. There seem to be two components to that quality. First, many weakly tied trustees have already established business and social circles and thus may not have the same need for one organization to provide them with many different opportunities. Second, weakly tied members are also peripheral to the board; therefore, there may be little incentive to make ECO central to their lives.

A third important difference concerns exclusivity—weakly ties trustees stress the need for the board and organization to *diversify* in terms of board composition, fundraising strategies, and marketing efforts. These recommendations may derive from their corporate management perspective; they may also derive from a desire to break up the strong tie network which is prohibiting weakly tied trustees from exercising much influence.

One of the first questions to raise regarding moderate ties is whether it is a useful distinction, particularly since it was the least robust category relative to the weighting scheme. On a theoretical level, designating a moderate tie category transforms a dichotomous variable into more of a continuous one. The content of these ties appears to substantiate the continuous quality: For example, moderately tied trustees displayed less of the social relationship characteristics of the strong tie group but more than weak tie members, and the organization and the board were important to their lives but not central.

Thinking of ties as a continuous variable, at least in the organizational context, also introduces two developmental dimensions to the theory. First, at this point in ECO's development, the moderately tied group may represent transitional characteristics of the board as it moves from a family and social orientation to a more professional and managerial one. Members of this group hold positions in the formal structure because of their personal connections to the strongly tied group as well as their professional competencies. They recognize, however, that the board needs even greater managerial expertise and community connections. It is unclear whether, as the board matures, these moderately tied trustees will maintain their formal influence or be replaced by some of the currently weakly tied members who possess these skills. This latter point raises a second developmental dimensions. Overtime, some trustees may move sequentially between tie groupings. This movement may take place in *both* directions—from weakly to more strongly tied or from strongly to more weakly tied. A longer history with the board, the development of new social relationships, or the opportunity to offer needed skills and resources may be important conditions for movement toward stronger ties. Reduced involvement due to a change in board composition, a change in the perceived mission of the organization, or heightened outside responsibilities might weaken the connections of some currently strongly tied trustees. The use of a continuous variable concept allows the researcher to track these movements in a more precise manner. The tracking provides an avenue for exploring shifting coalitions, changes in perceptions of board and organizational issues, as well as changes in organizational life cycle.

Adaptive and Nonadaptive Components of Ties

The second important piece of learning from internal board networks concerns their influence on the functioning of the board and organization, in particular, their adaptive and nonadaptive qualities. The data on strong ties suggest that they enhance trust, commitment, and attention to values and mission among early organization members. By the significant emphasis on social relationships and personal qualities, strong ties provide the glue that bonded trustees, staff, and musicians during the organization's early period. This bonding appears to have contributed to the high quality of ECO's artistic performances and created a distinctive niche for the new performing arts organization. More weakly tied trustees do not emphasize the unique values within the organization that represents this binding quality. People are less central to them as they focus on the need for problem–solving processes. These instrumental characteristics may not always be advantageous for an organization, particularly during its formative stages.

At this point in ECO's development, however, nonadaptive qualities of strong ties are also surfacing in several ways. First, the exclusivity pattern of these ties constrains the organization from recruiting and using trustees who are different from those strongly tied trustees. These differences relate to a more professional managerial orientation toward board work and trustee responsibilities. The organization's needs for management expertise and increased fundraising capabilities, agreed to by all trustees, are not being met at least in part because of strong tie members' reluctance to "turn a club into something more professional."

Second, ambiguity in the authority structure that both reflects and reinforces the strength of certain ties has led to increasing intra–office and office–board tension. Historical relationships and ties that connected some office staff to key trustees have changed, and no formal structure has taken their place. As a result, new staff are in danger of remaining isolated from powerful trustees and potentially of being scapegoated for the organization's problems.

Third, strongly tied members are raising questions concerning the ownership of the organization. A complex dynamic is taking place between Paul, the conductor, and Walter, the trustee who sees his role as one of ensuring that the board does not view ECO as "Paul's orchestra." In this instance, members of the strong tie group appear to be fighting among themselves for ownership. Ingroup tension is often an indication that the group perceives threats from the outside.

To summarize, this article has attempted to go beyond both the academic and practitioner–focused notions of nonprofit boards of directors as a single group within organizations. From an academic perspective, the research has shown the usefulness of analyzing the networks of a small group within the boundaries of an organization. For practitioners, the research has challenged the often suggested view that boards (should) function as a team. A unified board team may not be realistic, given the differing ties and connections among trustees and between trustees and the organization based on their backgrounds, interests in the nonprofits, and expectations from their board work. Finally, and in a more general sense, the research results may point toward an increasing tension within nonprofits between professionalizing and rationalizing their management structures and maintaining close interpersonal relationships among organization members. These social relationships perform important integrating functions for the nonprofit and, one could argue, for the community as well. An orchestra member describes,

> I don't care about playing the oboe much any more. I do care about making music. It is a tool where the goal is to make music in such a way that people in the audience will be mentally healed by it. With orchestra audiences, there are a lot of barriers—the coats and tails, the conductor, many out there who don't know what they are listening to. But a group can do that for a group if both parties are ready for it.
>
> If I can make a contribution to an organization that can create that feeling, that's it for me. Money is an enabling force, but philosophically it has little to do with it.
>
> No one can pay for that—it has to be a *free gift*. Money gets in the way, but someone has to handle that.

While much in this chapter has pointed to the nonadaptive qualities associated with overly strong ties between organization members, it is important to recognize the benefits of this integrating functions as well. Rationalization and professionalization are not integrating processes, but rather seek to differentiate persons from positions and persons from organizations. In the push to manage nonprofits more effectively, one should strive to maintain a balance between the positive aspects of social relationships for an organization with those of a better managed system and structure.

REFERENCES

Alderfer, Clayton P.
1977 "Group and Intergroup Relations." In J.R. Hackman and J.L. Suttle (Eds.) *Improving Life At Work*. Santa Monica, Calif: Goodyear.
1980a "Consulting to Underbounded Systems," in Alderfer and Cooper (Eds.) *Advances in Experiential Social Processes Vol. 2*. New York: John Wiley.
1980b "The Methodology of Organizational Diagnosis." *Professional Psychology*. 11:459–68.
Alderfer, Clayton P., L. Dave Brown, Robert E. Kaplan, and Ken K. Smith
In Press *Group Relations and Organizational Diagnosis*. New York: John Wiley.
Alderfer, Clayton P. and Ken K. Smith
1982 "Studying Intergroup Relations Embedded in Organizations," *Administrative Science Quarterly*. 27:35-36.
Aldrich, Howard E.
1979 *Organizations and Environments*. Englewood Cliffs, N.J.: Prentice–Hall, Inc.
Coser, Rose Laub
1984 "The Greedy Nature of Gemeineschaft." In Walter Powell and Richard Robbins (Eds.) *Conflict and Consensus: A Festschrift in Honor of Lewis Coser*. New York: Free Press.
DiMaggio, Paul
1982 "Cultural Entrepreneurship in Nineteenth Century Boston: The Creation of an Organized Base for High Culture in America." *Media, Culture and Society*. 4:33–50.
DiMaggio, Paul and Michael Useem
1982 "The Arts in Class Reproduction." In Michael W. Apple (Ed.) *Cultural and Economic Reproduction in Education*. London: Routledge and Kegan Paul.
Fenn, Dan H. Jr.
1971 "Executives and Community Volunteers." *Harvard Business Review*. 49:4ff.
Foa, Uriel G.
1971 "Interpersonal and Economic Resources." *Science*. 171:345–351.
Glaser, Barney and Anselm Strauss
1967 *The Discovery of Grounded Theory*. Chicago: Aldine.
Granovetter, Mark S.
1973 "The Strength of Weak Ties." *American Journal of Sociology*. 78:1360–1380.
1974 *Getting a Job: A Study of Contacts and Careers*. Cambridge, Mass.: Harvard University Press.
1984 "Economic Action and Social Structure: The Problem of Embeddedness." *American Journal of Sociology*. 91(3):481–510.
Hall, Peter Dobkin
1975 "The Model of Boston Charity: A Theory of Charitable Benevolence and Class Development." *Science and Society*. pp. 464–477.
Hyde, Lewis
1979 *The Gift: Imagination and The Erotic Life of Property*. New York: Vintage Books.
Kerlinger, Fred N.
1973 *Foundations of Behavioral Research*. New York: Holt, Reinhart and Winston, Inc.
Kohn, Patricia and Kenneth Mortimer
1983 "Selecting Effective Trustees." *Change*. July/August.
Mauss, Marcel
1967 *The Gift*. New York: W.W. Norton and Co.
Middleton, Melissa
1983 "The Place and Power of Nonprofit Boards of Directors." Working Paper #78. Program on Non–Profit Organizations, Yale University.

Nason, John W.
   1977   *Trustees and the Future of Foundations.* New York: Council on Foundations.
Pfeffer, Jeffrey
   1973   "Size, Composition and Functions of Hospital Boards of Directors." *Administrative Science Quarterly.* 18:349–363.
Pfeffer, Jeffrey and Gerald Salancik
   1978   *The External Control of Organizations.* New York: Harper and Row.
Price, James G.
   1963   "The Impact of Governing Boards on Organizational Effectiveness and Morale." *Administrative Science Quarterly.* 8:361–377.
Provan, Keith C.
   1980   "Board and Power and Organizational Effectiveness Among Human Service Agencies." *Academy of Management Journal.* 23:221–236.
Ratcliff, Richard E., Mary Elizabeth Gallagher and Kathryn Strother Ratcliff
   1979   "The Civic Involvement of Bankers: An Analysis of the Influence of Economic Power and Social Prominence in the Command of Civic Policy Positions." *Social Problems.* 26:298–303.
Salzman, Harold and G. William Domhoff
   1983   "Nonprofit Organizations and the Corporate Community." *Social Science History.* 7:205–216.
Zald, Mayer N.
   1967   "Urban Differentiation, Characteristics of Boards of Directors and Organizational Effectiveness." *American Journal of Sociology.* 73:261–272.

Concluding Thoughts on
Closing the Board Gap

Robert D. Herman

In this closing piece I intend to reflect on the chief message I find in the preceeding pieces. This reflection, while drawing on and consistent with the available evidence from systematic research, will necessarily encompass personal experience, conversations with many nonprofit chief executives, board members, technical assistance providers, consultants and researchers and the inferences I've drawn from them as mediated by my ways of making sense of nonprofit organizations. Thus, the conclusions and suggestions offered here I regard as interpretative and tentative.

It also important to note that term "nonprofit organizations" as used in this piece, almost always refers to 501 (c)(3) service–providing charities. Also, I believe the conclusions and suggestions provided here are most appropriate to established (i.e. organizations that no longer include founders on the board or staff), staffed organizations.

The accumulating evidence on the role and behaviors of nonprofit boards of directors suggests one obvious conclusion—that there is a frequently a gap between prescriptive ideal and actual practice. Though there is no uniform prescriptive model that all authorities accept and endorse, my reading of much of prescriptive literature convinces me that there is widespread support for the following prescriptive standards. (1) The nonprofit board of directors has and uses a systematic process for assessing the strengths and weaknesses of the composition of the current board. Strengths/weaknesses are usually assessed on demographic characteristics and expertise and skills, resulting in a board profile. (2) The board profile is used to identify the personal characteristics and expertise/skills desired in new recruits to the board. (3) Recruitment of potential board members is systematic and rigorous, in that potential members are thoroughly informed as to the mission and goals of the organization, its financial condition, and the time, effort and level of contributions expected of them. Similarly, potential members are interviewed by a board committee (and perhaps the full board) as to their motives and interests in volunteering for board service. (4) New board members receive additional, thorough training and orientation, beyond that provided during recruitment and selection. (5) Board members commit significant time to board duties, not only attending committee and board meetings, but also preparing for meetings and undertaking other assignments. (6) Board meetings are characterized by a process through which all are encouraged to participate and disagreement is welcomed, while relationships are collegial and consensual. The board works as a team. (7) The board undertakes and uses processes of assessing the performance of the board as a whole and of assessing the performance of individual members. The board has and follows standards for removing members who do not perform. (8) The board's chief tasks are to (a) select, evaluate and, if necessary, dismiss the chief executive, (b) define and periodically reevaluate the organization's

mission and major goals, develop a strategic plan, approve budgets and policy statements consistent with the plan, and (c) ensure that the organization obtains the
resources necessary to meet the plan. Such a set of standards represents a "heroic
model" of nonprofit boards.

There may be some boards that achieve this heroic model. Such paragons are
undoubtedly rare. Most nonprofit boards fall short, far short. If it is true that this
heroic ideal is seldom, if ever, achieved is it desirable, appropriate to continue holding it up? There are two arguments for doing so. First, U.S. and state laws clearly
place legal responsibility for a nonprofit corporation's affairs on its board. Since a
board is legally responsible, it behooves the members, through self–interest, to con-
scientiously discharge their duties. Indeed, the recent "crisis" in liability insurance
has led some board trainers to use legal responsibility as a "stick" to encourage more
responsible board behavior. Some are worried that such a stick will discourage board
service.

A second argument for continuing the heroic model holds that an ideal is necessary for improving performance. Without high standards nonprofit boards would not
know what is desirable and would have nothing at which to aim. I think this is an
important argument and believe challenging standards are useful in generating
higher levels of performance. Of course, standards that are unobtainable soon lose all
motivating force.

If there is usually a substantial gap between heroic ideal and actual experience, a
search for modification in the ideal needs to be based on an analysis of the forces
creating the gap. I am convinced that the board gap is typically the result of two
realities—the ownership issue and the structure of incentives for board participation
and performance.

The realities of ownership are much different in the case of nonprofit organizations
than in that of business firms. Owners of business firms have a claim on the assets of
the firm. They have an equity interest in the firm. This economic–legal reality has
obvious implications for psychological ownership. For nonprofit organizations
ownership realities are different. No one has the same economic–legal relation to a
nonprofit organization as is the case for business firms. The nondistribution constraint (Hansmann, 1980) prevents anyone from having an equity interest and IRS
regulations require that, in the event of dissolution, a nonprofit organization dis-
tribute its assets to other charitable organizations. Though lacking the same sort of
economic–legal ownership status as in business, the board of directors of a nonprofit
organization is collectively legally *responsible* for the conduct of the organization's
affairs. Individual members of a board may, in some circumstances, be held personally liable for the actions of a nonprofit organization. This corresponds to the financial risks of business owners, though there is no corresponding financial incentive.

The economic–legal ownership reality in nonprofit organizations has implications
for psychological ownership. Certainly, those who found a nonprofit organization
usually have a deep and continuing feeling of responsibility for the survival and
success of that organization, and there are usually a few people in all–volunteer
organizations who have an owner's commitment to the organization. Similarly,
highly ideological, social–movement–related nonprofit organizations will attract volunteers who feel a strong sense of ownership about the organization. For the great
majority of established 501 (c) (3) organizations, though, the paid staff, especially the
chief executive, have the greatest sense of ownership of and responsibility for the

success of the organization. The evidence for this statement is mostly impressionistic. For example, I'll always remember the statement, near the close of a three day conference and retreat for Kansas City–area nonprofit chief executives, of a woman universally regarded as a highly effective manager that she felt responsible for everything that happened in the organization and she had learned that every other chief executive felt the same way. My colleague, Richard Heimovics, and I have recently completed a study that provides more rigorous and systematic evidence for this assertion.

The study was designed to gather data necessary to assess the skills of highly effective nonprofit executives. During the course of the study interviews were conducted with fifty–one chief executives and each was asked to describe one recent event that was especially successful and another that turned out unsuccessfully for the organization. At the end of the interview each of the executives was asked to complete a short questionnnaire, which required the executive to assess the extent to which each of eight different factors contributed to the successful and the unsuccessful outcomes. The eight factors assessed were:

1. Your personal skills and abilities
2. Your personal hard work and effort
3. The skills and abilities of your subordinates
4. The hard work and effort of your subordinates
5. The skills and abilities of your board
6. The hard work and effort of your board
7. Positive circumstances beyond anyone's control
8. Negative circumstances beyond anyone's control

The scores that could be assigned ranged from "1–did not contribute at all" to "5–contributed greatly." We also obtained the chief executive's permission to send similar questionnaires, appropriately modified to fit their roles, to three subordinates who had been involved in the two events and the board president (on presidents) at the time of the two events. They provided scores (using the same 1 to 5 scale) on the same eight factors.

Analysis of the responses to these questionnaires provide some very revealing evidence about who takes responsibility and who gets assigned responsibility for both success and failure in nonprofit organizations. Chief executives assign themselves (through their skills and abilities and hard work and effort) greater responsibility for success *and failure*. In contrast to both subordinates and board presidents, chief executives take responsibility for unsuccessful events, assigning higher scores to themselves than to others or circumstances. Both subordinates and board presidents assign the responsibility for unsuccessful events to others and bad luck more so than to themselves. In both successful and unsuccessful events chief executives are credited by themselves, their subordinates and board presidents as contributing the most to the outcomes. (See Heimovics and Herman, 1987, for more details on methods and results.) This evidence suggests that chief executives are treated by their subordinates and board members as centrally responsible for organizational events, and it suggests that *chief executives take such responsibility*. Interestingly, though board members are legally responsible for organizational affairs, in this study board presidents assigned themselves relatively little responsibility for either success or failure. That is not especially surprising. What happens in the nonprofit organization occupies a much less central part of their lives than the same events do for chief executives and other staff.

In short, while a nonprofit board of directors is legally responsible for the conduct of a nonprofit organization, the chief executive is typically the person with the greatest sense of ownership of the organization, the person everyone (including him or herself) expects to take responsibility. This pattern of psychological ownership in nonprofit organizations contributes to the gap between ideal and actuality. Those with little psychological sense of ownership are unlikely to invest substantial time, energy and effort.

A board member's sense of psychological ownership is affected by the structure of incentives for board participation and performance. As the pieces by Widmer, Middleton and Fink in this volume demonstrate, people who participate in nonprofit boards usually have multiple motives or incentives, though the relative importance of the motives or incentives varies substantially among individuals. The literature on work motivation has long distinguished between incentives that induce participation in or joining an organization and incentives that induce varying levels of performance in an organization. I believe this distinction is very important in understanding the behavior of nonprofit board members. Many of the incentives people look for in board service are achieved primarily through membership and participation in meetings. For example, if board membership is thought to confer some prestige or is valued by one's employer, such incentives will motivate people to join and do enough—attend meetings—to maintain membership. However, such incentives will not, by themselves, motivate high levels of performance on board tasks. Sociability incentives can be expected to motivate membership and meeting attendance. Sociability incentives might induce high levels of performance if one or more board members from whom others seek approval and friendship condition such approval and friendship on contributions to board work. Those who hope to acquire or improve certain skills (e.g. fundraising or strategic planning) are likely to be motivated to performance beyond membership and attendance. Board membership is an exchange. Members contribute participation and sometimes performance in exchange for expected outcomes of value to them. Apparently, valued outcomes are often obtained mostly through membership.

Incentives for board participation and performance are not the same for all nonprofit organizations. Those familiar with the nonprofit sector in every community, and in the country, know that a hierarchy of desirable nonprofit boards exists. While such a hierarchy is admittedly not important to every actual or potential board member, the evidence (see the review by Galaskiewicz, 1985) clearly shows that a community's business and professional elites are well aware of the prestige hierarchy. Thus, those nonprofit organizations at the top of this hierarchy have more incentives and more of each incentive to offer in exchange, particularly to executives and professionals that most nonprofit organizations would like to attract. I am unaware of any research that attempts to compare the performance levels of boards in elite and non–elite nonprofit organizations, though my impression is the greater incentives for elite organizations are mostly effective in making membership highly attractive. With the exception perhaps of motivating fundraising performance, the greater incentives of elite organizations do not generally create heroic boards for such organizations.

If it is true that there is typically a substantial gap between the heroic ideal of board performance and actual practice, and if this analysis of why such a gap exists is correct, then what can be done—either to move practice closer to the ideal or to change the ideal? I believe that some modification in the ideal should occur. I also believe that what's required to improve board practice necessitates greater clarity about who—the chief executive—must usually take the lead in board development.

As for the modifications in the ideal, I suggest that boards should give greater priority to a person's interest in the organization's work than to his or her demographic characteristics, occupation or connections to a community's elite. I am not suggesting that nonprofit organizations set aside attempts to achieve greater social diversity on boards, nor am I suggesting that recruiting board members who have needed expertise, skills or connections is undesirable. Rather, I'm suggesting that the most important criterion become a potential member's interest, due to personal history, family circumstance or strong values, in the work of the organization. Such members are more likely to find the rewards of board service related to performance than to mere membership. Similarly, those potential members who desire to learn or improve skills related to board performance should be seriously considered. Creating a core of board members who are willing to work and who find some rewards in doing so, is not only useful in itself, the efforts of such a core group may be effective in setting a standards for other board members. As several pieces in this volume attest, the importance of clarifying expectations of board service cannot be over-emphasized. Discussion of expectations is necessary, but living examples of board work can be especially useful in giving expectations reality. Further, though there are people who are very willing to let others take on the work of a board, many people will, in the face of evidence that others are contributing more time and effort, due to a desire to achieve fairness or equity, increase their contributions to the work of the board.

Turning to the substance of a board's work, I suggest that the tasks included in the ideal ought to be modified. Clearly, the board cannot avoid the task of selecting, evaluating and, if necessary, dismissing the chief executive. Undoubtedly, many boards can improve the methods and procedures used in this set of tasks. However, the other tasks boards are expected to perform—defining and redefining mission and goals, developing a strategic plan, approving budgets and policies and procedures consistent with the plan, and ensuring that the required resources are obtained—are, on the evidence presented in this volume, frequently left to staff or considered the staff's job. Given the ownership reality and structure of incentives for board service, it is not surprising that boards are usually reactive—that is, boards take action on goals, plans, budgets, policies and fundraising in response to information, proposals and options developed and presented by the staff, especially the chief executive. Boards are necessarily dependent on the chief executive. Boards and chief executives can deal with this dependence in one of two ways. Either the work of the board can become highly pro forma and ceremonial, in which the board truly "rubber stamps" the decisions reached by the staff or the board and chief executive can take the extra time and effort to review information presented in comparative form (as illustrated in Bader's piece in this volume), consider real options and actually make decisions. A long line of research on group decision–making and performance tells us that people who have truly participated in making decisions will have more commitment to their implementation. The potential contribution of boards to organizational performance is too great for boards to become rubber stamps. On the other hand, that potential is most likely to be achieved only when the chief executive takes responsibility for the performance of the board. Thus I suggest that the ideal be modified to recognize that the board's tasks are most usefully performed when the chief executive accepts responsibility for the process of board decision–making.

These suggestions for modification in the ideal are hardly radical. Even in this modified form, the ideal remains fairly daunting. I believe that change in practice can move actual board performance much closer to the (modified) ideal. Research that Richard Heimovics and I have recently completed (see Herman and Heimovics, 1987) convinces me that many of the most effective nonprofit chief executives have learned that their boards contribute more when they (the chief executives) accept responsibility, if necessary, for leadership of the board.

This research was carried out as follows. Several individuals in positions (such as foundation heads, United Way officials, technical assistance providers) where judgments of nonprofit chief executive effectiveness are required were asked to name those they regarded as highly effective nonprofit chief executives in the metropolitan Kansas City, Missouri area. We selected executives for inclusion in the highly effective sample if each received at least two nominations. Thirty executives received at least two nominations. To randomly select a comparison group we used lists of nonprofit chief executives provided by referral centers and consortia organizations. After eliminating those who had received one nomination from the nominator group, we randomly selected thirty chief executives to form a comparison group. Of the sixty chief executives selected, fifty–three agreed to participate.

Each executive was interviewed by an interviewer unaware of which group the executive was a part. Interviews were conducted using the critical incident method. Each executive described two recent events, one an event he or she considered especially successful and the other an unsuccessful event. Our interviewers tried to elicit as much detail about the executive's behavior in the event as possible. The interviews were taped and later transcribed. The transcriptions were read by two trained raters or judges, working independently. The raters were unaware that they were rating behaviors from two samples of chief executives. The chief executives also completed questionnaires that asked for personal, organizational and financial data.

In order to investigate whether the chief executives regarded as highly effective behave differently from the comparison executives, we developed a set of behavioral items derived from previous studies of management competencies and from leadership research. After eliminating some items that failed to achieve acceptable levels of inter–rater reliability, we used a set of twenty-three behavioral rating items, scored as either absent or present in an event, to assess whether and in what ways the highly effective chief executives differed in their behavior from the comparison group. We found that the highly effective chief executives were rated as exhibiting more of the behaviors, in both kinds of events, than the comparison sample. In examining possible differences on each behavioral item we found the highly effective exhibited the following kinds of behaviors more frequently:

1) Facilitating interaction in board relationships;

2) Showing consideration and respect toward board members;

3) Envisioning change and innovation for the organization with the board;

4) Emphasizing accomplishments and productivity of the board;

5) Providing structure for the board (i.e. engages board in goal setting and role clarification, in providing feedback);

6) Maintaining structure for the board (i.e. maintains stability and flow of work through scheduling, coordinating and problem-solving); and

7) Providing information to the board.

Given these differences in the behaviors of the chief executives, it is not surprising that our raters more frequently found the boards of the highly effective executives to be active in policy matters than the boards of the comparison chief executives. In short, nonprofit boards that are actively doing their jobs are those whose chief executives provide substantial, continuing leadership for their boards. Interestingly, the highly effective and comparison chief executives, with one exception—envisioning change and innovation with the staff—did not differ in behaviors in relation to subordinates. Taking leadership responsibility for board activities is what distinguishes those chief executives widely regarded as highly effective from other chief executives. While the results of this research require further testing in other places with other methods and while we need to know much more about how boards encourage or discourage leadership from the chief executive, I believe the results provide strong evidence for explicitly adding board leadership to the duties of nonprofit chief executives.

REFERENCES

Galaskiewicz, Joseph
    1985   *Social Organization of an Urban Grants Economy: A Study of Business Philanthropy and Nonprofit Organizations*. Orlando, FL: Academic Press.
Hansmann, Henry
    1980   "The Role of Nonprofit Enterprise," Yale Law Journal 89:835–901.
Heimovics, Richard D. and Robert D. Herman
    1987   "Cross–Perceptions of Responsibility in Nonprofit Organizations," (unpublished manuscript).
Herman, Robert D. and Richard D. Heimovics
    1987   "Effective Managers of Nonprofit Organizations," Independent Sector Spring Research Forum *Working Papers*.

Index